Manifestos and Polemics in Latin American Modern Art

Manifestos and Polemics
in Latin American Modern Art

EDITED AND TRANSLATED BY PATRICK FRANK

University of New Mexico Press | Albuquerque

Library of Congress Cataloging-in-Publication Data
Names: Frank, Patrick, 1953– editor, translator.
Title: Manifestos and polemics in Latin American modern art / edited and translated by
    Patrick Frank.
Description: Albuquerque : University of New Mexico Press, 2017. |
    Includes bibliographical references and index.
Identifiers: LCCN 2016018378 (print) | LCCN 2016028305 (ebook) |
    ISBN 9780826357878 (cloth : alk. paper) | ISBN 9780826357885 (pbk. : alk. paper) |
    ISBN 9780826357892 (electronic)
Subjects: LCSH: Art, Latin American—20th century. | Art, Latin American—21st century. |
    Art manifestos—Latin America. | Art—Political aspects—Latin America.
Classification: LCC N6502.5 .M36 2017 (print) | LCC N6502.5 (ebook) | DDC 709.8—dc23
LC record available at https://lccn.loc.gov/2016018378

All document translations are by the editor unless otherwise noted.

Cover photo: Workers reading *El Machete* (detail), 1929. Platinum print, 7.95 cm x 10.46 cm.
    Tina Modotti. Private collection.
Designed by Lila Sanchez
Composed in Minion Pro. Display type is Bodoni.

Contents

PART FIVE
CONSTRUCTIVE AND INFORMALIST ABSTRACTION

PART SIX
MIDCENTURY ARCHITECTURAL PROJECTS

PART TWELVE

TOWARD A NEW CENTURY

Preface

Painting's Near-Death Experience

⸬ SHE ANNOUNCED IT WITH MORE CONVICTION AND CERTAINTY THAN you might expect from a twenty-four-year-old artist: "Easel painting is definitely dead. And buried." Marta Minujín said this on the opinion page of a news magazine in 1965, as one of her gallery-sized installations entertained, shocked, amused, and baffled visitors at the Di Tella Institute in Buenos Aires. She created a succession of spaces that included breeding houseflies, rabbits, and flashing neon silhouettes of sports figures, capped off by a playground slide that disgorged visitors onto the oversized face of a nude effigy of the newest glamorous actress of the day, Virna Lisi. Viewers reported that the huge doll seemed to give off gasping sounds as they landed on it. In answering the obvious question—"What is it!?"—the artist replied that she had created "a visual and spatial event." She called it *El batacazo*, a slang term from horse racing that means "the long shot." She hoped, she said, to administer a blow to people's habitual ways of approaching an art exhibition.

The times were simply not right for "the contemplation of something static," the artist said—meaning static like a painting is. "People today are too shaken up by what constantly whirls around them, at jet speed and intensity, to pause for even a moment . . . It's indisputable that easel painting can neither fathom nor communicate the changes that take place minute by minute." Comparing her art to an auto race or a soccer match, she said that creating experiences that were "dynamic, ever-changing, hallucinatory, infinite" was "the only way forward." Preferring to show her art in the streets, she seemed determined to take the next step, now that painting was past saving.

Such funereal pronouncements are surprisingly common in Latin American modern art; most movements and styles emerge accompanied by debates and discussion. Paying attention to these polemics widens our perspective on the meanings of art in culture, because most movements, and many artists' careers, have been accompanied by pronouncements, manifestos, assertions, or declarations. But in Latin America, many of the relevant documents are still difficult to access, buried in personal archives and libraries or sometimes-obscure periodicals, books, or manuscripts. This anthology attempts to mitigate that obscurity and bring some dynamic creators closer to contemporary awareness. Only a few of these artists considered painting dead; many of them are, in fact, painters. But all communicate in a spirited fashion about what they hope to accomplish, and what they feel is at stake in their works and innovations.

I have selected the artists and texts for this book with an eye toward education. The artists anthologized here are among the most widely known; they are already visible in textbooks and museum exhibitions. Rather than promoting new discoveries, this book should deepen and enliven our current knowledge. I hope that it accompanies university courses, museum exhibition catalogs, and the explorations of any curious reader. My intent is not to rearrange the canon of modern Latin American art, but rather to assist those who will do so in the future.

To be sure, the stature of Latin American modern art has risen markedly in the United States in this new century. Most of the increased visibility can be traced in a rising wave of museum exhibitions, most of them with significant catalogs. Marking a watershed in this regard was *Inverted Utopias: Avant-Garde Art in Latin America* at the Museum of Fine Arts, Houston, TX, in 2004.[1] This exhibition ranked with the most important ever staged on this subject, along with the 1966 *Art of Latin America since Independence*[2] and 1993 *Latin American Artists of the Twentieth Century* at the Museum of Modern Art.[3] As its title suggests, the Houston exhibition focused on avant-garde movements, and its capacious catalog included many primary documents. While it omitted certain well-known artists such as Frida Kahlo and Wifredo Lam, and its curatorial scheme has not gained traction, the exhibition remains pathbreaking in its depth and breadth. One nationally recognized newspaper critic responded to *Inverted Utopias* with enthusiasm, writing, "Stirring throughout, revelatory in parts, it's sensational."[4] The exhibition also marked the arrival of the Houston museum as a locus of innovative and important scholarship, as later exhibitions gave unprecedented attention to artists such as Carlos Cruz-Diez, Antonio Berni, Gego, and Hélio Oiticica, all in large solo shows. The museum also hosts a large online archive of research documents in their original languages at its International Center for the Arts of the Americas.

The Museum of Modern Art in New York has also begun a program of periodic retrospectives of canonical Latin American artists, under the guidance of a specialized curator. So far, exhibitions have been staged on the work of Armando Reverón, Lygia Clark, Joaquín Torres-García, León Ferrari, Mira Schendel, and photographers Horacio Coppola and Grete Stern. MoMA in 2015 staged the most comprehensive exhibition on Latin American architecture in several decades, *Latin America in Construction*.[5] The museum also sponsored a Wikipedia Edit-a-thon in its education building, encouraging scholars and interested parties to contribute pages on Latin American art to that online resource.

The Edit-a-thon was a joint venture with the Colección Patricia Phelps de Cisneros (CPPC), one of the latter's many activities in recent years. This collection emphasizes abstract art from Argentina, Brazil, Uruguay, and Venezuela. Several important exhibitions have been assembled from its holdings; the largest of these in North America was held at the Fogg Art Museum at Harvard in 2001.[6] Others have taken place at the Hunter College Art Gallery, the Blanton Museum at the University of Texas, and the Grey Art Gallery of New York University. These and other CPPC activities, including a series of published in-depth interviews, have greatly increased the visibility of Latin American abstract art.

Besides New York and Houston, Los Angeles is emerging as a center for exhibition of Latin American modern art. The city's Museum of Contemporary Art has staged several thematic exhibitions, including one focusing on light and space.[7] At the time of this writing, the Getty Research Institute is helping to fund *L.A./L.A.*, a constellation of approximately forty exhibitions in venues across Southern California in 2017–2018 that highlight connections between the region's modern culture and that of Latin America. Other museums in major cities have added specialized curators to their staffs or staged traveling exhibitions. Several US universities have added the study of Latin American works and their creators to their art curricula; as of mid-2016, approximately ninety-five have at least one Latin American specialist in their Art History departments. Over the period 2002 to 2012, the average annual number of dissertations dealing with Latin American art increased fourfold.[8]

This enumeration of progress in recent years should not lead to a conclusion that Latin American modern art has met with full acceptance, integration into the canon, or even sufficient understanding. The issues that this art raises about canon formation, the definition of an avant-garde, the political ingredient in modernism, and the role of geopolitics in art appreciation all remain cogent. For now, I hope that *Manifestos and Polemics* contributes to building a more cosmopolitan and inclusive sense of what modernism was, and is.

This book brings the voices of the art's actual creators toward the forefront of a quickening discussion. This is not a book of "readings" in the traditional sense. Here are neither critical reflections nor historical research nor formal analysis. Rather, it is a collection of documents from across the past hundred years, with a special focus on primary materials. Besides the usual autobiographies, manifestos, and artists' statements, this book includes material from videos, blogs, handwritten notebooks, flyers, lectures, and even an after-dinner speech. Two of the documents contain expletives that I have not softened in translation. All of the items gathered here were written by artists, or derive from interviews with them. More specifically, I intend this book to be a more complete and updated follow-up to the anthology that I edited in 2004.[9] About one-quarter of the documents in that book are held over in the present one, because certain manifestos must be included in any book of this sort. But the rest are all new, and all are primary, with the majority appearing in English for the first time. The selection here is broader, with sixty-five texts instead of sixty. It is more contemporary, stretching into the present century. It covers a larger percentage of women artists. It also includes more Latino/a artists from the United States, in recognition of certain demographic facts: according to a 2015 report by the Instituto Cervantes, the United States is home to the second-largest number of Spanish speakers in the world, counting both native and nonnative speakers—second behind Mexico and ahead of Colombia, Spain, and Argentina.[10] These and other data, such as increasing Latino/a school enrollments, are important factors that will continue to impel wider visibility for Latin American art.

The goal of this book is to unlock the history of modern and contemporary art in Latin America: to bring it to more vivid life by exposing the discussion surrounding the creation of some of the most important and compelling art of the last hundred years. Here, we will see just how interdisciplinary the rebels were who founded Modern Art Week in São Paulo in 1922; the multiple reasons why many Mexican artists remained aloof from the mural movement; how a local style of photomontage arose in Buenos Aires in the 1940s, and why abstract and figurative artists nearly came to blows in the same city in the early 1960s; why Fernando Botero suddenly began painting scenes of violence in the 1990s; and how Rafael Lozano-Hemmer uses the latest technology to transform public spaces and empower his viewers.

A few wider themes emerge from this array of voices. Many of the documents take up the question of the function of art in society. Given that politically motivated art is often a dominant trend in Latin America, this should be no surprise. Abstract art, and the many reasons for making it, are another important concern. These texts show that in Latin America, abstraction is often undertaken for different purposes than it is on other continents. We also get a new look at the art scene from artists' perspectives at various times in capitals such as Lima, Havana, and Buenos Aires. The often-contentious relationship between Latin America and the Europe/USA axis haunts many creators, from late-stage Cubists to architects to conceptualists. These matters, and a great many others, can only be truly understood by making a fair attempt to re-create their original context, thus putting their creative energy into higher relief. Much of the surging debate and vital cultural force of the times rises to view in the primary documents that accompany each movement and artist. I have selected these pieces because I believe that they best embody the essential vigor, vitality, and restlessly searching quality of modern art in Latin America.

Notes

1. Mari Carmen Ramírez and Héctor Olea, *Inverted Utopias: Avant-Garde Art in Latin America* (New Haven, CT: Yale University Press, 2004).

2. Stanton Caitlin and Terence Grieder, *Art of Latin America since Independence* (New Haven, CT: Yale University Press, 1966).

3. Waldo Rasmussen, Fatima Bercht, and Elizabeth Ferrer, *Latin American Artists of the Twentieth Century* (New York: Museum of Modern Art, 1993).

4. Holland Cotter, "Ready to Rumba," *New York Times*, August 27, 2004.

5. Barry Bergdoll, Carlos Eduardo Comas, Jorge Francisco Liernur, and Patricio del Real, *Latin America in Construction: Architecture 1955–1980* (New York: Museum of Modern Art, 2015).

6. Yve-Alain Bois, *Geometric Abstraction: Latin American Art from the Patricia Phelps de Cisneros Collection* (Cambridge, MA: Harvard University Art Museums, 2001).

7. Alma Ruiz, *Supra-Sensorial: Experiments in Light, Color, and Space* (Los Angeles, CA: Museum of Contemporary Art, 2011).

8. Adriana Zavala, "Latin@ Art at the Intersection," *Aztlán: A Journal of Chicano Studies* 40, no. 1 (2015): 125–40.

9. Patrick Frank, ed., *Readings in Latin American Modern Art* (New Haven, CT: Yale University Press, 2004).

10. Instituto Cervantes, "El Español: Una lengua viva," accessed December 17, 2015. http://cvc.cervantes.es/lengua/anuario/anuario_12/i_cervantes/p01.htm.

PART ONE

Early Modernism

The Mountain Reborn

Dr. Atl

———

From Dr. Atl (Gerardo Murillo), *Las sinfonías del Popocatépetl* (Mexico City: México Moderno, 1921), 127–41. Ellipses and capitalization retained from the original.

This intense and poetic text captures some of the enthusiasm Dr. Atl felt for the volcanoes that he explored and painted for most of his life. Among the most important symbolic meanings that he found in them was that their new fire seemed to echo the mythical Aztec ceremony that marked the rebirth of the world after its catastrophic destruction. Parallels to a hoped-for rebirth of Mexico after the revolution are also apt.

The Return to the Mountain

By the wide road, still blood-red, in the sad silence of a funereal quiet, I returned to the Mountain.

From its snowy peak, there arose in the blue sky an immense plume of smoke. The Mountain seemed to emote. Full of bitterness, I entered into its forests. I wandered for a long time, searching for the ancient trails that neglect had covered over during my years of absence. Climbing among the giant pines burdened by the fury of the wind, I rested at the edge of a sterile sandpit, before the gray tree-skeletons. They were beaten just like men, bent over by an unseen flow that has no pity, terrorized in the same immobility of death by the implacable fury of Fate.

What a strange analogy! The entire world is like this forest, with the same desolate aspect, with the same terrified giants, with all of its vigor cast down to the ground, with its hopes turned upside down, with the unavoidable threat of a lurking hidden force. It waits resignedly for a tranquility which, after the Destruction, will cover with its shawl of pulverized rock all Hope and Life.

But at the peak of the Mountain, at its collapsed crater which had been extinct for millions of years, I saw rise up an immense column of steam, a sign of regeneration.

In the Pit of the Crater

At some past time, the pit of the crater was as silent as an abandoned tomb. Its sepulchral silence was broken only by the fall of the boulders that the wind tore loose from its ridges. Today, this ancient sepulcher has become a furnace.

At the bottom, an enormous spout rises up like a flower of fire, and around it tall fumaroles, wavy wisps, form an unsteady crown. The forces within have opened the way between the boulders that covered its ancient mouth, and now lava boils between the stones with glowing splendor.

Violent explosions stir the smoldering liquid. Thick clouds of whistling steam rise up screeching, mixed with particles of lava, stones, and ash. Rocks and light rain down. A fearful thunder shakes the Mountain and in this enormous cavity the blood of the Planet glows and rumbles.

In the Heart of Anahuac

Stones, stones, stones! Stones pulverized, stones in fragments, rivers of stones coming down the canyons, stones broken loose and planted over the slope like immense crystallized flowers . . . massive blackish walls, rotten, shattered . . . heaps of boulders, covered with gray dust; enormous reddened walls the color of blood push out pools of frozen tears.

Tortured greatness—tragic resignation—harsh desiccation.

The Mountain resembles a heart pointing upward to the sky, frozen by the coldness of an indifferent and incandescent Destiny.

Fatal desolation—the enormity of death—resistance constantly defeated—and now, a new hope over the summit!

O Mountain! Your formidable home, like the heart of this people, has bled since the night of the most remote past. Your heart, battling against treachery, shaken apart beneath the greatness of your sparkling sky, can still hold out . . .

At times this tragic summit seems to me like the heart of a victim, placed by the heathen hand of an Aztec priest on the Stone of Sacrifice . . .

But no! It lives. From its cloven peak at the Summit, a new, throbbing force arises.

On the Glaciers

Among the red pools of the Great Heart on the wasted road, across dryness and death, toward the glaciers that keep the final catastrophe from the summit of the Volcano;

Amid glassy ice sheets, I feel the warmth return, which I lost between my overheated blood, the fury of the struggle, and the boiling infamy of my foul passions.

Greenish, glassy walls—enormous and twisting snowdrifts, smooth and sharp—caverns as clear as enchanted grottoes—turquoise grottoes—opaque tunnels of dense snow, which open beneath the massive glaciers where dark waters flow—frozen triangular masses between crystalline blocks—long cascades like torrents of tears crystallized in the cold; there is something even colder than your crisp and eternal iciness: the opaque and shattering sadness of human disasters!

In the deep and mysterious darkness of your frozen breast, in the transparency of your core, as luminous as dark crystal—under the formidable masses of snow that cover the backbone of the Volcano, with the sound that the drops of water make as they fall from long stalactites—a strange comfort caresses my pained members, and a vague hope wraps my tortured heart, just as the boulders shore up your coldness . . .

On the Summit

I saw it, blood-red and desolate.

Between the steaming ruins of the cities, and across the countryside, the peoples groan. Where there was once a forest, now was a cemetery; over orchards, human bones whitened; where once had been a tree now appeared a cross. The symbol of death rose everywhere, signaling destruction. Crosses on the roads, crosses in the fields, crosses on the hills . . .

Everything seemed to me unclear, even the Truth. All appeared absurd to me, even Love. And from everything emanated profound sadness and fatal despair. From every walk of life was born a sob, and the rhythms of death permeated even the molecules of matter. Over the world reigned desolation, and in the anguished human heart all was extinguished: love, wisdom, hope.

Suddenly, through my clouded vision, the Volcano shuddered. Its ancient entrails groaned and its mouth vomited fire. Beneath my feet, there surged a flame, and its ardent force warmed even my spirit, which had been changed into a frozen molecule of the Mountain.

ON THE ANCIENT TOMB
THERE IS A NEW FIRE.

Voices and Demons

Armando Reverón

—◆—

From Juan Calzadilla, *Voces y Demonios de Armando Reverón:*
Cuentos, Anécdotas, Pensamientos (Caracas: Alfadil, 1990), 125–36.

These statements capture not only the painter's approach and his passions, but
also his somewhat unstable mental state. They were collected over a period of
several years by poet and critic Juan Calzadilla on various visits to Armando
Reverón's compound on Venezuela's Macuto Beach in the 1940s and 1950s, late
in the painter's career.

Light

People ask why I am here, and I reply: Because of my commitment to light.

Do you know the light? No one has introduced me to it. Nobody truly
knows it. Light is like a lady; the lord is the Sun.

When I paint, I cannot break apart the colors of the light.

Light is such a serious thing! How can we master it? I have tried; this has
been my struggle.

Painting is truth. But it is a blind truth that torments you and drives you
mad, because no one can see the light.

I came [to Macuto] in search of simplicity and I found clarity.

I have been painting in Macuto for many years. I have succeeded in finding simplicity and the caress of simple things. I have been able to get to
know the light.

Colors

My paintings look this way because placing one white tone here and there is
enough to allow us to imagine color.

Colors do not exist in the tropics because the light has overwhelmed
them.

6

I paint with white to avoid resembling other painters.

A canvas painted white is already a painting. We are both the canvas. You are the subject to be painted; so am I.

Your palette should contain only white. To begin a drawing, first mark the points, nearly geometrically, and then draw and draw until the figure comes out.

The canvas is white, and every brushstroke is a piece of soul.

When I speak, I am god. When you speak, you are god. God is in colors. Don't you see?

Technique

I enjoy painting in the nude; clothing is inconvenient.

I am the canvas. And the canvas must be naked. I don't accept that one should prepare the canvas with those sizing pastes. The canvas must be natural, because if you fill it first with white [sizing], the intention is lost.

If you put something into a painting without understanding that thing, the painting is lost.

The physical strength that is required in confronting a canvas of large dimensions has to be balanced out with something. Also, there are those ideas that crowd together in the mind, hindering focused thought, and it's necessary to block them off so that they don't escape.

You have to stand before the canvas like a bullfighter faces the bull.

Love is everything. Put love into things. Like a child before a bull.

Painters repeat themselves. They attach themselves to one thing, and don't want to leave it.

The dawn was my only subject. But painting at dawn, I always forgot about the seagulls. This must be because at other times the color of their flight catches the light.

The Canvas

A canvas is not like a daily newspaper, which has boundaries on all sides.

Paintings don't live through their shocks or surprises, but rather through their tranquility and their lively harmonies.

Once you begin, you must keep working. A canvas is never finished.

You have to de-compose. When the canvas does not come out one way, it comes out another.

On Theater

In painting, you practice continuously; such practice is life. That is why I enjoy the theater, because every theatrical production reflects life itself.

Life is the largest theater. Along with you journalists and photographers, we all are characters who act in the scenery of life. And on this stage, all movements made under the cone of light must be taken into painting. Light in the theater, light on the canvas, light in the cinema: In cinema as in painting, light is fundamental.

Various Thoughts

Painters who are too preoccupied with publicity end up with more medals than works of art.

I don't know what others say about me, and neither can I say anything about others. I need to be like a painting. Paintings don't talk.

We should not groom ourselves. We are a mirror. If we see a windmill [in the mirror], we have a windmill in our heads. I leave my hair like the sea, and I would even like to paint it blue, because the sea is blue.

Every hour has a distinct color, and you feel the change from one to the other.

The sky is everything, and it can't be avoided. It holds all the beauty that exists.

Regional Autonomy

Pedro Figari

———❦———

Pedro Figari, "Autonomía regional," *La Cruz del Sur*, May 31, 1924, 1.

The artist sent this essay from his Paris studio to one of the leading cultural reviews in his home country of Uruguay in 1924. Widely respected at the time as a success in the Paris art world, Figari nonetheless here urges his readers to remain focused on their own Uruguayan culture. According to Figari, modern cosmopolitanism is part of the problem. Here he argues eloquently for a modern culture that is instead local and regional. He also embodied this call in hundreds of paintings that took up folkloric subjects.

We have lost our way. Cosmopolitanism has erased what is ours, replacing it with exotic civilizations, and we, dazzled by the brilliance of the ancient and glorious culture of the Old World, have come to forget our own tradition. We have become accustomed to dragging ourselves along with the laziness of a contented chameleon, as if it were not necessary, for reasons of dignity and conscience, to create our own civilization, the most authentic possible. All of this has led us to live for many years a reflected and almost ephemeral life. From our own environment we kept only the echo. The traditional values, our spiritual essence and heritage, lay in oblivion, as values with little import, or even despised.

Some efforts and initiatives have been sustained by "the gauchos," be they rural or urban. For me a gaucho could be one or the other, as long as they maintain faith in the attitudes of the American race and consider it at least as good as any other, and always profess affection for our environment and gratitude for its progenitors. Some industrious champions of our tradition, working alone and thus against greater obstacles, have struggled for the preservation of the traces of the criollo legends. This work will allow us to reconstruct the poem of America, and establish over the depths of this vein a civilization that is ours, and which, measured against the teachings of world experience, and as much as they may take advantage of them, will be able to equal them in brilliance, honors, and advancements while always keeping them as recognizably our own.

This awakening of the autonomous conscience must reach its fullest development, so that it can reach a comparable plane of fertility, and so that one can feel its vibrancy . . . But we must not forget that we are all charged with the task of watering and growing this plant; because it is ours, we must see that its roots are healthy and its heights honorable and auspicious.

It is not with ostentation that we have to create the work of America; it is with deeds, with enactments, and with works that are judicious, effective, productive, progressive, and promising. Neither is it with hasty imitations that we should place it in the best possible light, but rather with study, work, and integrity: that is to say, effectiveness . . . It is prudent to note that the young require preparation so that they can join all of the wholesome and fruitful paths of productivity. And it is likewise necessary to remember women, especially rural women, who have been neglected and thus lag behind, though they bear the destiny of our race . . .

Thus we must organize ourselves: not by imitating, but by educating. Only by means of an autochthonous consciousness ready to investigate the factors in the environment and balance the most appropriate resources for a rich, firm, and positive prosperity, solidly founded on the features of our surroundings and in the aptitudes and modalities of our race: Only thus will we be able to undertake this fruitful enterprise with confidence in its results. Until we have shaken off the stupor that befogs us, we will not be able to perceive the beauties of our own earth and sky, or the poetry of our own tradition, or the greatness of our mission. Otherwise our enviable riches will remain like unmined veins of precious metal, inert and stiff under the gaze of the uncivilized.

The Southern Cross must shine more brightly, according to the breadth of our accomplishment in individualizing our race and our region, and even more according to how attuned and rational the elements have been with which we individualize it. We must set to work, conscientiously and decisively.

PART TWO

The Avant-Garde of the 1920s

Modern Art Week

Complete Program, Municipal Theater,
São Paulo, Brazil, February 1922

———

From notices printed in *O estado de São Paulo*, February 13–17, 1922.

Herewith a complete program of one of the most important events in Latin American modern culture. It took place at the city's grandest venue, a formal, classical building that had been open for about eleven years. The organizers installed an exhibition of paintings and sculptures by contemporary artists in the lobby. Modern Art Week was both controversial and interdisciplinary, as music and poetry shared the stage with lectures on art.

I. Monday, February 13

Lecture by Graça Aranha: "Aesthetic Emotion in Modern Art."
Music played by Ernani Braga
Poems by Guilherme de Almeida and Ronald de Carvalho

Chamber Music: Heitor Villa-Lobos: Sonata no. 2 for Cello and Piano, Trio no. 2 for Violin, Cello, and Piano

Lecture by Ronald de Carvalho: "Modern Painting and Sculpture in Brazil"
Three piano pieces by Villa-Lobos: "Mystic Waltz," "Rolling," "The Spinner"
Octet by Villa-Lobos: *Three African Dances*: "Farrapos (Dance of the Children)"; "Kankukus (Dance of the Old Men)"; "Kankikis (Dance of the Boys)"

II. Wednesday, February 15

Lecture by Menotti del Picchia, illustrated with poems and prose excerpts by Oswald de Andrade, Luís Aranha, Sérgio Milliet, Tácito de Almeida, Ribeiro Couto, Mário de Andrade, Plínio Salgado, Agenor Barbosa. Dance by Yvonne Daumerie.

13

Remembering Modern Art Week

Emiliano Di Cavalcanti

———◦———

From Emiliano Di Cavalcanti, *A viagem da minha vida*
(Rio de Janeiro: Ed. Civilização Brasileira, 1955), 107–18.

*Here we get a close view of some of the machinations behind Modern Art Week
in São Paulo. The author participated in the organization of the event and
showed his paintings in the lobby of the theater where it took place. He gathered his recollections some thirty years later for his autobiography. His enthusiasm for the endeavor remains infectious.*

Returning to São Paulo in 1921, after several months in Rio de Janeiro, I
brought with me some paintings and a series of drawings that I titled
Fantoches da Meia-Noite [*Midnight Puppets*]. Ribeiro Couto, poet and author
of *Jardins das Confidências* [*Gardens of the Secrets*], supported the enterprise
of making a luxury edition of them, and wrote a preface for it. Monteiro
Lobato funded the publication, for a public who at that time seemed little
interested in that type of book. My dear friend Octalles Marcondes [Ferreira]
believed equally in *Fantoches*, but he thought that in order to cover the costs
of production, subscriptions should be sold to fund the deluxe edition. I
decided to exhibit the drawings at the O Livro bookstore and publishing
house, which was directed by the old man Jacinto Silva. It was then located
on 15 November Street, and it had ample space for showing works of art.

Our modernist group was formed from this, because in order to create a
favorable atmosphere for the launch of *Fantoches* in São Paulo, I went to the
homes of all my friends and to the newspaper offices, in an effort to both interest viewers and obtain good press. Four people led our group, each one with
his own tasks, united in solidarity in the hope of ending the provincial rigidity
of the city, which still held on through the dawn of the post–World War I
period.

Our small clan of souls was open to new artistic speculations, interested in new literary forms, already convinced of new philosophical doctrines. These came to us through surprising books announcing new aesthetic or political ideas, which were evidently not so new in Europe, but whose appearance in our Brazil had been held up by the war. The idiotic academism of the literary and art critics at the newspapers; the arrogance of these subliterate, hollow, and wordy individuals, who dominated culture and politics; and the dead hand of the foreign and national bigwigs, all polluted the intellectual atmosphere of the city. This depressed us, because the city was on the verge of a great progressive adventure as regards business and industry. In the midst of all this "comedic dance," as Mário de Andrade called it, I was striving to both improve my art and earn a monthly sustenance.

The four who led our modernist battle were Oswald de Andrade, Guilherme de Almeida, Mário de Andrade, and Menotti del Picchia. The four seemed to judge my work as a young designer and painter as unexpectedly original, in that impoverished environment of well-behaved disciples of [academic still-life painter] Pedro Alexandrino or [prize-winning landscape painter] Batista da Costa.

Anita Malfatti's 1917 exhibition had been a revelation of something beyond Impressionism, but because Anita had come from overseas, as had [Victor] Brecheret and Lasar Segall, they all had the stamp of Paris, Rome, or Berlin. My modernism was tainted by Brazilian cultural anarchism and, though it barely limped along, it at least possessed the advantage of birth among the errors, inexperience, and lyricism of Brazilians.

From the *mardi gras* of Rio I had taken a love of color, of rhythm, and of the sensuousness of virginal Brazil. From the neighborhood of São Cristóvão the gypsy touch, familiar from the literature of Machado de Assis. My political causes I learned in the pages of the satirical magazine *O malho*. From the Northwest, from my relatives in Pernambuco and Paraiba, I got my audacity, which would grow when I saw the agricultural zone in the interior of São Paulo province. This revealed to me the existence of a Brazil colonized by Italians, who built entire cities by industrializing the production of coffee. And this presence of a multifaceted, real country, arising before my naïve and fascinated eyes, soon made me laugh uproariously at the stiffness of the ancient academy of the University of São Paulo Law School, with its illustrious jurists who educated judges, prosecutors, cautious lawyers, and reactionary politicians. I soon abandoned my law studies.

With Oswald, Menotti, Guilherme, and Mário, we gradually selected, accepted, rejected, or satirized the modernists newly arrived to our group.

We were already a very strong team working together, in the office of Guilherme de Almeida, with Antônio Couto de Barros and Sérgio Milliet. The latter had just come from Switzerland, without bringing its fat cheeses or punctual clocks but rather books full of precious poetry, and a gift for winning over women in bars. Tácito de Almeida, young poet and brother of Guilherme, also joined us.

Menotti del Picchia then worked at [the newspapers] *Correio Paulistano* and the *Gazette*, skewering the patriarchal politics of the Paulista Republican Party with improvised orations or exaggerated articles in praise of modernism (modernism which he loved without, after all, getting married to it). He wasted there both enormous amounts of time and his innate lyrical gifts, without thinking about the political possibilities that could grow gradually out of his eloquence as an illustrious half-Indian. Oswald de Andrade had an instinctive boldness, with a visionary sense of a new world rising, which he picked up at the shirttails of Jean Cocteau, Blaise Cendrars, Guillaume Apollinaire, and all the other French authors newly arrived to world literature; he mixed these with Dostoyevsky, with Romain Rolland, the Catholicism of [Charles] Péguy, the popular tragedies of [Maksim] Gorki, and with [Gabriele] D'Annunzio, who announced the birth of Fascism, and the pacifism of [Georges] Duhamel . . . And, as a counterweight, we had Mário de Andrade with his group from Lopes Chaves Street, where they practiced creation as a search, and where the verb "to contemplate" was always at hand. Mário was usually accompanied by Luís Aranha or Yan de Almeida Prado, or Rubens Borba de Moraes, and we often went to see or hear him, either reciting or playing the piano. Mário gave all of us the impression that whatever burned brightest in our hearts could never be extinguished, and that our restlessness was only turning over the ground where a new future would soon be planted. Mário de Andrade had a professorial personality, but in his own way, sometimes unexpectedly disappointed in himself, but always attentive to his students. Unfortunately for Brazilian literature, only near the end of his life did Mário learn about the human condition, by being present at the social evolution of our age. But in the meantime, he was the perpetual coordinator, always glimpsing a new category, system, or direction; this explains the pleasure he took in being with the younger ones, taking the role of master. And he was, truly, a master.

With these men at the forefront, I experienced the modernization of São Paulo, where my restless Rio de Janeiro sensibility apparently counted at least for something.

At the O Livro bookstore in that year 1921, Jacinto Silva one day mysteriously called me over to a corner, where he told me that Graça Aranha was in São Paulo. Silva asked if I would do what I could to draw younger people to my exhibition, because that famous academic wanted to make contact with the new generation of artists and writers in the city. Graça Aranha was for me only a name in a schoolbook. He was the author of [the novel] *Canaã*, which I had never read, and moreover was unable to read. The last time I had seen his name was in a headline that announced his return to Brazil after completing some overseas missions, because he was also a diplomat.

Just as old Jacinto finished urging me to bring in the young Paulistas, Aranha himself walked up: handsome, elegant, and perfumed. Jacinto introduced me to the great man, and the great man looked at my paintings and drawings with a noble detachment. He saw the thinly veiled romanticism in my work, and resolved to remain in contact with me. He had already heard my name in Rio, because Ronald de Carvalho had spoken to him of me. Aranha then criticized the struggle in my paintings and drawings, and began to preach that in Brazil we needed strong men. He asked if I had ever read his books, and if I too felt that the war had put to rest a speculative world order, and that it was perhaps time for the dawn of a new civilization of synthesis, where humanity could move toward a more universal comprehension. That handsome man seduced me like a beautiful opera singer electrifies a balcony filled with fools . . .

At my exhibition, Aranha met Oswald, Mário, Guilherme, and Menotti. His diplomatic abilities, his worldly *savoir-faire*, and his authority as an elder worked like seductive music. He proposed to join our movement, and take it northward and southward to all of Brazil. In meetings either at the bookstore, or at Aranha's apartment, or at the Sportsman Rotisserie on Largo do Patriarca, we defined our program of lectures, exhibitions, and concerts; we only needed to fund it somehow.

Aranha was friendly with Paulo Prado, whom none of us knew, least of all as the scholar of Brazilian history and excellent writer that he was. Aranha explained both who Prado was and his disposition to favor our movement. Aranha then sent me to Rio with a letter of introduction from our modernist group, so that I was the first of us to get to know that noble figure, who besides his education and refinement, personally knew [Paul] Claudel, Oscar Wilde, the ballerinas from the paintings of Edgar Degas, and even Degas himself.

So I went to meet Prado, and from my conversations with that important man was born the idea of Modern Art Week. That night and in several meetings, we discussed other elegant weeklong events that took place in Europe, such as the "Grande Semaine" at Deauville. I suggested to Prado that our event, which would be a week of literary and artistic scandals, should stick the spurs into the sides of the São Paulo middle and upper classes. This pleased Prado immensely, because he could not stand the lack of sophistication that surrounded him. In São Paulo he moved among wealthy businessmen and magnates of high finance. We counted on monetary support from those people.

"This has to be a scandalous week, with nothing of the high-school atmosphere of festivals that we know," said Prado, the author of *Retrato do Brasil* [*Portrait of Brazil*], at our first meeting with Aranha, Mário de Andrade, Oswald de Andrade, and a few others whose names I can't remember. After a lot of hard work, we came up with a general plan for the week, and with great enthusiasm we began our preparations . . .

And when I read the announcement of our upcoming week in the newspaper, I laughed to myself: The finest flower of the right-wing conservative society of São Paulo was about to sponsor a cultural event that opposed everything that they cherished.

Anthropophagite Manifesto

Oswald de Andrade

From *Revista de Antropofagia*, May 1928, 3.

This important manifesto sets out a crucial concept for the relationship of Latin American to European modernism: anthropophagy, or cannibalism. In order to fortify their own art forms, Brazilian modernists would cannibalize Europe just as the native peoples allegedly cannibalized the first explorers. Though most reports of such early cannibalism lacked supporting evidence, they helped to inform early European conceptions of Brazil as a barbarous, wild place. With tongue in cheek, the manifesto's author enthusiastically recuperates the concept. There was one sentence in English in the initial printing of this document, paraphrasing Hamlet with the substitution of the name of one of the cannibalistic tribes, the Tupy. This was the indigenous group whom the Portuguese first encountered on colonizing Brazil. Not everything written here makes perfect logical sense.

Only cannibalism unites us. Socially. Economically. Philosophically.

The world's only law. The disguised expression of all individualisms, of all collectivisms. Of all religions. Of all peace treaties.

Tupy or not Tupy, that is the question.

Down with all catechisms. And down with the mother of the Gracchi.

The only things that interest me are those that are not mine. The laws of men. The laws of the anthropophagites.

We are tired of all the dramatic suspicious Catholic husbands. Freud put an end to the enigma of woman and to other frights of printed psychology.

Truth was hindered by clothing, that waterproofing separating the interior from the exterior world. The reaction against the dressed man. The American cinema will show you.

Children of the sun, the mother of mortals. Found and loved ferociously, with all the hypocrisy of nostalgia, by the immigrants, slaves, and tourists. In the country of the Great Serpent.

It was because we never had grammar books, nor collections of old plants. And we never knew what urban, suburban, frontiers, and continents were. We were a lazy spot on the map of Brazil.

A participating consciousness, a religious rhythm.

Down with all the importers of the canned conscience. The palpable existence of life. The pre-logical mentality for [anthropologist] Mr. Lévy-Bruhl to study.

We want the Carahiba revolution. Bigger than the French Revolution. The unification of all successful rebellions led by man. Without us, Europe would not even have its meager Declaration of the Rights of Man.

The golden age proclaimed by America. The golden age and all the girls.

Descent. Contact with Carahiban Brazil. *Où Villeganhon print terre.* Montaigne. Natural man. Rousseau. From the French Revolution to Romanticism, to the Bolshevik Revolution, to the surrealist revolution and the technical barbarity of Keyserling. We continue down our path.

We were never catechized. We sustained ourselves through sleepy laws. We made Christ be born in Bahia. Or in Belém, in Pará.

But we never let the concept of logic be born among us.

———◦———

The spirit refused to conceive of the idea of spirit without body. Anthropomorphism. The need for an anthropophagical vaccine. We are for balance, against religions of the meridian. And foreign inquisitions.

We can only pay heed to an oracular world.

Our justice became a code of vengeance, and Science was transformed into magic. Anthropophagy. The permanent transformation of taboo into totem.

Down with the reversible world and objective ideas. Deadened ideas. The prohibition of dynamic thought. The individual as victim of the system. The source of classic injustices. Of romantic injustices. And the forgetting of interior conquests.

Routes. Routes. Routes. Routes. Routes. Routes. Routes.

The Carahiban instinct.

The life and death of hypotheses. From the equation, "me as part of the Cosmos," to the axiom, "the Cosmos as part of me." Subsistence. Knowledge. Anthropophagy.

———◦———

We were never catechized. Instead we invented the *Mardi gras*. The Indian dressed as a Senator of the Empire. Pretending to be William Pitt. Or appearing in Alencar's operas, full of good Portuguese feelings.

We already had communism. We already had surrealist language. The golden age.

Catiti Catiti

Imara Natiá

Notiá Imara

Ipejú

Magic and life. We already had the relation and the distribution of physical goods, moral goods, and the goods of dignity. And we knew how to transpose mystery and death with the help of a few grammatical forms.

I asked a man what Law was. He told me it was the guarantee to exercise the possible. That man was called Gibberish. I devoured him.

———◦———

Determining progress by catalogs and television sets. They are only machines. And the blood transfusers.

Down with the antagonistic sublimations. Imported in sailing ships. Down with the truth of missionary peoples, defined by the wisdom of a cannibal, the Viscount of Cairú: —A lie repeated many times.

But they who came were not crusaders. They were fugitives from a civilization that we are now devouring, because we are strong and vengeful just like the tortoise Jaboty.

If God is the conscience of the Uncreated Universe, Guaracy is the mother of living beings. Jacy is the mother of all plants.

We did not speculate. But we had the power to guess. We had Politics, which is the science of distribution. And a planetary social system.

The migrations. The flight from boring states. Down with urban sclerosis. Down with the Conservatories and tedious speculation.

From William James to Voronoff. The transformation of taboo in totem. Anthropophagy.

The *pater familias* and the creation of the Stork Fable: real ignorance of things + lack of imagination + attitude of authority toward the curious offspring.

It is necessary to start with a profound atheism in order to arrive at the idea of God. But the Carahiba did not need one. Because they had Guaracy.

The created object reacts like the Fallen Angel. After that, Moses wanders. What has this got to do with us?

Before the Portuguese discovered Brazil, Brazil had discovered happiness.

Down with the Indian on the candlestick. The Indian son of Mary, godson of Catherine de Medici and son-in-law of Sir Antônio de Mariz.

Happiness is the proof of the pudding.

———

Down with Goethe, the mother of the Gracchi, and the court of João VI.

Happiness is the proof of the pudding.

———

Anthropophagy. Absorption of the sacred enemy. In order to transform him into totem. The human adventure. The mundane finality. However, only the purest of elites managed to become anthropophagous in the flesh and thus ascended to the highest sense of life, avoiding all the evils identified by Freud, catechist evils. What happens is not a sublimation of sexual instincts. It's the thermometric scale of the cannibalist instinct. Moving from carnal to will-ful, and creating friendship. Affective, love. Speculative, science. Deviation and transference. And then vilification. The low anthropophagousness in the sins of the catechism—envy, usury, calumny, murder. Plague of the so-called cultured Christianized peoples, against these we are acting. Anthropophagi.

———

Our independence has not yet been proclaimed. A typical phrase of João VI: "My son, put this crown on your head before some adventurer puts it on his!" We expelled the dynasty. We must expel the spirit of Bragança, the laws, and the snuff of Maria da Fonte.

Down with social reality, dressed and oppressive, registered by Freud— reality without complexes, without madness, without prostitution and with-out the prisons of the matriarchy of Pindorama.

PIRATININGA
The year 374 after the
swallowing of the
Bishop of Sardinia.

Manifesto of *Martin Fierro*

Oliverio Girondo

———◆———

From *Martin Fierro*, May 1924, 1–2.

This manifesto urges the severing of all umbilical cords connected with Europe, but—with its praise for Swedish toothpaste, French towels, and Hispano-Suiza luxury cars—it also shows a lower level of nationalism than do the Brazilian manifestos. The seemingly racist reference to "blacks" in the closing sentences is a slang term that also means "dolts"; it is also a term of affection in Argentina among close friends or married people. Preserving the word as "black" preserves the contrast between dolts and vanguardists (whites). The magazine in which this essay first appeared was the leading forum for avant-garde ideas in both art and literature in Buenos Aires in the middle and late 1920s.

Faced with the pachydermal impermeability of the "honorable public";
Faced with the funereal solemnity of the historian and the professor, who mummify all that they touch;
Faced with the cookbook that inspires the discourses of our "finest" minds and the devotion to anachronism and mimeticism that they show;
Faced with the ridiculous necessity to bolster our intellectual nationalism, swelling up false values that pop at the first prick like balloons;
Faced with the widespread inability to contemplate life without first climbing the library shelves;
And above all, faced with the terrifying fear of making a mistake that paralyzes the very impetus of youth and which is more paralyzed than any retired bureaucrat:
Martin Fierro feels the urgent need to define itself, and to call out to whoever is able to see that we find ourselves in the presence of a new sensibility and a new understanding, which, if we align ourselves with it, can lead us to unexpected horizons, new media, and new forms of expression.
Martin Fierro accepts the consequences and responsibilities of locating itself,

because it knows that its health depends on this. Informed by its ancestors, its anatomy, and the meridian on which it walks, it consults the barometer and the calendar before going out to the street to live and feel with today's nerves and mind.

Martin Fierro knows that "everything is new under the sun" if seen with refreshed eyes and described with a contemporary accent.

Martin Fierro therefore finds itself more at home on a modern transatlantic liner than in a Renaissance palace; it maintains that a good Hispano-Suiza is a much more perfect work of art than a sedan chair from the age of Louis XV.

Martin Fierro sees architectural possibility in an Innovation brand steamer trunk, a logic lesson in a telegram, a form of mental organization in a rotary press. Yet this does not keep us from possessing, as in the best families, a portrait album that it leafs through from time to time in order to find itself among its ancestors . . . or to laugh at their collars and ties.

Martin Fierro believes in the importance of the intellectual contribution of Latin America, after snipping off all umbilical cords. We support and spread to other fields of endeavor the linguistic independence movement that Rubén Darío initiated. Yet this does not imply that we are unaware that we still use every morning our Swedish toothpaste, French towels, and English soap.

Martin Fierro has faith in our phonetics, in our way of seeing, in our habits, in our own ears, in our own ability to digest and assimilate.

Martin Fierro as artist rubs its eyes every moment in order to wipe away the cobwebs constantly tangling around them: habit and custom. Let us give to each new love a new virginity! And let today's excesses be different from those of yesterday or tomorrow! This is truly saintly creativity! There are so few saints!

Martin Fierro, as critic, knows that a locomotive is not comparable to an apple, and the fact that everyone compares a locomotive to an apple and that some choose the locomotive, others the apple, proves for us the suspicion that there are far more blacks out there than one might think. Only blacks cry out "Fabulous!" and think that they have said it all. Only blacks need to be dazzled by whatever sparkles, and are not satisfied if they are not dazzled by whatever sparkles. Only blacks have their palms flattened out like scales so that they weigh everything, and judge it by its weight. There are so many blacks!

Martin Fierro only has appreciation for the blacks and whites who really are blacks and whites and have no intention of changing their color.

Do you agree with *Martin Fierro*?

Collaborate with *Martin Fierro*!

Subscribe to *Martin Fierro*!

The Great Serpent

Xul Solar

———◈———

From Alejandro Schulz, "Cuentos del Amazonas, de los Mosetenes y Guaruyús. Primeras historias que se oyeron en este Continente," *Crítica. Revista Multicolor*, August 19, 1933, 4.

Xul Solar was an avid collector of folktales, many of which inspired his paintings. This story is one possible source for his many works that include a large serpent with arrows. Xul alleged that it came from an anthropologist in north central Bolivia who carried out interviews among the Mosetenes in that region. Xul published the story under a pseudonym in a Buenos Aires magazine edited by his friend Jorge Luis Borges.

Once upon a time, a man and a woman wanted to domesticate an animal. They went into the rainforest but could find none. Finally, upon reaching a field, they found a worm named Ñoko, lying on a leaf.

"Let's take him back to our home and raise him," they said.

So they took the worm into their home and laid him on a saucer covered with dirt.

Soon it was time to feed him. They tried a banana but the worm did not like it. But the worm grew so much that they had to move him onto a plate. They tried to feed him with nearly everything, but he did not want to eat.

One day the man killed a bird. Ñoko did not want to eat it, but the man gave Ñoko the bird's heart, and he ate it.

Now they knew what the worm would eat. The man killed birds every day, and gave Ñoko the hearts. He grew so much that they had to make him a large serving dish to sit on. The man killed all kinds of animals: birds, wild boars, tapirs. The worm ate only their hearts. He grew so much that they had to set aside a large ceramic jug for him. The man killed as many animals as he could every day, and the worm, now grown as big as a serpent, still ate only the hearts. He grew still more, so that no vessel could hold him, and they put him in the dirt outside their hut.

Ñoko ate continuously, while growing and growing. The man kept hunting, but soon there were no more animals. The man began hunting people, and gave their hearts to the serpent. The man killed them with a spear as thick as a man's hand. Finally, he had killed all the people who lived in that region.

He went to a large village nearby, and there killed many people, giving their hearts to Ñoko. Everyone in the village wondered what could kill so many people; it could not be a jaguar. One day the man went back to the village to kill some more people. Before a hut was a little girl. The man killed the girl with his spear, and removed her heart. Her brother, seeing what was happening from inside the hut, made himself an arrow, leapt outside, and killed the man. The other men of the village came, and they took the man to the village square and shot him full of arrows.

After a few days, when the man did not return home, his wife began to worry. Ñoko was getting hungry. She wondered what could have happened to her husband, and she told the serpent that she was leaving in search of him.

At first, Ñoko did not move. But soon he began to raise himself. He raised his head high enough to stretch all the way up to the sky. When his head was in the clouds, his tail was still on the ground. He began to rise up at daybreak, and stretched himself until noon. Ñoko looked around, and saw the man in the village square, pierced with many arrows.

Ñoko then set out for the village. First he changed himself into several serpents of various colors. When one of the serpents entered a house, the village men would kill it, but soon another serpent of a different color came. Finally, Ñoko laid himself down, surrounding the village, so that no one could leave. The men shot the serpent full of arrows.

But Ñoko kept growing and growing, so that he grew larger than the entire village, and he crushed all the people in it. Then the serpent changed into a man, gave birth to another man, and between them they ate all the hearts of the people.

Ñoko is now the Milky Way.

Piano solos [by Guiomar Novaes]: "In the Old Seraglio Garden" by E. R. Blanchet; "The Little Pierrot's Pony" by Villa-Lobos; "Evening in Granada" and "Minstrels" by Claude Debussy.

Lecture by Mário de Andrade in the Atrium: "The Slave Isaura Who is Not a Slave"

Reading by Renato Almeida: "Perennial Poetry"

Three Songs by Villa-Lobos: "Pagan Festival," "Solitude," "The Rattlesnake"

String Quartet no. 3 by Villa-Lobos

III. Friday, February 17

Music of Villa-Lobos: Trio No. 3 for Strings; songs based on "Tales" by Ronald de Carvalho; Sonata No. 2 for Violin and Piano; Piano Solos: "Song of the Peasant Woman," "The Enchanted Cradle," "Infernal Dance"; "Symbolic Quartet (Impressions of Everyday Life)" for three instruments and chorus

Manifesto of the Grupo Minorista, Havana, May 7, 1927

From *Carteles*, May 22, 1927, 16.

Cuban artists began to paint in modern styles later than they did Brazil or Argentina, but modern currents of thought broke out in all these places at nearly the same time in the 1920s. The Minorista group manifesto was more broadly based than other manifestos, as it was signed by thirty-four poets, anthropologists, musicians, journalists, and even scientists. In the artistic realm, the alliance of vanguardism with political protest was also stronger in Cuba than in Brazil or Argentina. The roots of the Minorista group lie in 1923 protests against the purchase by the government of the secularized Convent of Santa Clara at a too-high price that favored the property developers who owned it. The chief tenet of this manifesto that interested painters was the call to focus on both new art and popular Cuban art.

In response to a certain statement by a local journalist and essayist, Mr. Lamar Schweyer, to the effect that the Grupo Minorista (Minority Group) does not exist, the undersigned, who consider themselves to be members of the said group, now deem it necessary to correct, once and for all, the misconception under which certain people, among them Mr. Lamar, are laboring.

What is the Grupo Minorista, how was it born, who belongs to it? Some years ago, on March 18, 1923, to be exact, a small number of intellectuals, artists, journalists, and lawyers happened to be present at the Academy of Sciences and carried out an act of protest and censure against the then Minister of Justice who was also present. They expressed the general public's repudiation of the government's infamous purchase of the Convent of Santa Clara contrary to the wishes of the majority of the population.

That action set a destructive yet apolitical pattern of behavior for young people interested in participating honorably in civic life, and provided Cuban intellectuals with a template for social protest and revolutionary activity.

This nucleus of protesters used to meet regularly to assess material and books for a proposed anthology of modern Cuban poetry, so a link was forged between artistic collaboration and civic, even legal, responsibility.

They immediately tried to organize and expand the group, and proposed the creation of the so-called Group for Cuban Action. This organization did not prove effective, but almost all its adherents, together with a broader spectrum of dedicated sympathizers, joined the ranks of the association known as the Veterans and Patriots, which was planning an armed movement against administrative corruption and government incompetence.

What was this symptomatic of? Why these frequent unofficial and spontaneous gatherings of usually the same people, almost all young, almost all connected with the arts? Why did the group's conversation revolve around mocking false values, jingoistic hucksters, incompetents in high places, and official "geniuses"? Why did they criticize ignorance of Cuba's problems, the government's subjugation to foreign demands, electoral farces, and the sheeplike passivity of the average citizen? This proved that there was rising a left-wing intellectual group in Cuba, not a legally constituted body, but an increasingly important group of people with identical ideals and a growing public profile, and a natural product of its environment. It was a historical factor fully determined by the social function it would fulfill.

The fact that some members of the group met for lunch in a restaurant every Saturday explains why friends who were not actually comrades sat with them, and that is how the confusion arose which mistook the so-called Minority Group for a mere casual and diverse gathering with no particular schedule or special purpose of its own.

Thus, the Minority Group is a group without rules, without a president, a secretary, or a monthly membership fee; in fact, without symbols of any kind. But this is precisely the most viable type of organization for a group of intellectuals. What has failed so many times in the past is the regimentation of similar groups in which the imposition of a single norm is all-important. The Minority Group does not have the drawbacks of a formal, external, and procedural structure.

As the experience of other countries has shown, there is an undeniably new ideology and a shift leftward in such groups. The Minority Group knows that it is a group of intellectual workers: authors, painters, musicians, sculptors, etc. Its name, given it by one of its adherents, refers to its small number of operative members, but in reality it is a majority group because it is the effective voice, the platform, and the reflection of the majority of the population. It is only really a minority as far as its artistic judgments are concerned.

In the course of the year, the group has interpreted and reflected Cuban public opinion by protesting against the invasion of Nicaragua, against Washington's policy on Mexico, and against the ransacking by police of both the offices and the house of [former vice president and professor] Enrique José Varona. It in no way detracts from the group's unity and purpose if people who are not members of the core group sometimes appear at our demonstrations and sign our manifestos.

Collectively or individually, our nucleus has fought and is still fighting:

For the revision of false and outmoded values;

For popular art and, in general, new art in all its diverse forms;

For the introduction and spread in Cuba of the latest artistic and scientific doctrines, theories, and practices;

For the reform of public education. Against the corrupt system of University appointments. For University autonomy;

For Cuban economic independence and against Yankee imperialism.

Against political dictatorships anywhere in the world, in the Americas, or in Cuba;

Against the scandals of our pseudo-democracy, against electoral farce, and for the people's effective participation in government;

For improved conditions for the farmer, the peasant, and the worker in Cuba;

For the friendship and unity of Latin American nations.

Criollismo and Its Visual Interpretation

Carlos Enríquez

———❦———

From *Grafos*, December 1935, 16.

Carlos Enríquez did not sign the Minorista Manifesto—he was in New York City at the time—but his painting embodied many of its propositions. He embraced certain techniques of surrealism to aid in capturing typical Cuban subjects. In the Cuban context, "criollismo" means whatever is traditionally Cuban, apart from modern, cosmopolitan influences. The life and myths of the guajiro, *or rural dweller, interest him the most.*

The interpretation of Cuban reality in visual terms must necessarily be either objective or subjective. The various techniques, styles, and schools of art do not capture the essence of things, but only their own techniques. Within the subjective realm of interpretation, we find all the feeling that the artist has experienced, either in the culture or in the subtlest details of the landscape. He feels them not as an objective reality but rather as a spiritual essence that has played an important role in the evolution of his life.

Let us assert, then, that an objective transcription lacks value as interpretation. Any half-brained bureaucrat who is able to read gas meters could style himself a painter and acquire—why not say it?—a visual language. But he will never, I assert, capture the spirit, that marvelous force that escapes the casual onlooker, but that artists feel intimately because it is part of their emotional makeup.

It is true that a foreign-born artist could paint Cuban subjects; a tourist might think it sufficient to merely snap the shutter on his camera in order to later awe his compatriots. And even a Cuban artist, after receiving one of those long-term travel grants that the State gives, returning after his years spent abroad, may think his palette adequate to happily come to terms with what is ours. But it finally will be obvious that his position is untenable because he lacks the sensitivity necessary to realize his goal. In such cases the painter will capture a graphical or mechanical representation of the subjects, their exteriors, or their objective aspects. For us, on the other hand, what is essential is to sense the environment, submerge ourselves in it, and then express in an eloquent and sincere manner the inner realities that come to mind, just as the *guajiros* in Sunday dress come to town.

Creativity and imagination are the natural gifts of an artist, and they cannot be supplanted by pure technique. Technique is secondary in the process of artistic creation; it is the only way to realize a work, but it is neither the beginning nor the end of a work. We can be sure that if a painter faces a canvas motivated only by technical preoccupations, he will do everything except create a serious work of art. The painter must be more than a trained seal or a circus horse that surprises with its abilities the enthralled spectators at a provincial circus.

The question of Cuban art can be viewed from two angles: the "habanera" [Havana] side, and the rest of the island. The latter includes village, rural, and woodland life, and is saturated with myths and fantastic legends, spirit appearances, river gods, weeping women, and "voodoo." The habanera version, on the other hand, includes a mixture of cosmopolitan and folkloric elements, uprooted, hybridized, and without national relevance.

The artistic essence of nearly everything is found in its primitive aspects. In my trips through the interior of Cuba, I have found curious missing links to previous Cuban expression, today largely forgotten, which harken back to the heroic days of [bandit] Manuel García and [poet Juan Cristóbal] Cucalambé. The simple *guajiros* rightly say, "From the Little War to the Great Storm, no one has planted yucca around here." To find the people's culture, it is necessary to travel in the backlands of Cuba. It is a difficult search, if we recall that English is spoken in the sugar fields, and the workers can repeat from memory their geography lessons. I admit my attraction for rural life. I know from my childhood the regions of Guaracabuya, Pirindingo, Mayajigua, and Casimbas. In me, the Jungian collective unconscious completes itself.

Havana scorns the vernacular; observe how our sextets now play sentimental tangos of the Argentine slums, while they have traded the maracas, the güiro, and the bongo for instruments to use in playing the foxtrot. Paintings by the professors at the San Alejandro Academy resemble academic works from other countries. Our national literature wears a top hat, having traded our cool and wide straw *sombrero* for Italian felt. This does not mean that Havana lacks interesting subjects. I believe it has a great many of them, but they must be carefully selected and stripped of all fictitious and phony overlays before you can see them. We must do the same sort of work in the countryside, where we will intuit more than we actually see what remains pure, protected from all cosmopolitan influence by a blessed and healthful isolation.

PART THREE

Politically Committed Muralism and Indigenism

Manifesto of the Union of Mexican Workers, Technicians, Painters, and Sculptors

David Siqueiros

From *El machete* (Mexico City), June 15, 1924.

This manifesto reflects a Marxist version of the role of art in society, rooted in contemporary events. As the 1924 general elections approached, President Álvaro Obregón encouraged voters to choose Plutarco Elías Calles as his successor. This spurred a group of rightist generals led by Enrique Estrada and Guadalupe Sánchez to rise in revolt, as they promoted their own candidate in Adolfo de la Huerta. This document ties the ideology of the Mexican mural program to that political struggle, which was resolved in March 1924 with the exile of all three coup leaders. All of the principal Mexican mural painters signed it.

To the Indian race humiliated for centuries; to soldiers made into executioners by the generals; to workers and peasants lashed by the greed of the rich; to intellectuals still uncorrupted by the bourgeoisie.

COMRADES:
The military coup of Enrique Estrada and Guadalupe Sánchez (the most significant enemies of the aspirations of Mexican peasants and workers) has been of transcendental importance in defining and clarifying the situation in our country. This, aside from a few details of a purely political nature, stands as follows:

On the one hand the social revolution, ideologically better organized than ever, and on the other the armed upper classes. Soldiers of the people, peasants, and armed workers defending their rights, against soldiers dragged by deceit or force by the politico-military leaders who have sold out to the bourgeoisie.

On their side, the exploiters of the people, shacked up with the traitors who sell the blood of soldiers who fought in the Revolution.

On our side, those who demand the end of an antiquated and cruel order—an order in which you, the peasants on the land, fertilize the soil so that its harvest can be swallowed up by the rapacity of profiteers and politicians while you starve; in which you, the workers in the city, operate the factories, weave the cloth, and produce with your own hands the modern comforts that service prostitutes and layabouts while your skin shrivels in the cold; in which you, the Indian soldier, in a heroic selfless act, leave the land you till and give your life to fight the poverty that your race and class has endured for centuries, only for a Sánchez or an Estrada to take advantage of the generous gift of your blood by favoring the bourgeois leeches who suck away your children's happiness and rob you of your land and your work.

Not only is all labor good; all that is virtuous is a gift from our people, especially our Indians: Every manifestation of the physical and spiritual existence of our race as an ethnic force springs from them; moreover, so does the extraordinary and marvelous ability to create beauty. The art of the Mexican people is the greatest and most vital spiritual manifestation in the world, and its Indian tradition is the best of these. It is great precisely because it is of the people and it is collective. That is why our primary aesthetic objective is to socialize artistic creation, in an effort to destroy all traces of bourgeois individualism. We reject so-called easel painting, and all the ultraintellectual salon art of the aristocracy. We exalt all manifestations of public art because they are useful to the people. We believe that any work of art that is alien or contrary to popular taste is bourgeois and should disappear, because it perverts the aesthetic of our race. This perversion is already almost complete in the cities.

We proclaim that because our society is in a transitional stage between the destruction of an old order and the foundation of a new order, the creators of beauty must struggle to make their labor into clear ideological propaganda in favor of the people. This will make art, which at present is mere individualist masturbation, into something of beauty, education, and commitment for everyone.

We are all too aware that the advent of a bourgeois government in Mexico will mean the corruption of our race's popular indigenous aesthetic, which at present is found only in the lower classes but which was, however, beginning to penetrate and purify intellectual circles. We will fight to prevent this coup from happening, because we are sure that victory for the working

classes will bring a harmonious flowering of ethnic art of cosmic and historical significance to our race, comparable to that of our admirable ancient
native civilizations. We will fight tirelessly to bring this about.

Victory for de la Huerta, Estrada, and Sánchez will be, in aesthetic and
social terms, a victory for typists' taste; a victory for the all-corrupting criollo
and bourgeois approval of popular music, painting, and literature; the reign
of the "picturesque," the North American "kewpie doll," and the official
establishment of "l'amore e come zucchero." Love is like sugar.

As a result, the counterrevolution in Mexico will prolong the pain of the
people and crush their admirable spirit.

The members of the Painters' and Sculptors' Union have for a long time
supported the candidacy of General Plutarco Elías Calles because we believe
that his decidedly revolutionary fervor, more than that of any other, will
guarantee a government that will improve conditions for the working classes
in Mexico. We reiterate our support in the light of the latest politico-military
events and put ourselves in the service of his cause, which is the cause of the
people, in whatever way he may need it.

We now issue a general appeal to revolutionary intellectuals in Mexico to
forget their proverbial centuries-old sentimentality and laziness, and join us
in the social, aesthetic, and educational battle we are waging.

In the name of all the blood shed by our people during ten years of revolution, with the threat of a reactionary coup hanging over us, we urgently
appeal to all revolutionary peasants, workers, and soldiers in Mexico to
understand the vital importance of the impending battle and, forgetting our
tactical differences, form a united front to combat our common enemy.

We urge all ordinary soldiers of the people who, unaware of recent events
or deceived by their traitorous officers, are about to shed the blood of their
brothers in race and class: Remember that the deceivers will use your own
weapons to steal the land and livelihood from your brothers, which those
same weapons gained through revolutionary struggle.

The Revolution in Painting

Diego Rivera

———

From *Creative Art*, January 1929, 27–30.

This essay catches Diego Rivera at a good moment: before he came to the United States and became a celebrity embroiled in art controversies. As he wrote this, he was working feverishly on murals at both the Secretariat of Education in Mexico City and the agricultural school at Chapingo, works that some critics believe to be among the best he ever created. The basic point of this essay is the Marxist one that every type of art serves some class interest or other, and that by choosing a style or a subject, an artist necessarily takes sides in the churning economic struggles of the day. Rivera made his choice, and apparently found it deeply energizing for his creativity.

It would have been very easy for me, twelve years ago, to write several thousand words on the subject of my own painting. If anyone had asked me then, as *Creative Art* does today, to write 1,700 words, I would have felt it too little to express everything that I believed it essential to proclaim. I remember that Marius de Zayas often made a similar request to me and that at that time I filled a good many pages in my own handwriting. Today I can hardly remember the words I wrote. But since then I have worked a great deal, and, to tell the truth, today I do not know exactly what to say about my own art. Seven years ago I returned to Mexico, but during the preceding ten years I had gorged myself with the works of all the masters. Little by little I found that, as far as I was concerned, certain laws presented themselves in all their works. I achieved my work guided by my own intuition and relying on my knowledge of certain elemental qualities of form and color necessary to the craft of painting.

During that time I could have delivered lengthy disquisitions on the esthetic problem of my own work, but today I can no longer do so. Everything that appeared to me then upon a theoretic plane now comes to me as familiarly as a ruler, a t-square, and an angle come to a carpenter.

But the carpenter does not believe he makes chairs and tables in order to learn the nature of his compass and his angle, nor to demonstrate why a graduated circle exists for measuring angles. On the contrary, he understands these utensils thoroughly, but knows how to use them, and he does use them to make chairs which can be useful for men to sit upon around tables where they take their meals or play at a game of cards.

For a long time I have observed that the more useful a work of art is, the more humble, the more beautiful and pure it becomes, as for example the wooden figurines of Egypt, Tanagra statuettes, and the sculpture of Negroes and Mexicans. But in spite of all the good will in the world I was not able to find enough prowess to achieve painting that was truly humble. I now realize that this was because I worked too little and because I believed too blindly in all the words which one writes down in capital letters: Pure Art, Pure Lyricism, Pure Poetry, and so forth.

It was first necessary for me to work night and day in order to arrive at a point where I could honestly call myself a workman. Only then did I attain the right to make my work itself serve the interests of my class with enough of the joy and the ardor that are capable of attainment only when one is defending not just one's self but one's own self multiplied by an equal number of all of one's comrades, of the workers as a mass. If I try to speak of my painting, I do not know how to do it unless I speak of the life of those comrades of mine. And I feel also that to speak of that life as the cause of my art is almost despicable. I find my only justification in painting. Probably that is why I have been able during the last seven years to paint buoyantly, without fatigue, fifty easel pictures, any number of drawings, a quantity of watercolors, and 150 mural paintings in fresco.

A few years ago, before the Great War, I often discussed the role which art would assume once the power of the State was in the hands of the working class. After the Mexican Revolution, my revolutionary confrères—then living in Paris—thought that if they gave modern art of the highest quality to the masses this art would immediately become popular through its instant acceptance by the proletariat. I was never able to share this point of view, because I always knew that the physical senses are susceptible not only to education and development, but to atrophy and desuetude; and also that the "esthetic sense" can only be reached through the physical senses themselves. I had also observed the indubitable fact that among the proletariat—exploited and oppressed by the bourgeoisie—the workman, ever burdened with his daily labor, could cultivate his taste only in contact with the worst and vilest portion of bourgeois art which reached him in cheap chromos and the illustrated papers. And this bad taste in turn stamps all of the industrial production which his salary commands—public expositions being difficult of access for him because he is at work day in and day out.

Popular art produced by the people for the people has been almost wiped out by this kind of industrial production of the worst esthetic quality throughout the world. And I also believed that a popular peasant art could not achieve an effective substitute in modern industrial production of fabrics, utensils, illustrated books, and so forth.

It was therefore evident to me that the proletarian stomach was not ready to assimilate, nor even to receive—as a form of nourishment too refined in quality and also somewhat gamey—the bourgeoisie's artistic esthetic menu. If one tried to give the proletarian too much of it, he would simply be sick to his stomach, and the attempt would provoke a reaction in the popular taste towards the direction of academic art subjects that might happen to interest it. Unfortunately, this has been confirmed by the experience of Soviet Russia. The magnificent results obtained in their other activities as opposed to the field of plastic art, confirm this tendency which I had foreseen since 1913. Is such a disaster the fault of the proletariat? Certainly not! It is the problem of the revolutionary artists to be capable of furnishing a fitting form of esthetic nourishment, and this is of great importance because in order to direct public taste and the popular consumption of esthetic goods, there is only taste to guide our choice. Taste therefore becomes the extremely important economic factor.

Only the work of art itself can raise the standard of taste. Art has always been employed by the different social classes who hold the balance of power as one instrument of domination.—Hence, as a political instrument. One can analyze epoch after epoch—from the stone age to our own day—and see that there is no form of art which does not also play an essential political role. For that reason, whenever a people have revolted in search of their fundamental rights, they have always produced revolutionary artists: Giotto and his pupils, Grünewald, Bosch, Breughel the Elder, Michelangelo, Rembrandt, Tintoretto, Callot, Chardin, Goya, Courbet, Daumier, the Mexican engraver Posada, and numerous other masters. What is it then that we really need? An art extremely pure, precise, profoundly human, and clarified as to its purpose.

An art with revolution as its subject: because the principal interest in the worker's life has to be touched first. It is necessary that he find esthetic satisfaction and the highest pleasure, appareled in the essential interest of his life.

I have therefore arrived at the clearest and firmest conviction that it is necessary to create that kind of art. Is it necessary therefore to discard all our ultra-modern technical means, necessary to deny the classic tradition of our *métier*? Not at all. It would have been as foolish to believe that in order to construct a grain elevator [or] a bridge, or to install a communal cooperative, one should not use the materials and methods of construction achieved by the industrial technique of the bourgeoisie. It is on the contrary the duty of the revolutionary artist to employ his ultra-modern technique and to allow his classic education (if he had one) to affect him subconsciously. And there is absolutely no reason to be frightened because the subject is so essential. On the contrary, precisely because the subject is admitted as a prime necessity, the artist is absolutely free to create a thoroughly plastic form of art. The subject is to the painter what the rails are to a locomotive. He cannot do without it. In fact, when he refuses to seek or accept a subject, his own plastic methods and his own esthetic theories become his subject instead. And even if he escapes them, he himself becomes the subject of his work. He becomes nothing but an illustrator of his own state of mind, and in trying to liberate himself he falls into the worst form of slavery. That is the cause of all the boredom which emanates from so many of the large expositions of modern art, a fact testified to again and again by the most different temperaments. That is the deception practiced under the name of "Pure Art," two new resounding words which attest to nothing more in the work of talented men.

Lyricism and also "pure lyricism" is no less than any other form of art a form of social expression, because it corresponds to the preoccupations of a certain class who as a class are more interested in the individual man than in the collective interests of the mass—typical, that is, of the upper bourgeoisie, and the small intellectually bourgeois minority. The proletariat, in the midst of its struggle to unseat the dictatorship of the capitalist classes, cannot accept either pure lyricism or pure art as anything relevant to its life. On the contrary, it needs an epic form of art to aid its organization and express its struggle in social reconstruction. If bourgeois individualism seeks more and more profoundly the "I" in its egoistic quintessence, the proletariat needs an expression of the beauty of the masses. It needs great surfaces of walls, masculine and simple methods of fresco and encaustic, effective in public buildings or places where men congregate to deliberate, and at the same time to enjoy art.

I searched my soul profoundly in order to see if I had the necessary qualities to attempt that kind of artistic expression in proof of my convictions, and I found that instead of possessing merely a certain amount of residue left from my previous habits and point of view, I had attained sufficient strength to be a workman among other workmen. I chose my subject: the same subject that would have been chosen by any other Mexican workman fighting for class justice. I saw with a fresh eye the beauty of Mexico, and since then I have worked as indefatigably as I have been able. I believe that this experience of mine, realized in Mexico, under extremely unfavorable conditions, may be significant to artists everywhere.

The Syndicate of Painters and Sculptors

José Clemente Orozco

From José Clemente Orozco, *Autobiografía* (Mexico City: Occidente, 1945), 89–96.
All quote marks and ellipses retained from the original.

Orozco never fully subscribed to the leftism of his fellow muralists. Here, in autobiographical reminiscences written years later, he describes his discrepancies in sometimes drily ironic terms. There is a chronological error in his mentioning of the anarchist Abelardo Saavedra del Toro, who died years after the Syndicate was founded, but the rest of this excerpt reads very well.

One of the most curious manifestations of the painters' critical attitudes was the organization of the "Syndicate of Painters and Sculptors," whose ideas congealed into a very important "Manifesto." From this document came the influence which has been both felt for decades and fruitlessly resisted by younger artists.

The Syndicate in itself had no real importance, because it was not a group of laborers defending itself against an oppressive boss, but still the name served as a symbol for the ideas that were gestating, based on contemporary socialist theories, about which Siqueiros, Rivera, and Xavier Guerrero were the most knowledgeable.

Siqueiros put together, and we all accepted and signed, the Syndicate's manifesto, which was aimed at "The soldiers, workers, peasants, and intellectuals who were not in the service of the bourgeoisie." To summarize, it made the following proposals:

- Socializing art.
- Destroying bourgeois individualism.
- Repudiating easel painting and any other art form that emerges from aristocratic or ultraintellectual circles.
- To produce only monumental works for public viewing.

- Because this historical moment was a transition between a decrepit age and a new era, to create an art of value for the people, rather than catering to individual pleasure.
- To produce beauty that both emerges from the struggle and encourages it.

These proposals were amended somewhat for the final document, but not in their basic meaning.

Siqueiros had gathered these radical ideas in Europe. As a military attaché to the Mexican consulate in Barcelona, he gave a subversive lecture at the funeral of the Mexican anarchist [Abelardo Saavedra] del Toro, who had been killed by the police [in 1938]. Siqueiros was expelled to Argenteuil, France, where he attended communist workers' meetings. There he absorbed the ideas contained in the Manifesto, and when he returned to Mexico in 1922, invited by [Secretary of Education José] Vasconcelos, he already had in mind a plan for revolutionary art, which he proposed to us.

Naturally, the socialization of art was a very long-term goal, which could not be realized unless the underlying social structure also changed radically. Moreover, we needed to define more precisely the meaning of the word "socialize" in relation to art, because it was subject to many varied interpretations.

The repudiation of easel painting never really happened. We saw that it was not reasonable, because easel painting is not in itself opposed to mural painting; rather, it is only a different medium, and it could be just as useful for the people and the laborers as mural painting. We thus called it "portable painting," though it was still easel painting. But we considered that not only easel paintings but also small prints could be very useful in order to provide each working-class household with a work of art. We also saw that not all painters had equal abilities for mural painting; their talents might be better applied to the creation of small works.

Condemning all easel painting as aristocratic would be to condemn a large part of art from all periods. Works by Rembrandt, Titian, and El Greco, for example, would all have to be burnt.

By this path we arrived at the so-called "proletarian art," the true product of the Syndicate of Painters and Sculptors. Proletarian art consisted of the representation of workers at their tasks, and which we supposed would be created for the workers. But this was a mistake, because a worker who has spent eight hours on the job is not pleased to return home to find *Workers Laboring* in his house; rather, he might prefer to see something that has nothing to do with work, which thus might afford him some ease. The funniest fact was that this proletarian art was bought at very good prices by the bourgeoisie, against whom it was supposed to be aimed, while the workers, if they had enough money, eagerly bought bourgeois art. Those who lacked funds contented themselves with colorful calendars showing aristocratic women reclining elegantly on bearskins, or a very elegant gentleman kissing a countess by moonlight in a castle tower. Meanwhile, the homes of the bourgeoisie are filled with proletarian furniture and objects, such as mats, seats woven with rushes, earthenware jars, and tin candle holders. The workers, in contrast, if they had enough resources to furnish their homes, would buy "Pullman couches" lined with thick velvet, and stock their "breakfast rooms" with nickel-plated furniture, thick crystal glasses and beveled mirrors. The shoe factories of León and Guadalajara produce huge quantities of peasant shoes for the bourgeoisie of the United States, just as our servant girls are sighing for high-heeled shoes and silk stockings. Madero and Juárez Avenues are lined with shops selling proletarian objects. To find silk fabrics, one must go to the Lagunilla [open-air market]. The truth is that good taste is not innate, nor even determined by one's class or race. Only education can create, guide, or degrade it.

At the height of the Indigenist period, the Indian was identified as proletarian, ignoring the fact that not all Indians are proletarian, nor are all proletarians Indians. Still there arose the school of Indo-Proletarian painting, which was also born from the Syndicate. Most of these paintings went to the United States into the hands of white people. No Indians on either side of the border took the least interest in these paintings that supposedly exalted their race. In North America it was believed that Mexican painters were as immensely popular among the native masses as [agrarian revolutionary leader Emiliano] Zapata, while Zapata himself could be absolutely unknown among the indigenous people of [the provinces of] Durango or Quintana Roo.

The Manifesto also promised an art of struggle, to inspire the oppressed to work for their liberation. But this point is still too vague to allow a precise definition. When is a painting or sculpture truly able to provoke in viewers the mental processes that lead to revolutionary actions? When is art truly subversive? It is true that the Roman Catholic church has used all of the arts, especially painting and sculpture, to awaken faith and devotion; believers generally respond to the sight of a Crucifixion or a Virgin Mary. But it is also the case that in many Protestant churches and in mosques there are no images, yet the faith is still equally lively.

As to whether art can have a decisive revolutionary influence on a viewer, this is often influenced by unknowable circumstances, or by the mere occasion. It is not the same to hear "The Internationale" or the National Anthem sung by twenty thousand people in a public place while flags fly, as it is to hear it alone in one's home on a phonograph.

It is also worth remembering that the ridiculous and the sublime are often separated by a thread, and that many works, instead of evoking a shout of indignation or enthusiasm, often provoke only laughter.

The Manifesto laid much emphasis on the "content" of a work of art; that is to say, on the sum of ideas and feelings that it expresses. But this too is confusing, because this path leads to purely illustrative or descriptive painting, or to impersonal photographic documentation, or perhaps to literary painting that neglects questions of form to focus on storytelling or anecdote.

In regard to abolishing "bourgeois individualism," Siqueiros and Xavier Guerrero came up with the idea of teams: groups of painters who would work by common consent on a project, sharing the tasks according to the abilities of each, following a preconceived plan. Even before the teams came about, it was agreed that no Syndicate member would sign a mural painting, as they were supposed to be the product of a master and his helpers, with critical input from all the painters on the team. This idea failed, because no one wanted to keep to the plan.

Later, some teams did really function, but not often enough to demonstrate predictable results. It is possible that in certain cases, collective work is the best way to create a certain piece of painting or sculpture, and the result would be quite different from a work produced by an individual. But individual work cannot completely disappear, as the Manifesto intended that it should.

Another version of this idea holds that the artist should create while taking account of the collective taste, or of the society of which he is a member, and not merely to please one or a few individuals. But here, too, is confusion. Good art may indeed interest everyone, but unfortunately, bad art is equally interesting, and may be even more interesting to some. The world is filled to bursting with vulgarities, known and enjoyed by millions of people across the world. The worst movies stay longest in the theaters.

The question can be put another way: Should an artist's works be imposed on the public "by reason or by force," as the Chileans say? Or should the public impose on the artist its tastes and preferences? First we must determine which public we are talking about: which social class, which race, which age group, and what level of education. It would also be interesting to know if the public itself will dictate its taste to the artist, or if this will be done by the people's representatives. This begins to complicate things: Who represents the public? And how faithfully will they interpret the taste of the public? Before all else, one would have to figure out if the public even has a clearly defined taste.

Of course, the public does have such a taste: The majority very much enjoys sugar, honey, and caramel: diabetic art, in other words. The sweeter it is, the more successful it will be . . . commercially.

Religion, Revolution, and Painting

An Interview with Francisco Goitia

Anaya Sarmiento

———⚫———

From Anaya Sarmiento, "Entrevista con Francisco Goitia,"
Revista Mañana, July 27, 1957, 33–34.

As a staff artist in the army of Francisco "Pancho" Villa during the Mexican revolution, and later as a chronicler of indigenous culture in the region of Oaxaca, Francisco Goitia always lived a solitary life of voluntary poverty. This lifestyle, and his refusal to join the mural movement, delayed wide recognition of his powerful art. Here, in a brief interview granted a few years before his death, he explains some of his motivations.

Goitia: All of my work is religious. I look back to the Early Christian days for inspiration in the struggle. All of my paintings are influenced by religion. For me, even [Pancho] Villa is the armed scourge of Divine Providence who strengthens the arm of the chosen few, spreading great social movements. But I do not forget Villa the bandit and adventurer, or Villa the just and benevolent. These religious and secular thoughts motivate my art. It is difficult for an atheist to understand, but that is the fundamental difference between me and them.

Q: What do you think of the mural movement?

A: I cannot join the muralists because as presently constituted, the movement promulgates a socialism that I do not share.

Q: Are you a socialist?

A: I have always felt myself to be both a socialist and a communist, but also a Christian. That is, I practice a communism that is much more complete than that of the atheists. The atheist movement will take you to materialism, a doctrine that St. Francis of Assisi opposed. I try to follow the path of St. Francis, and I believe that my solitude is the culmination of that path.

Q: Do you express your ideology in your works?

A: Yes. I consider my work to be essentially Christian because it is concerned above all with the soul. [Archaeologist Manuel] Gamio commissioned me to paint the Mexican people in their exterior, physical appearance, but I presented him with work that also included the religious aspect. Therefore it was a more complete work of art. As I am telling you, the communism that I profess incorporates both the left and the right.

Q: Both the left and the right?

A: Yes, because I choose what is best from both, and I prefer this—the center—over the radical extremism of either side. I am also against the capitalists, ever since I learned that it was easier for a camel to pass through the eye of a needle than for a rich person to enter heaven. The capitalist must first become a human being, and understand that in reality he owns nothing. Unless he changes his attitude, he will fall into biblical condemnation.

Q: Would it be better to force him to change his attitude?

A: Divine justice is more powerful than the human kind. This is why I fight on the Christian side. Christianity has remained viable for twenty centuries, while atheistic materialism is a newborn that does not merit my support. If my works are ever gathered into one place, you will better understand their religious nature. I wish the government would take an interest in realizing the plan drawn up by the architect [Benedictine monk Gabriel Chávez] de la Mora, and erect it to house all of my works on my plot in Xochimilco. That is my hope.

Art, Revolution, and Decadence

José Carlos Mariátegui

———

From *Amauta*, November 3, 1926, 3–4.

Marxist philosopher and literary critic José Carlos Mariátegui is one of the more important non-artists who wrote about art in modern Latin America. In this essay he is at pains to point out how not all new art is revolutionary: if artists withdraw into purely formal explorations, he asserts, then they cease being both revolutionary and new. He cites as examples the Futurists in Russia and Italy, whose political programs were inseparable from their artistic practices. That he wrote this essay in the first year after he founded the magazine Amauta *indicates the important role he imagined for art and artists in society.* Amauta *generally supported the indigenist painters such as José Sabogal, but it also covered other modern movements.*

It is important to denounce a mistaken idea that confuses some young artists. We need to establish, by clarifying certain hastily formed doctrines, that not every new art is revolutionary, nor is it even truly new. In our world there are two spirits, the revolutionary and the decadent. Only the presence of the former guarantees that a poem or a painting is truly new.

We cannot accept as new an art that brings only a new technique. To do so would be to fall into the most fallacious of the current misconceptions. No aesthetic can reduce artistic creation to a mere matter of technique, because any new technique should correspond to a new spirit as well. If not, then the only thing that changes is the surface, the décor. And no artistic revolution is content with mere formal innovations.

The distinction between these two sorts of artists is not easy to draw. Decadence and revolution, such as they exist in the world of today, can coexist in the same individuals. The conscience of the artist is the site of struggle between these two frames of mind. The comprehension of this battle often, or nearly always, escapes the artist himself. But finally one of the spirits will win out, leaving the other lying in the dust.

The decadence of capitalist civilization is reflected in the atomization and dissolution of its art. In this crisis, art has lost its essential unity because each of its principles and elements has proclaimed its autonomy. Secession is its most characteristic attitude. Schools of art are multiplying to infinity because only centrifugal forces animate them.

But the present anarchic situation, which has irreparably split and shattered the spirit of bourgeois art, is also the preparation and prelude to a new order. We live in the transition from the sunset to the dawn. In this crisis, we already see widely dispersed the elements of an art of the future. Cubism, Dadaism, expressionism, and the rest, just as they give evidence of a crisis, also point to a renewal. None of these movements makes a contribution in isolation, but each brings an element or an idea to the coming regeneration.

The revolutionary aspect of these schools and tendencies lies not in their creation of a new style, nor in their overthrow of the old techniques. It is in the rejection, repudiation, and jeers that they suffer from the middle classes. Whether we recognize it or not—and usually we do not—art is always nourished by the spirit of its times. Our contemporary artists, in most cases, have empty souls. The literature of decadence is a literature without an absolute; thus we can take only baby steps. People cannot march ahead without faith in something, because to lack faith is to lack a purpose. To proceed without faith means to spin our wheels. The artists who describe themselves as the most exasperated and nihilistic skeptics are the ones who most need a myth to live by.

The Russian futurists were mostly communists; the Italian futurists mostly adhered to fascism. Is there a better proof that artists cannot remain aloof from politics? [Italian futurist author] Massimo Bontempelli said that in 1920 he was nearly a communist, and that in 1923, the year of Mussolini's march on Rome, he felt like a fascist. Now, he seems fascist all the way. Many have made fun of Bontempelli for his admission, but I defend him, because at least he was being honest. The empty soul of the poor Bontempelli had to adopt and accept the Myth that erected the altar to Mussolini. (The Italian vanguardists are all convinced that fascism is revolutionary.)

[Peruvian poet] César Vallejo writes, and [Peruvian political theorist] Haya de la Torre thinks, that the *Divine Comedy* and *Don Quixote* have a political quality to them, while [Chilean poet] Vicente Huidobro pretends that art is independent of politics . . . In these matters and others, I naturally stand with Haya de la Torre. If, for Huidobro, politics extends no further than the royal palaces, then we can allow his art all the autonomy that he claims for it. Both Haya and I may have raised politics to the level of a religion, as [Miguel de] Unamuno says, but this much is true: politics is the actual unfolding of history itself. In certain classical eras, in the peak years of one order or another, politics can be confined to the parliaments or to the offices. But in romantic times and in times of crisis, politics is the front page of life. This is the proclamation from Louis Aragon, André Breton, and their compatriots from the "surrealist revolution," the greatest minds of the French vanguard, as they march toward communism . . .

We need to clarify the question, and dispel all misconceptions. It is a difficult task, with many points to reconcile. The signs of decadence in vanguard art are many, and must be overcome until art transcends its sickening subjectivism and proposes real revolutionary goals. [Alberto] Hidalgo, writing about Lenin in a complex poem, says that the social equality of women is foreshadowed in untrammeled breasts and tomboy haircuts. This should not surprise us. There are even poets who believe that the jazz band is the harbinger of the revolution.

Fortunately, there are still artists in the world such as [George] Bernard Shaw, who are able to see that art is great only when it promotes an iconography for a living religion, and that it is completely despicable only when it imitates the iconography of religions that have declined into superstitions. This latter path has tempted many new artists in the literature of France and other countries. But future generations will laugh at the consecrated stupidity of those critics who call such creators new or even revolutionary.

In Defense of Indigenist Painting

José Sabogal

———

From José Sabogal, *Del arte en el Perú y otros ensayos*
(Lima: Instituto Nacional de Cultura, 1975), 109–13.

*This is the bulk of a brief speech that Sabogal made at a testimonial dinner in
1943, upon his retirement from the directorship of the National School of Fine
Arts, which had been a hotbed of the indigenist movement. As the decade of
the 1930s progressed, attacks on indigenism mounted. See, for example, the
article by César Moro in the next section. In this speech, the chief founder of
the movement defends it from its critics.*

At the end of the Great War of 1914–18, Peru entered an interesting period of
recovery and renewal. As a country with an ancient artistic tradition, the
visual arts flowered as essential ingredients in our national development.

In 1919, I returned to my homeland after ten years of travel and study in
Europe, Africa, and the Americas. I arrived with an exhibition of canvases
that I had painted in Cuzco. I did not want to make my debut in Lima with
the usual trite scenes of the Seine River, nor with golden impressions of Italy,
nor even with the stridently sunny landscapes of Spain or North Africa. My
intent was to portray Peru, and, camped out among the primordial walls of
old imperial Cuzco, I began a pictorial adventure that later took me all across
the country. I hoped through my canvases to reveal hitherto unexpected
beauties: the high, snowy peaks and rocky Andean crests, the hushed flat-
lands laid out under bulky clouds, the silvery light of the slopes, the shrouded
tonalities of the coastal plains, and also the people who inhabited this land
of both magic and pain, from the marvelously coppery faces of the Aymara
and Quechua peoples, to the yellow-jasmine shades of the Lima women,
passing through all the picturesque racial mixtures of our varied land: these
were my preferred subjects because they attracted me. And such was my
position in the art world, beginning in 1919.

The following year, I was invited to work alongside the founders of the School of Fine Arts. I already grasped the admirable astuteness and judgment of our illustrious [director, Daniel] Hernández, who founded the school in that fragile and delicate environment. Upon his death I assumed the difficult job. From the beginning, the public attitude was impatient. Soon, harsh diatribes rang out, sometimes in organized campaigns; but these only swelled the ranks of students who entered our silent and serious halls. We were called "cultivators of ugly art" by those whose tastes ran to pale and washed-out Romanticism. They considered themselves in the right, but their pillowy blows were launched from a belief that has no foundation in the soul of the people, and the people have no use for them. Some of the attackers lacked spiritual foundation as well—which might harmonize better with the people—but they came from the ranks of those we might call "tacky."

Then they labeled us Indigenists, but with malice and surprising ill-will; they accused us of promoting an impossible restoration of Inca ways. But by tarring the Indian races, these upstarts aligned themselves with the Spaniards of the days of the Viceroyalty.

Yes, we are Indigenists, in the true sense of the term; even cultural indigenists, because we seek our identity in our own soil, our own humanity, and our own times. We do not believe any race to be superior, but we do believe that a new type of person has been born in America. In today's Peru and alongside the group of artists whom I have the honor of defending, we attempt to express that theme, by presenting the genuine physical appearance that defines our nation, just as artists did in ancient times through their own resounding and enduring art.

Our artistic ancestry lies in the era of pitiless aesthetic conflict between the styles of two cultures: Neither the Inca empire nor the empire of the invaders succeeded in dominating Peru. The new humanity that emerged from those two currents first arose in the colonial period, with artistic manifestations that fit neither an Incan nor a Spanish mold, yet with a marked flavor of each. These manifestations of popular art grew up together with the Peruvian identity. They gradually become more defined and resolved, reaching works of high distinction such as the *Toritos de Pucará* in ceramic, the engraved gourds of the Mantaro region, decorated horse bridles of the northern coast, and the painted altarpieces of Ayacucho: in sum, so many pieces showing simple feeling that speak for a surging popular culture as strong as our ancestors who produced it.

With Pancho Fierro, the mixed Peruvian culture reaches a peak of maturity; the nineteenth century sings in his graceful watercolors. He is like the bard of his people, revealing to the world the typical characters of that time. Living in close harmony with his society, this determined indigenous artist gave this culture its true face.

Also out of this cross-cultural breeding ground came a man with deep Peruvian characteristics and a French name: Paul Gauguin. His art defines itself with the warm blood and spirited temperament of his controversial grandmother, Flora Tristán.

We find another high point on our artistic relief map in the work of Francisco Lazo, the sensitive painter of the late nineteenth century. His canvases of rich blacks and transparent washes of delicate grays communicate the deep melancholy of our land, along with the sharp restlessness of the Spaniard. Lazo carries within himself an identity from Peruvian soil, and he expresses it using the subtleties of the art of both races.

At this memorable event, you who attend honor our work in the difficult but beautiful cause of an art endowed with an identity from our soil. I have felt it appropriate in this aesthetic confession to clear up certain points of confusion and certain twisted interpretations. As in all potent movements, these debates may even be necessary because their heat tempers us.

This, then, is our aesthetic position, which rose up in our country after World War I. Its defining characteristics originated in the complicated times of ancient Tahuantinsuyo, continued during the Spanish invasion, and lasted up to our days. Judging by the size of the audience here present, this view has taken root in the consciousness of a good number of Peruvians.

We should thus undertake, with understanding and sympathy, another stage of evolution, which coincides with yet another world war. Now a new generation of artists has risen up who have done nothing but work with passion and sincerity, and they have added a more modern artistic prestige to the legendary name of Peru.

The New Realism

Antonio Berni

————◆————

From *Forma*, August 1936, 8.

Berni here takes aim at the quest for formal innovation that motivated many modern artists; he also attacks the flights of fantasy-based surrealism. He wrote just after returning to Argentina from Europe, where he had experimented with surrealist techniques and found allies among the more politically-oriented surrealists such as Louis Aragon. The New Realism that he proposes here would unite the resources of modern art with a lively sense of the drama and tensions of the current historical moment. Though he wrote this essay in the middle 1930s, most critics hold that he best expressed these beliefs in the 1960s, when he developed his series of works around the characters of Juanito Laguna and Ramona Montiel.

A fever for visual art seems to have broken out among large sectors of contemporary society. Thousands of painters debut in every season in European cities. In our country, an incalculable number of artists are making an appearance, along with the birth of art magazines and art galleries. I can say without reservation that no other century has enjoyed such sheer numbers of paintings and artists. But this enormous wave of easel painting has brought along with it something that nobody wants: a decline in technical skill and sensitivity, and what is yet more shocking, a growing incomprehension among the public regarding what makes great art and great thought. Several explanations have been offered for this phenomenon. The most simplistic attributes this plague to the sheer quantity of work, taking the debatable formula "wider spread means shallower depth" without seeking the roots of the problem among a bundle of complex issues whose solution may require generations of corrective work. It cannot be denied that modern art is passing through an anemic phase, boosted by a public who are great in number but without conviction or true feeling, and propped up by a diet of official injections, which as sustenance meets its biological needs only poorly. The current confusion of aesthetic ideas, where the subversion of values is the dominant tone, complicates and worsens the situation. Almost anyone can present himself as a painter. All have ideas, whether their own or borrowed, which they express as much as they please by exhibiting in whatever gallery, where they generally escape ridicule for their preposterous or vacuous poses. In "modernism," everything is permitted as long as it has "*l'esprit*"; lacking this, perhaps the work in question is "fauvist." Almost anyone can learn to paint an apple or a figure according to the criteria of "serious" or "academic" critics. If an artist possesses a few of these traits, and some well-placed friends, the road ahead opens.

On a daily basis, the press spits out so much verbiage that all artists, no matter how inferior, get their corner of the page along with a self-proclaimed or unscrupulous scribe to praise them. Every large city boasts a population of artists without training or commitment, who paint just because it is an easy way to make a living. They widen the avalanche of scrap that floods the galleries. There are also those who began seriously and, after getting meager encouragement, gave up serious work and now dedicate themselves to pleasing the "public." Pleasing this gallery-going public requires little mental effort. A certain range of color and looseness of brushwork will suffice to meet the demands of most viewers. Meanwhile, the saner public, who can actually be influenced by ideas and deeper thought, stays away because of the difficulty of finding the diamonds among so much rough.

What has happened to cause this breach between the public and the artists? And why has this divorce led to the decadence of art? Artists themselves are certainly one cause of this rift. Since the end of the nineteenth century, painters have sealed themselves up in their own art, deliberately removing themselves from all the social and psychological problems of the moment. The estrangement has become unsustainable. Some artists today have noticed their error and begun to analyze their means of expression, finding that they have done a poor job of both communicating with the public and meeting their own needs. Life in the ivory tower of "pure art" is uncomfortable and insupportable. Removed from reality, artists feel attacked by a disease; they know that they need to recover the health and vitality that previous generations had.

Let us set forth some concrete proposals; let us elaborate a technical and theoretical basis that could ground our art. This will naturally force a break with the current decadence and withdrawal, and put artists back in contact with the public at a deeper and more genuine emotional level.

The art that we now call modern, which was born in Paris just before World War I, devotes its thought and imagination to purely artistic questions. In their hurry to disconnect themselves from everything that could represent or relate to the real world, artists created a world of shapes and colors so abstract that today, in the hands of its leading exponents, painting has become a merely frivolous and superficial decoration. These searches for pure form and color, or a lyrical composition, are pathways that lead us directly to the cubism of Picasso and the expressionism of Matisse. This is the endpoint of an evolutionary trajectory that began with the realism of Courbet, which established the split between the subject and its representation, and ends in our day, with the triumph of pictorial values and the suppression of the subject or its transformation into a mere pretext for the composition. But every bad thing contains its own negation; that is, the negation of that dualism and the possibility of synthesis. We can thus begin to discern a new language that expresses our need for a more substantial art. All the philosophical and aesthetic ramblings about pure art can now be replaced by more realistic reasoning that is in better accord with the social and collective psychology of our moment. And viewpoints that were formerly rejected by the modern sectarian opinions are coming back strongly, pushed on by their sheer irrepressible vitality. Social realities, and the dramatic world in which we live, are breaking out of their shells and claiming their place in our art, contradicting the critical literature of this century, which has been dominated by impressionist or expressionist ideas.

We had thought for a moment that the subject matter, or the reality in a given work, had been forever banished from the domain of the visual arts. But since the times of the cave paintings, through the Egyptians, and up to modern times, humanity has always felt a need to express feelings in pictures. Nature and social life were the two key elements that made up this dramatized world. Only in the twentieth century have painters removed themselves so far from the world, heading toward the realm of pure form and color, as if on a flight of Icarus. But we know the results of that quest: Icarus's wings burned and the law of gravity took over, returning him to the world he hoped to escape.

This avoidance of the objective world and visible reality has allowed imagination and improvisation to rise in uninhibited lyrical flight. Painters can invent or create their own worlds of images in their own styles, giving the most capricious interpretations of people and things. But we already recognize these pretentions for the pipe-dreams that they are. Creation becomes a cliché, and invention an obvious gesture. Painting becomes vulgar and empty decoration. An entire generation of young artists remains under the sway of these sterile illusions; their false conceptions of reality lead to mere improvisation and to a false modernity. Imitating one or the other outmoded style of creation or modernity makes one neither creative nor modern. We cannot follow the examples of Cézanne or Picasso by imitating their manner of working, but rather only by interpreting, as they themselves did in their times, the new forms of our reality, new theories that impact the mind, and the novel aspects of the moment in which we live. The true art of a person or a nation is the one that opens new paths, pushed along by the shifting, living world. On the other hand, art ceases to be such when artists work merely according to established clichés, clinging to passé and outmoded forms that in no way relate to current artistic or social reality. A new order, a new discipline, supported by a new criticism inspired by our concrete moment, needs to supplant all of the obsolescence that we put up with today. A new and splendid horizon of novel and unexpected sensations is available to our young artists. There they will find nourishment for their enthusiasms and an outlet for their energy and talent.

The search for such realism has led to all the great art of past civilizations. In those centuries, both objective reality and current ideas gave form and vigor to art. We cannot, therefore, promote or establish the absolute supremacy of the subject on the one hand, or of the play of technique and composition on the other, because both of these form an indivisible whole. Studying the works of Giotto or Pieter Brueghel the Elder, we may take an interest in the painting itself apart from its subject, because the former is always there and the latter is remote in time and fades away. But we cannot overlook the dramatic content and the truth that such works express, because they are the essential elements that give life to the work and constitute its very reason for being. In the new realism arising today, the construction of the action is the most important, because it does not consist merely of transcribing people and things; it includes as well their activities, their life, their ideas, and their misfortunes. New realism is not merely rhetoric or declamation without foundation or objectivity; it is the suggestive mirror of the great spiritual, social, political, and economic reality of our century.

PART FOUR

Surrealism and Related Modes

DOCUMENT 18

On Painting in Peru

César Moro

———

From "A propósito de la pintura en el Perú,"
El poder de la palabra, December 1939, 3.

Here the first Latin American to actually join the surrealist movement takes on the indigenist movement of his own country in dense and sarcastic language. This attack was probably one of the motivators of José Sabogal's 1943 defense, document 16 in the previous section. Although Moro abstains from proposing an alternative to the indigenist movement, his prescriptions do show surrealist influence. He was living in Mexico City at the time that he wrote this; early the following year he, along with André Breton and Wolfgang Paalen, would there organize the International Exhibition of surrealism.

The problem of Peruvian painting has taken on some repellent characteristics in both its form and its content. A vagueness or mental weakness shrouds any clarity in its goals or purposes. We need to see clearly past the imposing scrolls of the new esoteric sect: *indigenist painting*, whose crusade has taken on alarming potency in my country.

There are those who would pretend to alleviate the great misery and total ostracism that the Indians suffer in Peru by energetically portraying them in made-up canvases or in tourist-trade knickknacks, thereby sanctioning all of the stigmas with which the well-heeled ruling classes of the West would gratify our worthy people of the colored races.

In Peru, a country without a pictorial tradition, this contemptible yet conventional throng takes it upon itself to busily create, out of our paucity of resources, a style of painting that supposedly has nothing to do with European art. That is, in place of chubby subjects from Brittany, Holland, or even Switzerland, we now have Indians by the bushel. And, as anyone can see, indigenism is not restricted only to painting. An entire gamut of Peruvian intellectuals would like to erect a new Great Wall of China to isolate us from

Europe, which our ever-wise readers of translations of Spengler call decadent. They fail to realize for one instant that if Europe is decadent, then we are intellectually only a pale reflection of that decadence, following years behind it with a lack of vitality that is uniquely ours. Our weakness comes in part from our poverty of thought, which is widespread across the Spanish-speaking world, including Spain, of course. We all know, or should know, that the Spanish language has been frozen in time since the Golden Age [of the 1600s], and that neither philosophy nor poetry have produced those best representatives who are numerous in many other languages. Among us, what abound are intellectuals who speak of everything and nothing as they suffer from literary indigestion after having read the fraudulent translations from that famous Chilean publishing house and a publisher that is not the summit but rather a typical example of the dominant culture of our "stupid continent," as it was described brilliantly some years ago by [Spanish novelist] Pío Baroja. A stupid continent, despite our burbling intellectual capitals that some locate in Buenos Aires and others elsewhere depending on their impoverished regional sentiments. It is evident that Buenos Aires is the capital only of the tango, and it spreads its influence on our continent's poetic productivity.

But let us return to our greenhorn Peruvian painting, which has a maddening tendency to dissolve into thick clouds in the minds of optimistic viewers who decide to take it on. We need to take as many precautions when thinking about it as we might in descending past the doorway of the convoluted labyrinth of a freshly uncovered ancient Egyptian tomb, all without losing our sense of distance. Woe to you who, in my country, dares to look at the world through eyes other than those of a daring indigenist painter or folkloric writer. You are immediately labeled as foreign, Francophile, and the intransigent enemy of the Indian, enemy of this fabulous cardboard myth that gives you a living, including, doubtless, "friends of the Indian," those early North European tourists who, watercolor pad in hand, devoted themselves to capturing the "soul of the Andes," thus speaking like perfect indigenists, giving us *ad nauseam* the well-known image of the Indian in his fetal position, with his reed flute in his hands like an obvious symbol compensating for his lost masculinity. Such is the song that is sung by poets in the service of the exploiter caste that has always existed in Peru.

Indigenism is a yardstick. Either you are an indigenist, or you are a charlatan. Either you paint in the most basic and unpainterly way, with the most backward mind, your hollow Indians, your Indians like market dolls, or you are the most hopeless Francophile that our "gentle homeland" has been able to produce in all our millennia of oppression.

It was difficult for us Peruvians to think for ourselves under the provocation of the Inca ruler who once a year took up the ritualistic trowel in order to stir the devotion of his forced laborers, while he spent the rest of the year preparing for the next annual feast. It is true that in the Inca period we at least had the advantage of being ignorant of the efforts of the "Salvation Army." . . . Human dignity had at least reached a certain level. Then came the Spanish with their horrible parade float of Christian virtues. Our present age, which embraces great schemes of subjection that, as soon as they conquer a territory, try to colonize and channelize the turbulent and surging waters of true culture, which they energetically attack through their movies, books, compromised and corrupt press, etc., etc. . . . Our age, in which Hitler and Stalin are the ferocious enemies of culture, is characterized by precisely the same castrating fury, in which the swastika and the hammer join forces.

From the iron hand of the Incas we pass to the claws of the [Spanish] conquerors: pig farmers, fanatics, illiterates, voraciously hungering for gold, yearning to wallow in that perfect excrement, and with that well-known inferiority complex that led them to assassinate [the Inca ruler] Atahualpa when he figured out that [the conqueror Francisco] Pizarro was unable to decipher the signs that represented the idea of God, while the Inca's own soldiers could easily read a word written even on his fingernail. We owe this Atahualpa a splendid homage for being the first in the New World to throw the Gospels on the ground, thus restoring them to their rightful place. Was it not the Spaniards who, through the mouth of one of their own, Father Aranda (a Jesuit, naturally), boasted of destroying six thousand manifestations of the devil in one day (referring to the splendid and marvelous Kero cups)? Those ignorant conquerors could have brought to our people a valid new manner of thought, but they thought only in terms of the Church. Thus they replaced the Temple of the Sun with a Roman Catholic church, scraping away even the foundations of the solar temple.

On gaining our independence from Spain [in 1821], we only ended up with worse Spaniards: hispanophile mestizos and mulattoes with Castilian titles, under the guise of a republic, who muzzled thought and refused to implement the most elementary tenets of democracy.

And thus, naturally, we come to describe the essentially poetic and therefore universal expression of our pictorial language, in terms that take account of the problem of the contemporary Peruvian mind. We find it in a closed and uninviting alley of arbitrary or just representation of the Indian, his wife, his in-laws, his children, and all of his relatives, all dressed in those garments which, as if maintaining some dead thing, are the only ones that the exploiters of their lands permit them to wear even today.

To this steady stream of larcenies subscribe all of those who, consciously or unconsciously, adore the dominant classes by painting for them and only for them, painting in the worst taste deformed Indians whom this class accepts in their houses, on the condition that they come in already framed and without that peculiar odor of wool they say characterizes the Indians. These patrons prefer the odor of embalming fluid that indigenist painting gives off. These paintings serve the Aryan fat cats as proof of the supposed inferiority of the races of color.

The National School of Fine Arts is the strongest citadel of this insipid tendency. From there emerges year after year *ad nauseam* the band of supporters of this stupefying art, those who believe themselves to be fulfilling the profoundly disruptive function of art as they devour their daily ration of painted Indians. I do not believe it necessary to defend myself against the stupid charge that could be made, that I write under the influence of personal antipathy or hatred, nor other charges that such imbeciles in their moral poverty will doubtless lay on me. Their own words will both judge and define them. That said, I can affirm that I do not believe in the Utopian future of the Indian; I do see their undeniable current conditions, but I also see that any intent to confine them in anecdotal paintings shows the workings of a reactionary mind. I see, as anyone can, their greater or lesser degree of exploitation, along with that of the mestizos who populate the coast. The indigenist painters believe neither in the Indians' future nor in their past, which they are unaware of. For them, the Indians have always and only been Quechua. The other highly developed civilizations of the coast do not exist for them. They do not perceive their extraordinary influence, which, far from waning in influence and impact, does not cease to stir up, with the powerful force of dreams, the miserable reality that oppresses and surrounds them. The indigenists see only the decrepit Indian that the poisonous memories of the colonial period have left behind, the Indian dressed in multicolored rags.

But there is another Indian: the beast of burden who competes with the llama. The Indian who resembles any exploited person. The Indian who has, in many cases, an impeccable and classical beauty. The Indian who works unceasingly in hostile climates with only a handful of corn for food. The

Indian who takes refuge in coca leaves and alcohol. This Indian should spit scornfully on those who paint him to look like a farcical creature. The indigenists prefer to ignore this Indian because he is not distinctive enough in appearance. This Indian is not picturesque. It would be better if they took as subject some of the cruder coastal peoples. They could, for example, paint the Lord of the Miracles procession.

The indigenists do not paint the present reality of the Indian, because that reality implies the fading of bright colors and the loss of the picturesque. Rather than lose their subject matter, they prefer to aid at any cost the perpetuation of the state of things that will guarantee them future frescoes and pleasant scenes ready for easy export.

I have no suggestion for a replacement school of painting. My only principle is total freedom for art. I oppose these styles that offer only formulas to better attract and entertain buyers, disturbing neither their sleep nor their digestion. Art begins where tranquility ends. I favor any restless art over that which puts us to sleep.

DOCUMENT 19

An Approach to a Reality
That We Do Not Understand Yet

An Interview with Leonora Carrington

Hans Ulrich Obrist

From *Leonora Carrington*
(Dublin: Irish Museum of Modern Art, 2013), 155–68.

Leonora Carrington was notoriously reclusive and reticent about giving interviews, but this excerpt takes the best from the best available. Among the many subjects discussed are her relationship to the surrealist movement and its members, and some of the sources of her art. The initial question contains an editing error: Carrington described an imagined surrealist exhibition in a letter to André Breton that was noted in a 1991 book by Marina Warner (not Marina Mono).

Q: When you were in London in 1959, you told Marina Mono about this 1959 exhibition of surrealism by André Breton which was unrealized. You said that you visualised a room somewhere between a cathedral and a Swiss clock. It's a surrealist exhibition that never happened, so I was wondering if you could tell us about this unrealized room.

A: What, the cuckoo clock? It was pretty visual. We had bishops instead of the cuckoo coming out of the clock. You know, when the bird comes out and says "cuckoo," a bishop would gallop out.

Q: So it's an unbuilt room and it never happened?

A: Never happened.

Q: Do you have projects that are too big to realize?

A: I really don't make too many projects, to be quite honest. I don't make projects, the projects make themselves.

Q: Do you think that there's a self-organization that happens?

A: An organization that happens, or doesn't happen.

Q: Are there public art projects, like monuments, that were proposed, that couldn't be realized?

A: There is a monument of a very big crocodile in Chapultepec [in Mexico City].

Q: That was realized?

A: Yes, it was realized. The model I made here, and then several other models were made. The crocodile was made originally from a drawing. The person who organized the project was Dr. [Isaac] Masri.

Q: Are there some public art projects that are not yet built, but that could be in the making?

A: No. Except for the one thing that is coming: an exhibition, as far as I know. I did the sculptures of this [for] Dr. Masri, who wanted me to do the sculptures, and [my son] Pablo did the paintings and also the bells that are in [the Paseo de la] Reforma. Did you see them?

Q: No, I have to see them.

A: Pablo did a bell, a very beautiful one. And I did one, which is a bat that is in front of El Seguro Social [building], and Pablo made another in front of La Diana, close to the corner where the statue of Diana is.

Q: And that bat? Is it like a flying bat?

A: No, it's a sitting bat and unfortunately it's not upside down. It's a public project.

Q: Could you tell me how the idea of animals came about? Maybe because you were surrounded by animals?

A: I don't think so. I think that a lot of things occurred, but I don't know why. And it's usually something that I don't want to do.

Q: But it is one element that comes out, again and again, isn't it?

A: You tell me, because I don't remember.

Q: Like horses?

A: Yes, horses, because I like horses, dogs and cats. And I also do human animals, because I think that we are also animals.

Q: Do you think that animals are also persons?

A: I hope not. Imagine what kind of world we'd get. I don't know, but I hope not.

Q: You said in an earlier interview that the paintings of Bosch have been somehow important to you.

A: Very important. I saw them when I was in Spain, in the Museo del Prado in Madrid.

Q: Can you tell us more about the recurrence of horses?

A: Oh, I can. I used to ride a lot. My mother was Irish and it is well known that the Irish have a tradition with horses. This is a logical reply and I don't think it's really true. I don't think it is that simple, but I don't really know.

Q: Whistler once said that "art happens," and you're basically telling me the same thing.

A: Yes, I think he's right . . .

Q: I was very fascinated by the first text that I read by you, it was called *The Debutante*. I read it, and I found that it has a lot to do with you going to the zoological gardens, and with the first question that I asked you, about animals. Can you tell me a little bit more about *The Debutante*?

A: The zoo in London is very big and has a lot of animals. As I've always liked animals, I liked to go to the zoo a lot and look at them.

Q: Was the London zoo an inspiration as much as the museums?

A: Well, I've always liked animals. We had dogs and cats, and horses and cows and pigs and hens, chickens, ducks, and fish.

Q: Do you think that animals have spirit?

A: I think that animals have everything, maybe a little bit more than we have, but I believe that human beings are animals. I don't think that we make a decision like animals [do]. We both live the best we can and then we die, and we don't know anything about what happens after death, maybe nothing. We are in the same situation as animals. Animals sometimes have certain faculties that we don't normally have, such as a kind of telepathy . . . There are some faculties that we haven't admitted or recognized, because we're frightened that somebody might think that we are also animals, which we are.

Q: They're like a source of knowledge.

A: Tremendous knowledge and no pretension, other than the dominant males of course, they always have big pretensions.

Q: Animals also lead us to the question of reincarnation. So I was wondering if we could talk a little bit about religion and your interest in Buddhism and in reincarnation.

A: I'm not an expert on religion. But I think that all religions have something, plenty of goddesses and gods. I think there are thousands of them, and I also think that we don't know the meaning of the word "god." I think there are animal gods, there are microgods of all the subatomic worlds. I have found very strange things about the subatomic world—you should know about it.

Q: You mean quantum physics and parallel reality? I met Albert Hoffman, the man who invented LSD. He's one hundred years old, so perhaps LSD was good for him.

A: What is LSD?

Q: It's like the Mexican mushrooms. Is that something that you're interested in?

A: I've never taken them. The worst drug I've been addicted to is cigarettes.

Q: One of the things that I'm fascinated by is your "encounters." I would like to know about your encounters with [spiritual teacher George Ivanovich] Gurdjieff.

A: I never met Gurdjieff. I read his book [*All and Everything*], but I never met him.

Q: Is it true that he inspired [your novel] *The Hearing Trumpet*?

A: Oh, there was a wonderful place, here in Mexico. I think it was in Tlalpan, a very big house, and all these Gurdjieff people all gathered there, but Gurdjieff never came to Mexico as far as I know. I don't think so. But there were all these people who followed Gurdjieff and they all got together there and they were utterly humorless, and I thought they were very funny.

Q: Where was it?

A: I invented most of it . . .

Q: I want to ask you about the relationship between your work and the city, because in your autobiography you talked about different cities.

A: Well, I was born in England, my mother was Irish, my father was English. I went to a convent when I was nine. I was sent into a convent. I didn't go willingly, I went kicking and screaming into the convent, but I quickly left; I didn't like it there.

Q: How did Mexico enter into this relationship?

A: That was when the Germans invaded France. That's how I got to Mexico, running away from the Nazis.

Q: And was Max Ernst with you when you came?

A: Yes, but Max was in a concentration camp. He didn't come here, but I came with Renato Leduc, who was a very kind man, so I could get into Mexico. The Germans disliked the surrealists very much, and the surrealists didn't like Hitler. I continue to dislike Hitler; I'm sure we all do. And then the Mexicans kindly accepted me as a sort of a semi-Mexican because I married a Mexican, Renato. Do you know him? He wrote some poetry. The only bad thing about Renato was that he liked bull-fighting, which horrifies me . . .

Q: I would like to come back to your beginnings. You studied in London. I was curious: Could you tell us a little bit more about the Ozenfant Academy in London, where you studied?

A: There was a mixture of people: There were two English women; there were two Egyptians. The Egyptians were quite talented, Hamed Said and I forgot what the other one was called. Also Ernö Goldfinger. Does the name Goldfinger mean anything to you? He was an architect. That is actually where I met Max, with Goldfinger and Ursula, who was Miss Blackwell before she married. That was Ursula's family name before she married Goldfinger.

Q: How was [Amédée] Ozenfant as a teacher?

A: I think he was an excellent teacher.

Q: What did he give you?

A: He gave me drawings of fur coats where he put people when they were naked and then he called them fur coats.

Q: Was he also a writer?

A: I never read a thing he wrote. I know he called himself a purist. What was pure about him, I don't know. But he was a very good teacher.

Q: About the city of London, which is the home of the British Museum. I was curious about which was your favorite museum.

A: Probably the British Museum—I like the mummies, the Egyptian mummies—the National Gallery and the Tate Modern Gallery.

Q: My favorite museum is the National Museum of Anthropology by [Pedro] Ramírez Vázquez, in Mexico [City]. Is that a museum that you like?

A: El Museo de Antropología, it's an extraordinary museum.

Q: What other museums do you like?

A: Well, I don't know. In Florence, the Uffizi.

Q: Florence is very important because, if I'm not wrong, you lived there when you were very young.

A: I was fifteen. I was discriminated against by the American girls because I dressed very sloppy, very English. Eventually, we became very good friends. I was in school with about twelve other girls; it was a very small school.

Q: And what were your impressions? Was there any picture that shocked you? At that time in Florence, what struck you the most?

A: What struck me the most was the Italian lessons. We had a woman called Daisy who taught us Italian and we had an hour of Dante and an hour of *Pinocchio*. That's how I learned Italian. I remember that very clearly: *Pinocchio* and Dante.

Q: Do you have a relationship with any particular museum?

A: I think I remember the Prado in Madrid better than the others, probably I was a little bit older and probably because they have a lot of Bosch in the Prado. They have an incredible collection of Bosch. I went back and back to the Prado when I was in Madrid.

Q: Was the Prado the most important?

A: I don't know if it was the most important. I think that the British Museum is important and I think the National Gallery is important. Each museum, I think, has something excellent . . .

Q: You often refer to the kitchen and to food as something analogous, and you put it in relation to painting, as an analogy.

A: That's just a thing that came into my head because my grandmother had an incredible kitchen; it was huge, it was ancient, and I still like cooking. I made tapioca once with squid ink, and squid ink with tapioca comes out looking like caviar. [Film director] Luis Buñuel came over and he thought it really was caviar; Buñuel had no sense of taste.

Q: He came to your house and ate your caviar?

A: He came to the house lots of times, and then I made like a bucket of caviar, and here's what he said: "This is a scandal to waste so much money on caviar; we have to call Gayoso [funeral directors] and give it a burial." But I think it cost me maybe twenty pesos.

Q: I want to ask you about Buñuel. Did you see him a lot? Did you have a friendship?

A: Yes, we were very good friends.

Q: Did you collaborate?

A: I was an extra in one of his movies. I think I was a widow.

Q: I was also wondering if you had any interest in making films.

A: No, never, absolutely not.

Q: I just saw Dalí's retrospective in Rotterdam and they reconstructed his animated film. I was wondering if you ever thought about animating or drawing a film.

A: No, never. But I made a lot of theater. I wrote *Penélope* and *Seven*. I also made the décor for another play.

Q: And you made a play with [director Alejandro] Jodorowsky, you told me.

A: But that was my play, it wasn't for Jodorowsky. Jodorowsky made a play of mine and I did the décor for my play, not for Jodorowsky. I actually allowed him to do my play.

Q: And is it preserved? Does it still exist?

A: I don't think so, but the sketches still exist . . .

Q: How do you feel about surrealism?

A: Well, it depends on what surrealism. I was doing it long before I met the surrealists. The person who really introduced me to the surrealists was the most unlikely person: my mother, who was totally into art of any kind. The book that really amused her was the one by Herbert Read [titled *Surrealism*] with the Max Ernst drawing. When I saw it I thought, I have an affinity with these people. But I didn't become a surrealist. I wasn't like [André] Breton.

Q: You said, "It depends on what kind of surrealism," so I was wondering, what is your definition of surrealism?

A: I said, "Which surrealist?" I said, "Which one of them?"

Q: How would you define surrealism today [2005]?

A: I would define it as an approach to a reality that we do not understand yet . . .

Q: I would like to talk more about exhibitions. You participated in the surrealists' exhibition; could you talk a little more about it?

A: I used to be sent out to buy cigarettes for Miró, so I didn't fancy it too much. He used to give me one franc for getting him ten packs of cigarettes on different occasions on the same morning.

Q: You were involved in some of Marcel Duchamp's shows also?

A: Marcel and I arranged an exhibition [*First Papers of Surrealism*, 1942]. I was a good friend of Marcel. We got very bored putting up all those strings.

Q: Can you tell me a little more about that experience, because I was very fascinated by that show.

A: We just put a lot of string around everything. That was Marcel's idea, not mine.

Q: But you realized it with him?

A: We made it together.

Q: How did you put up all that string? Was it improvised, or was there a drawing?

A: No, no drawing. He also made the faked photographs; they were very funny. In the catalog he put photographs of all the painters but using different people. They were very funny, like monsters.

Q: Is there any special memory of an exhibition that you'd like to share?

A: Perhaps the last surrealist exhibition; it was in Paris. Dalí did a taxi. It was raining inside the taxi and it was full of plants.

Q: That was in 1938. What did you do in the show?

A: I told you, I went for cigarettes for Miró. I think I had one rather small, insignificant painting.

Q: What was your relationship with Peggy Guggenheim? Did you find her with Max Ernst in London?

A: They were in Marseille and I was on that plane to New York. At that time I thought she was a good person, Peggy. I met her in New York. I went to her house several times. I liked Peggy.

Q: Did she buy your work?

A: I think so. Yes, she did. I think in Venice she had a couple of paintings of mine.

Q: You told me the other day that you did a mural for [fashion designer] Helena Rubenstein?

A: Oh, yes. But that was in 1968; there were a lot of people involved in it, everybody that went to Breton's place.

Q: At that time did you know Frida Kahlo?

A: I knew Frida very briefly because Jacqueline Breton introduced us. She was a very kind person, but her condition was rather terrible, she was suffering constantly. She was in so much pain that she didn't like to talk that much.

Q: What did you talk about? Did you talk about art?

A: We certainly didn't talk about art; she was in too much pain to talk about anything.

Q: Did you appreciate her work?

A: Yes, I did appreciate Frida's work.

Speaking of One of My Paintings

Frida Kahlo

From "Hablando de un cuadro mío," *Así*, August 18, 1945, 70–71.

Frida Kahlo was recruited for the surrealist movement by André Breton, but she never fully joined it, preferring to maintain that she was more Mexican than surrealist. We know the often pained self-expression that animates many of her works, but this essay exposes other sides of her: intellectually curious, assertive, and down-to-earth. Here she discusses a rather small but interesting work: Moisés [Moses], *from 1945. As this text was transcribed from a speech, it has many slang expressions in it, some of which are in quotation marks here as they also appeared in the original magazine. The work discussed is in a private collection, but is viewable online at several websites.*

This is the first time in my life that I have tried to "explain" one of my paintings to a group larger than three persons, so I hope you will excuse me if I take on "balls" and show some rough edges. About two years ago, José Domingo told me that he would like for me to read *Moses and Monotheism* by Sigmund Freud and to paint my interpretation of that book, however I wanted. This painting is the result of that short conversation between José Domingo Lavín and I.

I read the book through just once before I started to paint, working from the first impressions that it gave me. Yesterday I just reread it, and I should confess to you that I now find my painting quite incomplete and rather different from what appears to be Freud's marvelous analysis of Moses. But now, because I can neither add to the work nor take from it, I will describe it just as it is, and as you can see it for yourselves. Naturally, the general theme is "Moses, or the Birth of a Hero." But I interpreted the facts and images that most impressed me from the book in my own admittedly mixed-up manner. Because I am finally responsible for all this, you can tell me if I have stuck my foot in my mouth or not.

What I wanted to express most intently and clearly was this: The reason that people need to invent or create heroes or gods is out of pure fear. Fear of life and fear of death. I started with the figure of Moses as a baby. The word *moses* in Hebrew means he was taken out of the water, and in Egyptian it means baby. I painted him as he is described in many legends, abandoned in a basket and floating on the waters of a river. I tried to have the basket, with its animal-skin covering, resemble a womb because Freud says that the basket is the exposed womb and the water is the maternal source that gives birth to a newborn. To highlight this fact I painted the fetus [in the womb just above] in its final stages of development in the placenta. The ovaries, which resemble hands, reach out toward the world. Just to the sides of the newly created child, I placed the elements of his creation [above on either side], the fertilized egg and the first cell division.

In a way that is very clear, but too complicated for my mind, Freud analyzes the important fact that Moses was not Jewish but rather Egyptian. In the painting, I portrayed him as neither Jewish nor Egyptian, but just as a boy who could represent Moses, or anyone who could have had this legendary beginning, transforming himself later into an important person or leader of his people, which is to say, a hero. (The "all-seeing eye" shows that he is wiser than others.) Similar cases include Sargon, Cyrus, Romulus, Paris, and others.

Freud's other interesting conclusion was that Moses, not being Jewish, gave to the people who chose him as their leader and guide, a religion that was not Jewish, but rather Egyptian: the religion of Amenhotep IV, or Akhenaten, who revived the cult of Aten, or the Sun, which is rooted in the ancient religion of Heliopolis. Thus I painted the sun as the center of all religions, as the first god and as creator and propagator of life.

There have been and will be in the future a large number of "crazy visionaries" like Moses, who transform religions and human societies. We could say that they represent a certain kind of messenger between the people that they lead and the gods that the leaders have themselves invented to aid in their leadership. These gods are quite numerous, as you know. Naturally, not all would fit in the painting and so I inserted them on either side of the sun, at least those that have a direct relationship with the sun. On the right are the Western gods, and on the left the Eastern ones.

[On the right] the Assyrian winged bull, Amen, Zeus, Osiris, Horus, Yahweh, Apollo, the Moon, the Virgin Mary, Divine Providence, the Holy Trinity, Venus, and the Devil. On the left, the Thunderer, the bolt of lightning and its trace, which is to say [the pre-Columbian gods] Huracán, Cuculcán, Gukamatz, Tlaloc, the magnificent Coatlicue, mother of all the gods, Quetzalcóatl, Tezcatlipoca, Centéotl, the Chinese Dragon and the Hindu Brahma. I needed to add an African god, but I could not find one anywhere, so you can mentally allow him a space. I cannot tell you much about these gods, because of the shocking lack of information available about their origins, importance, etc.

Having painted in all the gods that would fit, in their respective heavens, I wanted to divide the heavenly world of imagination and poetry from the earthly world of the fear of death. So I painted the two skeletons, human and animal, that you see here [on either side above the heads]. Mother earth encloses them in her hands. Between death and the group of "heroes" below there is no division, because the heroes die and the earth swallows them all up, dependably and without prejudice. On the earth itself [below the skeletons], I painted the portraits of other heroes, with their heads a little larger than the masses below. They are few in number but carefully chosen: Transformers of religions, inventors or creators of religions, conquerors, rebels; that is, the "movers and shakers."

On the right you see Amenhotep IV, who was later called Akhenaten, young ruler of the Eighteenth Dynasty of Egypt [1370–1350 BCE]; I had to paint him with much more importance than any other. He imposed on his subjects a new religion that broke from the tradition of polytheism, establishing a strict monotheism that was based on traces of the ancient religion of Heliopolis, the religion of Aten, that is, the sun. They revered the sun not only as a cult object, but also as the creator and preserver of all living things, in or out of Egypt; his energy showed itself in rays, anticipating the modern scientific discoveries about solar power. [James Henry] Breasted [in *The Dawn of Conscience*] called Amenhotep IV "the first individual in human history."

Next is Moses, who in Freud's analysis gave his adopted people the same religion of Akhenaten, adapted somewhat according to local interests and circumstances. Freud came to this conclusion after a very close study of the intimate relationship between the religion of Aten and the religion of Moses, both of which were monotheistic. It proved impossible to translate this very important part of the book into my painting.

There follow Christ, Zoroaster, Alexander the Great, Caesar, Mohammed, Tamerlane, Napoleon, and that other "lost child," Hitler. On the left, the marvelous Nefertiti, wife of Akhenaten. I imagine that besides being beautiful she must have been the "lost key" and a highly intelligent collaborator with her husband. Then come the Buddha, Karl Marx, Freud, Paracelsus, Epicurus, Genghis Khan, Gandhi, Lenin, and Stalin. The order is messed up, but I painted it according to my historical awareness, which is also messed up. Between them and the mass of humanity, I painted a sea of blood, which symbolizes warfare, the inevitable and inexhaustible.

And finally, the powerful and "never well-regarded" mass of humanity, which is made up of all sorts of critters: warriors, pacifiers, scientists, ignoramuses, monument-builders, rebels, flag-wavers, medal-wearers, orators, the crazy and the sane ones, the happy and sad, the sick and the healthy, the poets and the fools, and all the rest that you can think of, who live on this massive orb. Only the nearest ones are seen a little more clearly; as for the rest, well, you can't hear them over the noise.

In the left foreground is man, the builder, in four colors which signify the four races. On the right is woman, the mother figure, the creator, with a baby in her arms. Behind is an ape. The two tree trunks form a type of rainbow/triumphal arch, representing new life which always springs from the old. At the bottom center is the most important item for Freud, and for many others: love. It is represented by the snail and the shell, the two genders which unite to create new and thriving races.

This is what I can tell you about this painting. I invite any kind of question or comment; I won't get upset. Thank you.

Genesis of *La jungla*

An Interview with Wifredo Lam

Antonio Núñez Jiménez

———

From *Bohemia*, June 4, 1982, 16–19.

Wifredo Lam associated with surrealists in the 1930s. In fact, he left Europe in 1939 on the same boat as André Breton, as both fled the Nazi takeover. His 1943 painting La jungla *does not depict a jungle, but rather a sugar cane field. This is an important distinction that helps to define the work's anticolonial message. This article was written for a mass-circulation magazine, but it reveals important information about Lam's intellectual environment in Havana and the work that he created there.*

In 1981 (forty years after his first return to Cuba), Lam recalls that in 1941, after eighteen years of absence in Europe, he returned to Havana as just one more refugee:

> Helena and I lived on Calzada de Jesús del Monte. Through our window we could see the ocean; the bay was always active, and the streets were noisy. We spent hours just looking at the Cuban scenery; it was like rediscovering the sun and its dazzling light. Even now, just as at that time, I come under the spell of Cuban light.

In the street they ran into their friend, the writer Lydia Cabrera, and she offered some assistance. The most urgent need was a larger house, and Lydia, on one of her visits, told them that she had seen one on Panorama Street, in Marianao, with a gateway, a patio, and a garden. At that house they planted a small orchard, adding a few trees to what they found there. They grew bananas, papayas, and okra. The exuberant okra flower became a theme in many paintings, and a suite of sixteen etchings titled *Apostroph'*

Apocalypse, which accompanied a poem by their friend Gherasim Luca. The bananas in that garden in Marianao became a symbol of optimism for them . . .

On Sundays they entertained many visitors, both old friends and new. Alejo Carpentier, Pierre Loeb and Silvia with their children, Albert and Florence, Peter Watson, Carlos Steinberger, Pierre Mabille, and Benjamin Péret, all came to visit. Virgilio Piñera brought [José] Lezama Lima and [José] Rodríguez Feo, directors of the magazine *Orígenes*, and also Oscar Hurtado, who became a great friend. They talked incessantly of philosophy, literature, and painting, of course. A few times Fernando Ortiz honored them with a visit; at that time Lam was very much influenced by that important Cuban thinker.

The war had been left behind. They followed its course by reading the newspapers, but it no longer involved them: France and Italy invaded by Nazis; the siege and blockade of Leningrad; Hitler's invasion of Russia. Such was the news.

In those years, Lam attended a great many concerts, especially those conducted by Erich Kleiber, with music by [Cuban composers] José Ardévol and Edgardo Martín: "I was surprised one day to read in the program that I had been named Vice-President of the Chamber Orchestra of Havana; I owed this honor to Ardévol, who had dedicated some compositions to me."

Some famous musicians came to Cuba and wanted to meet him, among them Jascha Heifetz and Igor Stravinsky; Lam received them in his home:

> My house was made of plaster with very thick walls, but the ceiling was in terrible condition. Stravinsky came along with his wife. He had a head wound, covered with a bandage. The conversation became animated with various themes, some of them more personal. Stravinsky's wife had an art gallery in San Francisco, a distraction while he was composing. But I could not pay close attention; my eyes kept going up to the ceiling from Stravinsky's head and I thought: If a piece of plaster falls and splits his head open, people will think I tried to kill him.
>
> This worried me, because just a few days before, I had gone to visit a babalawo [Afro-Cuban diviner] with Lydia, Loeb, and Mabille. The diviner told me to be careful of accidents. When I got home I began to worry about the living room ceiling, that the plaster might fall. After Stravinsky's visit, I spent the next day working, and late at night I went to bed. About a half hour later, a racket like two trucks colliding made

me leap up. The entire ceiling had suddenly fallen down. The babalawo had warned me! When I told Lydia about this disaster, she just smiled without saying anything . . .

They used to call me, in discriminatory terms, a black painter. In this, they showed their inability to obstruct the path that I had taken. The well-off are too weak in spirit to appreciate true art. I could say, along with [Francis] Picabia: 'I will die content because my works have not pleased those whom I detest.' From my Paris days, I had an idea: to take African art and put it to work in its own environment, in Cuba. I wanted to express in a work the resistance and combative energy of my ancestors.

It occurred to him to wet down the packing papers that he had brought from Europe, and prepare a panel by layering them and gluing them atop each other. Then through one long night, he drew on the surface. As the work progressed, he began to feel that the intricate structure that he was creating resembled a forest. In less than twenty days he painted his key work: *La jungla.*

The background of the work was at first somewhat reddish. Pierre Loeb, who was very astute about painting, told him that this would not harmonize with the chosen theme. So he went over it again and made it greenish blue, much more in accord with the Cuban scenery. Loeb has written,

> In the three years that I have watched him live and realize his message, I witnessed the birth of a work that day by day grew both more legible and more mysterious. More legible as a composition and more mysterious in a spiritual sense, even though nothing in today's world resembles the signs he created. If occasionally some shape jogs the memory, it has been subjected to such a vigorous transformation, mixing with other shapes, that we find ourselves in the presence of a work that little resembles those of the past.

Fernando Ortiz has written about possible economic and social interpretations of *La jungla.* Other interpretations have also been offered, but Lam said,

> *La jungla* gives form to the revenge of a small Caribbean country, Cuba, against the colonizers. I placed the shears [in the upper right] as the

symbol of the cutting necessary to resist all foreign impositions on Cuba, against all colonization. We are already big enough to march ahead without assistance: Here are the shears.

Lam had seen much African sculpture in Europe, and he knew the intellectual commotion that they had created; those sculptural works had revolutionized Western art. But on seeing them, he thought of the blacks uprooted from their home continent, pitilessly enslaved, and how in the twentieth century the exploitation of their art continued.

In *La jungla* the African myths function within the Cuban landscape of the cane field. Cuba's entire destiny down to the present has revolved around the cultivation of sugar cane and its economic ramifications. My conversations with Picasso showed me that it is necessary to use all intellectual manifestations to forward a truth . . .

I have been considered a painter of the School of Paris, and a surrealist painter, and I don't know what other tendency, but never as a representative of the painting that I actually do and that which I believe I reflect in great measure: the poetry of the Africans who arrived in Cuba, and who still show so much pain in their songs and tales. I have put my feelings into forms, always following a poetic urgency . . .

Lam painted *La jungla* in a period of intense introspection. He relates that when he first saw *The Martyrdom of Saint Maurice*, by El Greco, a work that he considers "the marvel of marvels," he reflected on the fact that the artist painted it at about age forty. At the time that Lam saw it, he was twenty-two. As he neared age forty, he said to himself: "The moment has come to do something important."

To paint *La jungla* I made maximum use of what I learned from studying the classics. And if that work is now widely renowned, it's because I did not paint it just casually, but rather seriously, with all my effort. I worked as if in a ritual, supported by my experiences in Spain and France. Into that work I put all my analytical abilities, which were never in conflict with my feelings. My interest in African and Polynesian art inspired me, and led me to unfold a series of subconscious motivations and observations; these did not follow sentimental pathways. I wanted to follow the insightful path opened by those primordial art forms, although without forgetting the compositional rigor that I had observed in Poussin and Cézanne.

As he painted, it upset him to see that for many Cubans his work seemed to mean nothing. Those were times in which every foreign creation was published, promoted, and honored. He said, "I have never seen a country so remote from its own reality as mine is."

In those days of penury, he was surprised to read his own name in the company of Fidelio Ponce and Víctor Manuel, in the context of a government grant to the three artists who best represent Cuba:

> I paid it no attention, but Helena, with her European upbringing, said that I should go find out about it. So I went to the Ministry of Education, a useless trip: I met up with a friend from Sagua, and after long discussions with secretaries and assistants, we were able to nearly force our way into his office. The minister, with evident sarcasm, asked what we wanted. I informed him of my curiosity about the situation. He answered that he had proposed the grants, but that nothing had yet been firmly decided. I later found out that they went to a few political lackeys.

He sold the painting for three hundred dollars . . .

Notes on Photomontage

Grete Stern

———◦———

Text read at the Foto Club Argentino, Buenos Aires, 1967.

This is testimony from one of Latin America's few photomontage artists. Grete Stern had no connection to the surrealist movement, but in photomontage she created a body of work that analyzed dreams, sometimes a surrealist preoccupation. She gave this lecture late in life, but at the time that she made the montages discussed, in the late 1940s, she was associated with the Madí abstract art group, hosting exhibitions in her home. The Julio Cortázar story that she refers to at the very end, "Las babas del diablo," was the basis for Michelangelo Antonioni's film about photographers, Blow-Up. *In today's age of digital image manipulation, this lecture reminds us how labor-intensive photography and its related arts were in the past.*

Some years ago the magazine *Idilio* (published by Editorial Abril) devoted one page in each issue to the interpretation of dreams, titled "Psychoanalysis Will Help You." At this time, psychoanalytic ideas penetrated nearly all levels of society, and this page was eagerly read by the magazine's predominantly female readership.

I recall that the scholarly and analytical part of this section was under the direction of Dr. Gino Germani, who was well-known in intellectual circles, and signed his notes with the pseudonym Richard Rest. The Abril publishing house invited me to illustrate the interpreted dreams through photographs, and I proposed the use of photomontage for this.

The work proceeded more or less along these lines: Germani would send me the text of the dream, which was usually a faithful copy of one of the many letters that Abril received requesting interpretation. Sometimes, before commencing my work, I discussed the interpretation with Dr. Germani. Often, he requested specific characteristics in the illustration: that it be horizontal or vertical, with the foreground darker that the background, or perhaps that it show unbalanced shapes. At other times, he would specify that a figure should appear doing this or that thing, or requested floral or animal forms.

What is a photomontage? Here is a quick definition: It is set of different photographs, either already existing or specially shot, united to create a new photographic composition. This manner of working suggests numerous possibilities for arrangement, among them the joining of vastly divergent elements. For example: A woman in a bathing suit at a dance hall leading an elephant. Moreover, one can distort the proportions of the elements used in the photomontage. Thus, it is easy to have a child sitting on a housefly that might represent an aircraft, flying above a forest of cabbages. The perspective, as well, can be distorted: a man photographed from above examining some towers, or trees photographed from below. The distorted perspective will always give the effect of uncertainty or of strangeness. I should add that, in contrast, a correct perspective is essential for other cases, such as the child riding on the housefly, because in that case the correct perspective increases the image's visual credibility.

There are various techniques for rendering photomontages. For example, you can project the various elements of the composition directly onto photographic paper using an enlarger. This involves moving the enlarger forward or backward to achieve the desired size, or moving the paper that receives the projection according to where the image will be located. Or you can mask parts of a negative or the photo paper to prevent the entire negative from projecting, or in order to leave parts of the paper blank for other projections, or in order to keep one image from covering another, unless (as frequently happens) that is the desired effect.

The montages that I exhibit here [at the Foto Club Argentino] were realized in another manner: First I prepared a sketch, a pencil drawing, which is a diagram of the elements and their locations on the montage. For example: a cloudy background, a sandy beach in the foreground, on which we see a glass bottle with a girl trapped inside. I enlarged the negatives according to the sketch. The clouds and the beach came from negatives in my archive; I took the picture of the girl seated in the position indicated, and enlarged it and placed it behind a real bottle. In order to give the illusion that the girl is in the bottle, I photographed the juxtaposition and cropped it. Next, I adjusted the background tone of both the sky and the beach, so that the bottle stands out properly. Then I adjusted the size of the bottle relative to the background, to arrive at the best tonality and relative sizes. I prefer this method because it allows me to make choices visually, rather than through thought, adjusting or changing the photographic elements until I arrive at a satisfactory composition. Next, I attach the photographs in the preferred arrangement. If necessary, I may add other elements, such as shadows, lined borders, or others. Touch-ups are also useful in a montage, highlighting or suppressing what I want. In this case, the result consisted of both graphic and photographic elements.

Another way of working, more complicated than the one I have just described, but which yields better effects of space, light, shadow, and ultimate veracity, goes like this: I place the various photos that will make up the montage, either loose or between glass plates, attached to sticks or boards, in their corresponding locations, as if this were a scene on a stage. If necessary, I can leave some elements out of focus. In the background, the clouds; the beach, closer to the camera; and at the edge of the beach, between sand and sky, the bottle with the girl. No photo actually touches another. This method makes possible new effects by shifting the lighting. Finally, I photograph the entire arrangement.

Photomontage can also serve other purposes. Architects, sculptors, decorators, and especially theater set designers, use it often. Photomontage demands close regulation of perspective and proportion . . . It can also be used for advertising publicity. These days it is used less often than it was ten or fifteen years ago [in the early 1950s]. But it is always interesting to use for book covers, posters, and notices . . .

Discussing whether or not photography is an art form seems to me to be a waste of time, because the task of defining art is endless, stale, and controversial. No definition of art can deny the importance photography has in the social, political, and expressive life of people today. In any case, photography is for me a medium of personal expression, and it requires, as Julio Cortázar said in his story "Las babas del diablo," discipline, aesthetic training, and steady hands.

A World Created by Magic

Excerpts from a Conversation with André Pierre

Donald Cosentino

———◆———

From *Sacred Arts of Haitian Vodou* , ed. Donald J. Cosentino.
(Los Angeles, CA: UCLA Fowler Museum, 1995), xx–xxi.

When André Breton visited Haiti in 1945, he found an active art scene at the Centre d'Art in the capital, Port-au-Prince. Many of its artists were current or former practitioners of Vodou, the indigenous religion, and this animated many of their subjects. André Pierre, a priest of Vodou, came to the Centre a few years later. Here, he discusses the impact of Vodou on his imagery.

The Vodou religion is before all other religions. It is more ancient than Christ. It is the first religion of the Earth. It is the creation of the World. The World is created by Vodou. The world is created by magic. The first magician is God who created people with his own hands from the dust of the Earth. People originated by magic in all countries of the world. No one lives of the flesh. Everyone lives of the spirit.

People who are not aware of this are not profound in their studies. They write and they read, but their study is not profound. It is not sufficient to read from a book. You must study nature. You must study people. You must study your neighbors. You must study that all is dust, and will return to dust. You must study that people possess nothing. One should eat well. Drink well. Sleep well. Enjoy your soul. Wait for the last day.

My life is very simple. I've been alone since I was five. I have no father. No mother, no grandfather nor grandmother. I have been the master of my personality since the age of fourteen. I am the protector of my life: me, God, the Spirits and the Dead.

I paint to show the entire world what the Vodou religion is. Because three-fourths of the terrestrial globe thinks that the Vodou religion is diabolical, I paint to show them that Vodou is not diabolical.

The Vodou religion is purely Catholic, apostolic, but not Roman. It is not directed by men. It is directed uniquely by God. Since all people are liars, no one is a Catholic. Only God and his spirits are Catholic. The spirits of Vodou are the limbs of God. God is the body and the spirits are the limbs. To use Vodou, you must be an honest man. One who likes his neighbor. Because it is your neighbor who is God. You receive nothing from God. You receive everything from your neighbor. God passes everything through the hands of your neighbor. If you do not know your neighbor, you do not put your faith in your God who loves you. To love God, you must pass through your neighbor.

Love, love. Those who do not love are nothing. Love of God. Love of neighbor. Love of work. Love for doing some good. When we have to do something, love of doing it well. You must not judge anyone. One does not know. For God told you, "You will not see me, but you will see the poor always with you." When they come to your home to ask for charity, have the courtesy to say, "I have nothing this morning. Pass by in a few days and I will leave something for you." But don't ignore them. Don't deceive them. Why not love the poor? Why do you not have the poor live with you? It is only Vodou which welcomes the poor.

Vodou allows you to walk with your head held high. Religion makes you walk with your head low. But with Vodou you can fight any war. All men are warriors. But with religion, No. Men are slaves. It is always, Yes, Yes. You don't have the right to say anything but "Yes" to everything they tell you. Slaves of slaves. You don't have a personality. But with Vodou, you keep your personality: "I want," or "I don't want." But in religion, there is neither "I want," nor "I don't want." That's what personality is: the return of the Guinea spirits.

After Haiti's independence, in 1804, they returned, guided by the Star of the Messiah. Guided by the Star, and the Cross of Christ, Judah's tribe, the roots of David. Ogou returned with a red and blue flag. And the woman saint brought the Kongo Paket [bundle of spiritual objects]. Ogou took away the white, and left a bi-color. He changed the country. He took the white away from the French flag. He said, "I am giving this land back to you, and I am coming home."

I am going with my big horse behind me
The river brought me and will take me back
Two feet and two arms led my horse
My bags are packed and tied
And my flag is deployed

My bongo is on my back
Forward, riflemen!

Before I paint, I take this canvas and I put it on the easel. I wait for an inspiration, before describing it on earth. Then an inspiration comes. I sing a song, and then I describe what I sang. I describe the song on the canvas.

Hell is on earth. Paradise is on Earth. Purgatory is on Earth. All is on earth. Nothing is in the sky. Nothing was made in the sky. No one needs to speak of the sky. Instead of talking about the sky, talk instead of the earth. God has said, "If you don't believe me when I tell you about terrestrial things, how will you believe when I tell you about celestial things?" God does nothing in the celestial. Even to create the sun and the moon he put his foot on earth; all was created on Earth.

For me, the mother of the terrestrial is the Virgin Mary. Honor the saints. Honor the relics of the Saints. But honor the holy Virgin more than the angels and the saints. The Virgin Mary is Ezili Danto. Not Freda, for she is the mother of pain, going up to Calvary. The mother of suffering. Freda is Elizabeth. The Mother of John the Baptist. John the Baptist is the Word. The Breath which comes out of the mouth of God. All the saints are *lwa*. St. John the Baptist is Ti-Jean Petwo, called "Bacalou Baka." I am married to Ezili Danto. I sleep at her altar on Tuesdays:

Ezili Danto, lend me the chick of your black hen
I am going to make my magic work
It is you who walks
It is you who sees
Ezili Danto, lend me the chick of your black hen

I have confidence in the spirits. I love the spirits. I live with the spirits. I respect the spirits. I do what I want with the spirits, and they do what they want with me. Because they have confidence that I will never betray them. That is why I have confidence in the spirits.

PART FIVE

Constructive and Informalist Abstraction

The New Art of America

Joaquín Torres-García

———◦———

From "Nuevo arte de las Américas," *Apex*, July 1942, 11–16.

Always a persistent polemicist, Torres-García's call for an autochthonous art form grew even more urgent in the 1940s. His Americanism was founded on a primitivistic appreciation of certain pre-Conquest art forms, expressed in an abstract language that he regarded as universal. This combination was his own creation, yet it had great influence across the continent. His continental idealism is worth comparing with that of his compatriot Pedro Figari, document 3. The urgency that he felt led Torres-García to a certain prolixity, which has here been condensed.

Today's artists have understood that art cannot be separated from the human problem. Therefore, they should select what each age requires, but only, in my opinion, what it requires in a universal sense; that is, what can unite humans rather than divide them. And in realizing this, art must preserve its purely visual and nondescriptive aspects, because visual creation belongs to a universal order, being based on universal laws. In this way, there is no longer any disparity between the form and what is expressed, for everything joins in perfect unity. Perhaps some artists have misunderstood this urge, in trying to approach human life, because they have believed that the human was only to be found in the anecdotal. But we don't believe that; we have resolved the problem in another way. And by resolving it in this way, we see that we enter fully into the great universal tradition that demands, just as we demand, that both the life and the aspirations of man, along with those of art, should be founded on the pure laws of thought. We establish thereby an objective law that will raise humans above the level of their individuality. This individuality separates humans, while the universal law unites them. Hence, thought of a geometric sort should direct our art and our life.

Well, then, on our continent, many centuries ago, there was an amazing and perfectly good culture, founded on just those principles. And that is reason enough why we should not search far afield for something we already have close at hand, and in a form that is both more understandable and more appropriate to our world . . .

Across the Americas, a great desire for unification is rising. And although some interpret this urge in a narrow political sense, we ought to contribute to this movement, without losing sight of the primordial, while distancing ourselves from the merely political. We must explore deeper realms, disregarding the purely material aspect and keeping it out of our thoughts.

We are faced with the human problems of all countries, which interest us because they are human in the universal sense. However, without being selfish, we should be even more interested in our own problems. Here we have been given our own ground to cultivate and we must complete our own tasks. For this reason, we already inverted the map, indicating that our North was the South, and so, in a way, breaking our ties to the spiritual tyranny of Europe. Let us reintegrate ourselves, then, into the great Indo-American family.

What we are proposing is not pan-Americanism, but a spiritual union based on a profound relationship that transcends the concept of States. We need an objective toward which to orient our production, and also one to serve as a basis. This would not only define us, in that sense, for ourselves, but also for others. Under the sign of Indo-America, we can march in perfect harmony, basing ourselves on something real, since the artist too must take from the earth. We must be, then, artists of the Americas . . .

Our generation should be a new one, which attempts to relate to this land by penetrating into its depths. Therefore, we disregard and repudiate the superficial, which, as it has no roots, does not survive here; and this means everything foreign. We must also reject colonialism, the invaders, and the pseudo-culture they created: it is a bitter drink brewed from the worst kinds of alcohol. To be precise, if we want to find stature, nobility, measure, order—that is, what should be called culture—we can find it in the ancient cultures of this continent; there is everything that could elevate, regenerate, and purify us . . .

Let us build. Form ourselves. Create. A true culture must replace what is commonly called culture here. Not, then, an amalgam of diverse kinds of knowledge and principles, incoherent and random, but something mature and unified: a structure. Something integral, based on a fertile idea, realized in harmonious conjunction.

In recent years, we have already carried out an initial task. The idea of structure, of construction, has been launched, and works have been created in accordance with it. The geometric principle has appeared, and this is already a reintegration into the archaic culture. The idea of the cosmos, of universality, has also been introduced. And, because these ideas did not previously exist among us, we can say that the return to the tradition of the continent begins now—and not through archaeological studies, as in other parts of America, but through the essence of that tradition . . .

Falling into the archaeological, making South American pastiches, would be an extreme danger that we must avoid at all costs. That is what everyone who has tried to make an autochthonous art has fallen into: Chileans, Mexicans, Peruvians, etc., even including figures such as Diego Rivera. If not that, another stumbling block is just as dangerous: falling into folklorism. For now we seem to have freed ourselves from that pitfall, and I am sure that we will remain free of it. We are equally untouched by the values and qualities of European art that we studied so devotedly. Let Cézanne and Picasso, Matisse and Renoir, remain over there. Let Cubism and Neoplasticism remain over there. And even the masters of all schools. And why not Egypt and Greece, and Byzantium as well . . . because we have here an art as strong and as profound as theirs. It is better for us to study our own, in order to understand its essence . . .

Let us start from this: We here are not in Western Europe. This is a reality. And although this land was colonized by Europeans, that means nothing; we are in South America. Their European problem, then, does not have to be our problem. Our culture must have a different origin. This continent is younger; its chronology is not that of the Old World; our prehistory comes later than European prehistory. So the origin of culture here is more recent. Besides, at a certain moment its normal evolution was interrupted by the invaders, which is to say that it was buried for almost four centuries.

Well, then, I believe that if the autochthonous culture is to continue, we must pick it up where it was left off, ignoring a false culture that was formed later: false in the sense that it could never be more than a transplant. And that hybrid, mixed, and deformed thing is what we call our culture today. Poets, philosophers, artists, musicians, statesmen, legislators, educators, everyone, for the moment, has that illusion and is in that false position . . .

The lack of character of these South American peoples is only apparent, for underneath the slight European veneer lies the true autochthonous character. Now what happens is that, due to the European overlay, the true character does not thrive. But with a different consciousness of the situation, it can grow and develop, and this is what should happen. This true character is also threatened by the bastard culture to which I have referred, a sort of covering scar that leaves no outlet for the genuine. One lives in that shadow and ignores a reality whose hour has come. It is time for it to manifest itself. Above all, any exaltation of the invaders and their grotesque manifestations should cease. Because the Indian was a geometer. And that means culture. And through that comes a manifestation of Universal Humanity. With the Indian (and one can hardly speak of the contemporary Indian), we can have a dialogue. His monuments and his cosmic concept of the world, which determined his social system, his calendar, his mythology, and his art: these speak to us eloquently. But such fundamentals, which are similar to those of other lands, here are marked with their own particular structure and qualities. Through them, we must follow the great Tradition of Humanity, but in our own Indo-American way.

Inventionist Manifesto, Salon Peuser, Buenos Aires, March 1946

———

From *Arte Concreto-Invención*, August 1946, 8.

This manifesto, which has sixteen signers, was written by the members of the Concrete-Invention group in 1946, near the time that the Madí movement split away from it. The divisions were both personal and philosophical, as Concrete-Invention remained devoted to pure painting. The polemic here is against illusionistic art of any sort, no matter how loosely based on reality.

The artistic age of representational fictions has reached its end. People everywhere are becoming less and less sensitive to illusionistic images. That is to say, they have progressed in their feeling of integration with the world. The old phantasmagoria no longer satisfy the aesthetic needs of the new person, who was formed in a reality that demands total participation, without reservation.

Thus the prehistory of the human spirit comes to an end.

Scientific aesthetics will replace speculative, idealist, and utopian aesthetics. Considerations regarding the nature of beauty have lost their reason for being. The metaphysics of beauty have died of exhaustion, to be replaced by the physics of beauty.

There is nothing esoteric about art; those who style themselves among the "initiated" are only liars.

Representational art shows abstractly framed static "realities," when in fact all representative art is an abstraction. Only an idealistic misunderstanding has caused people to label nonrepresentative aesthetic experiences as "abstract." In truth, these experiences, whether we realize it or not, have taken us in the opposite direction from abstraction; the results, which have included an elevation of the values of pure painting, prove it irrefutably. The battle begun by so-called abstract art is fundamentally the battle for concrete invention.

Representational art tends to sap the cognitive strength of viewers, rendering them unaware of their true powers. The raw material of representative art has always been illusion:

Illusion of space.

Illusion of expression.

Illusion of reality.

Illusion of movement.

A formidable play of mirrors that leaves people cheated and debilitated.

In contrast, concrete art exalts Being, because it practices Being. An art of the act generates the will to act.

Let a poem or a painting not serve merely to justify a retreat from action, but rather let both contribute to placing the human in the world. We concrete artists are not above any controversy. We are on the front lines of all controversies.

Down with art that reinforces our differences. We favor an art that serves, using its own methods, the new union arising in the world.

We practice the technique of joy. Only exhausted techniques feed off melancholy, resentment, and conspiracy.

We favor creative delight. Down with the disastrous plagues of Existentialism and Romanticism. Down with the minor poets with their minor wounds and minor introspective dramas. Down with all elite art. We favor a collective art.

The surrealists have said, "Down with optics." They are the Last Mohicans of representation. We say, "Exalt Optics."

This is fundamental: to surround people with real things and not phantasms. Concrete art accustoms people to a direct relationship with things, and not pictures of things. A particular aesthetic demands a particular technique. The aesthetic function opposes "good taste." It is the pure function. Let us neither seek nor find; let us invent.

Madí Manifesto

Gyula Kosice

————◆————

From an exhibition brochure, 1946.

Madí is presented here as surpassing all preceding art, and the manifesto takes certain special pains to separate it from its contemporaries in the Concreto-Invención group. Of the two groups, Madí was generally more hospitable to three-dimensional works and to work in other disciplines, as they point out here.

Madí art can be identified by the organization of elements peculiar to each art form across the spectrum. It contains presence, movable dynamic arrangement, development of the theme itself: clarity and plurality as absolute values. Madí art is, therefore, free from contamination by the phenomena of expression, representation, and meaning.

Madí *drawing* is an arrangement of dots and lines on a surface.

Madí *painting*, color and two-dimensionality. An uneven and irregular frame with a flat, curved, or concave surface. Articulated surfaces with linear, rotating and changing movement.

Madí *sculpture*, three-dimensionality without color. Total form and solid shapes with contour, articulated, rotating, changing movement, etc.

Madí *architecture*, environment and mobile interchangeable forms.

Madí *music*, plotting of sounds in the golden section.

Madí *poetry*, invented proposition, concepts and images that are untranslatable by means other than language. Pure conceptual event.

Madí *theater*, movable scenery, invented dialogue.

Madí *novel and short story*, characters and events outside specific time and space, or in totally invented time and space.

Madí *dance*, body and movements circumscribed within a proportional environment, without music.

In highly industrialized countries, the old bourgeois realism has almost completely disappeared. Naturalism beats a hasty retreat, defending itself halfheartedly.

It is at this point that abstraction, essentially expressive and romantic, takes its place. Figurative schools of art, from Cubism to surrealism, are caught up in this order. Those schools have responded to the ideological needs of the age, and their achievements are invaluable contributions to the solution of problems of contemporary culture. Nevertheless, their historic moment must be considered finished. Their insistence on themes beyond their actual physical properties is a return to naturalism, rather than to the true Constructivist spirit that has spread through all countries and cultures and is seen, for example, in Expressionism, surrealism, Constructivism, etc.

With Concrete Art—which is in fact a younger branch of that same abstract spirit—we began the great age of nonfigurative art, in which artists, availing themselves of elements in their respective continuum, create the work in all its purity, without hybridization or objects without essence. But Concrete Art lacked universality and organization. It fell into deep and irreconcilable contradictions. The great voids and taboos of old art were preserved: in painting, superimposition, the rectangular frame, lack of a purely visual theme; in sculpture, stasis and the interference between volume and environment; in poetry, epistemological statements and images translatable into graphic language. The result was that Concrete Art could not use an organic theory and disciplinary practice to seriously combat the intuitive movements, such as surrealism, that have won over the world. From the latter triumph has come, despite adverse conditions, the victory of instinctive impulses over reflection, of intuition over consciousness; of the revelation of the unconscious over detached analysis and the artist's thorough and rigorous study using the laws of the object to be constructed; of the symbolic, the hermetic, and the magical over reality; of metaphysics over experience.

Regarding the theory and appreciation of art, subjective, idealist, and reactionary description still rule.

To sum up, pre-Madí art was:

A scholastic, idealist historicism.
An irrational concept.
An academic technique.
A false, static, and one-dimensional composition.
A work lacking in essential utility.

A consciousness paralyzed by insoluble contradictions and impervious
to the permanent renewal of technique and style.

Madí rises against all this. It confirms man's firm, all-absorbing desire to
invent and construct objects within timeless human values. It labors alongside all humanity in the struggle to construct a new classless society that
liberates human energy, masters time and space in all senses, and dominates
matter to the limit. Without basic descriptions of its total organization, it is
impossible to construct the object or bring it into the continuity of creation.
Thus we define the concept of invention in the field of technique and the
concept of creation as a completely defined essence.

For Madí-ism, invention is our internal, controllable method, and creation
is our unchangeable reality. Therefore, Madí INVENTS AND CREATES.

Madí and Concrete-Invention

Gyula Kosice

————

From *Autobiografía* (Buenos Aires: Asunto Impreso, 2010), 45–47.

Here the principal founder of the Madí group, writing years after its founding, recalls its origins and how it diverged from the proposals of Concreto-Invención. The story of the creation of the first Madí poster is of minor histori-cal interest, but it did give him an important idea for light as a medium, which he also sets forth here.

The year 1946 continued the feverish rhythm of the previous one. My creative activity went hand in hand with the necessity of defining more coherently the goals of the group and giving it a clear and defined identity in the world.

Certain divergences of a personal, artistic, and ideological nature grew wider among us, and led eventually to a split. Thus it was that a group of companions ([Tomás] Maldonado, [Ennio] Iommi, and soon [Alfredo] Hlito, [Edgar] Bayley and a few others), who felt more closely identified with the previous projects of concrete art after the manner of Max Bill, split off and formed the Asociación de Arte Concreto-Invención. They held to an orthog-onal vocabulary, within a rectangular format that they treated in the classic two-dimensional way, under the premise of "exalting optics."

This split reinforced the necessity for us to work toward the launch of another movement, unanimous and clearly distinct. When the time came to think of a name for the group, we needed a designation that would differenti-ate it from the Movimiento de Arte Concreto-Invención, under which we had all gathered previously.

It's important to point out the reasons why we could not continue with the original name. We thought that an obvious contradiction existed between the defining concepts of our two groups. If we proposed "invention," then we could not speak of "concrete art," because we understood the former term to exclude the latter. And we were not making concrete art; rather, we were undertaking pure invention of the art object. At that time the term "Madí" came up, an invented word that nonetheless was based on "Madrí, Madrí . . ." the war cry of the Republican cause during the Spanish Civil War [as they defended Madrid from the invading Fascists].

The name is copyrighted as Intellectual Property No. 238.535. The appropriations and falsifications of the origins of the term Madí that [Carmelo] Arden Quin later disseminated were the precipitating causes of his departure from the group in 1947, the year that he moved to Paris. He also intended to claim for himself the invention of the shaped canvas, when this was the undeniable creation of [Rhod] Rothfus. But I will leave these polemics to one side.

In mid-1946, Grete Stern and I created the famous inaugural poster for Madí. At the intersection of Avenida 9 de Julio and Corrientes there was an enormous sign that promoted Movado watches; it was made from large letters outlined by neon tubes. Grete and I went up to the roof of the building where the sign was located and photographed it against the background of the obelisk. Later we made a photomontage to which we added the remaining letters in smaller scale. In this way, the word Madí with its large capital M was framed against the unmistakable Buenos Aires cityscape with the obelisk; this showed the origins of our growing movement in the River Plate region.

The initial idea had been to photograph the sign at night to take advantage of the neon glow, but Grete did not then have the appropriate equipment. In any case, the linear dance of those neon tubes stayed in my mind as a powerful presence. In that same year, I thought of the idea of using neon as material for a piece of sculpture. At that moment, I was making linear sculpture with joined strips of metal. Why not use a material that had light within itself, and thus incorporate the magic of luminosity? That is how the first neon sculptures were born. This also marked the first appearance of neon in an art work; I cannot fail to underline the importance that this event had (and still has) for me.

Finally the day came when Madí was ready to be launched into the world, but we still had no access to art galleries. Once again, my friend [Robert] Weibel Richard, cultural attaché at the French embassy, came to our aid. Through his assistance we obtained the use of the auditorium of the Instituto Francés de Estudios Superiores, which was located behind the Galería Van Riel on Florida Street, near the offices of the Asociación Amigos del Arte.

At the entrance to the exhibition we passed out flyers that were printed with phrases expressing our basic beliefs: "Against static painting and sculpture. The non-rectangular frame and articulated movable sculpture, abstract and linear, are absolute inventions of Madí." Participants in the show included Valdo Wellington, Martín Blaszko, Elizabeth Steiner, Ricardo Humbert, Alejandro Havas, Esteban Eitler, Paulina Ossona, and Diyi Laañ and myself. In our works we unveiled the full range of what we were proposing: the articulation of colors and planes, the introduction of curved edges and surfaces, the shaped canvas, flexible sculpture, the proposal for movable and disposable architecture. We had the will to transcend the limits of art as recognized at that time, and we launched into creative exploration of a continent of new artistic realities.

Art Has to Be an Adventure

An Interview with Fernando de Szyszlo

M. Isabel Guerra

———

From *Las Burbujas Recargadas,* http://burbujasreloaded.wordpress.com/2005/06/09/.

Here, a prolific abstract painter expresses his thoughts on Latin American identity and surrealism. This interview also offers valuable oral history on the transformation of Peruvian art after the decline of indigenism. Like César Moro (see document 18), Szyszlo looked to surrealism in his early days.

Q: Many Peruvian artists whom I have interviewed believe that for a Latin American artist, the artisanal traditions of our continent, and our history, amount to an obligatory point of reference for their work, even if unconscious, during the creative process. What is your opinion on this?

A: Well, I will tell you that in Peru it is only recently an obligatory point of reference, because up until the 1940s no important Peruvian artists made mention of pre-Conquest art. Indigenists spoke of indigenous art, and at times popular craftwork or folklore, but never of the pre-Columbian past. Thus, when you say "the artisanal traditions" I do not know if you are referring to the living folkloric traditions, or the traditional creations of Peruvian artists from the beginning of our history.

Q: I refer to the latter, to [pre-Columbian] artistic creation.

A: I do not think that all Peruvian artists feel particularly linked to that, nor do I think that it is necessary to feel a linkage to the pre-Columbian tradition in order to create good works; but there are some who have treasured this cultural storehouse, this other facet of our culture, the authentic or the local one. And of course, some have made use of this, and prospered. But I repeat, I do not think it is necessary for a Peruvian artist to link his work to it. For example, [painter] Sérvulo Gutiérrez knows pre-Columbian art better than almost anyone, but has no intention of using its motifs.

Q: Critics have written a great deal about your art. Most seem to agree in describing it as a union of the Peruvian cultural heritage with certain modern tendencies in European painting. After dedicating your entire life to painting, how would you analyze your own work?

A: I sincerely believe that whatever one produces is practically involuntary. What is certain is that just as I studied European art and probably allowed myself to be influenced by it on a conscious level, I equally admired pre-Columbian Peruvian art, and surely this entire vocabulary of forms that was created in the past in Latin America also became part of my own vocabulary. But I have never wanted to use any source directly, and I have never done so. Picasso and Matisse took ideas from African art, but they did not want to make African art; they observed the discoveries of African artists regarding the treatment of forms, and they used those discoveries to their own advantage, for their own culture. Such has also been my relationship with Peruvian pre-Columbian art.

Q: [Novelist Mario] Vargas Llosa wrote that all of your works are variations on one theme: metamorphosis.

A: Yes, undoubtedly; I have said the same thing myself many times. I will tell you that I belong to a certain type of painters. We feel within ourselves, rather vaguely, that we search through a thousand different forms and many different paintings, for a certain "feeling of a painting." Through our entire career we try to reach this, without success. For all of my life I have pursued a certain sensation in my painting, and this links all of my works together. They are all sincere attempts to capture something fleeting.

Q: Is this a sensation?

A: It is a sensation, because it is not a form. A search for certain shapes or defined things would be easier: a certain play of light or a shadow, for example. [French art historian] André Malraux said once, "To be a painter is to place works that do not yet exist alongside works that do." That is, confronting the paintings of others, and trying to find one's own painting. Caravaggio said the same thing when confronted with works by Renaissance painters: "I am also a painter," which means "I also have something to say." That's what it means to be a painter, in the end: to bring forth, from yourself, an image or a form which is yours.

Q: Is it this search for an unreachable image that has led you to create paintings in series?

A: Yes, without a doubt. I have never intended to create a series of works.

I start work on a painting, and it ends up being a *Black Sun*, for example, which captures a certain sensation. Then, when the work is finished I notice that it is not quite what I wanted; there is a disjunction between what I wanted to do and what I have just done. Then I try to reach the sensation again in another work. And the same problem arises and I keep trying, approaching the idea from various angles, and the end result is a series of paintings with the same title, born of the same sensation, but different.

Q: You once told me that when you returned from Europe in the 1950s, you found the country very much behind the times in regard to art.

A: Well, from my adolescence I have been very attracted to literature, probably for family reasons because my house had a very large library, on the one hand belonging to Abraham Valdelomar, my mother's brother who was a writer, and on the other to my father, who was a highly educated European man who spoke fourteen languages. Thus I was always very interested, very attracted to literature even before I took up painting. When I finished high school [in 1943] I already knew that Peruvian literature was very rich; I was unaware that Peruvian painting had not yet reached the same level. When I took up painting after having studied architecture for a while, I immediately connected with artists from my generation, such as [Sebastián] Salazar Bondy, [Javier] Sologuren, and [Jorge Eduardo] Eilson, and also with some from the previous generation, such as [Emilio Adolfo] Westphalen and [José María] Arguedas; they all became friends of mine. Around that time I began to learn about contemporary art, and I found that Peruvian painting had actually developed very little. Sérvulo had not yet made his best works; Ricardo Grau was the best of the independents, but he had trouble finding a place for himself because of the domination of the indigenists. The panorama of painting was actually very depressing; there was not a single gallery. I held my first exhibition at the North American Cultural Institute, which at that time was next door to the church of La Merced. And it was not just because I was young that I exhibited there; everyone did, including Sérvulo and [José] Sabogal, because there was no other gallery. It was the only one. In the Bach Academy they occasionally had exhibitions, and there was a small salon on Palacio Street whose name I can't recall, but the fact is that there was nobody who took care of the task of being the intermediary between the artist and the public. That is, nobody made a living selling paintings, and therefore nobody helped painters to live.

Q: So are you saying that there was no market for art?

A: There was none; it all had yet to be developed. And it was a long struggle.
    It began with the creation of Francisco Moncloa's Galería Lima [in 1948],
    which was the first gallery in Lima in the modern sense of the word. We
    also began to have magazines such as *Las moradas* [in 1947], which was
    fantastic and up to date with what was going on in the world. They pub-
    lished articles on Kafka, Proust, and contemporary music. In the same
    year, the group Espacio [Space] was formed, which labored on behalf of
    contemporary art and architecture, and staged conferences and exhibi-
    tions. It produced a tremor in the cultural life of Lima and without doubt
    changed it forever. Then in 1955, with the foundation of the Instituto de
    Arte Contemporáneo, the climate changed radically. They not only
    staged lectures, they tried to educate the public by bringing artists and
    shows from abroad, such as Armando Morales and Alejandro Obregón.
    We also brought in exhibitions from England in the form of the English
    contributions to the São Paulo Biennials.

Q: You and Ricardo Grau were the ones who tried the hardest to modernize
    painting in Peru. I imagine that there were many polemical discussions
    in those years.

A: Well, Grau was older and he led the charge at first, in the early 1940s,
    before I took up painting. Ricardo Grau and the critics Juan Ríos and
    Raúl María Pereyra had a magazine called *Nuestro tiempo*. There they
    published the first serious articles against indigenism and its domina-
    tion. My crusade began a little later, and it was more famous because we
    were younger and full of energy. Because *Nuestro tiempo* had a small
    circulation, we crusaded in the newspapers. Fortunately one member of
    the group Espacio was the architect Luis Miró Quesada, who designed
    my house, and who was a great champion of modern art. Because he was
    the son of the editor of the newspaper *El comercio*, he got them to give
    us a page every Thursday. And on that Thursday page we unleashed a
    great battle for modern art, along with some great polemics.

Q: And yet, in later years you began giving your works titles in Quechua
    [the language of the Inca].

A: Yes, I took an interest in Quechua culture. I was always interested in pre-
    Columbian art, but thanks to José María Arguedas, a very close friend,
    I found links to contemporary Quechua culture. We used to go on
    Sundays to see things in the theaters. And he introduced me to Quechua
    poetry, above all that marvelous poem *Apu Inca Atawallpamam*, which

is an elegy on the death of the Inca ruler Atahualpa. It is believed to date from the seventeenth century and was preserved by oral tradition; it was later taken down in Quechua and Arguedas translated it. In 1962, I staged an exhibition at the Instituto de Arte Contemporáneo, which was a series of paintings on that poem. It consisted of thirteen works, each titled after a line of the poem. The poem begins, "What a rainbow is this black rainbow" and that was one of the paintings. And there was also a beautiful line that read, "His grinding teeth are already biting the barbarous sadness." All the lines sounded very modern and very beautiful. The poem gave me a lot of motivation, and that show was certainly where I began to find my own language . . .

Q: I understand that when you were in Paris [1949–1951] you had contact with the circles of André Breton. What memories do you have of that time?

A: Oh, it was marvelous, marvelous. They were unforgettable years. I made some lifelong friends. [Mexican poet] Octavio Paz, for example; I saw him about four times a week. Now that he has passed away I miss him dearly, because he was a leader, a person of great ability and intelligence, and great cultural sensitivity. Thanks to Paz I got to know Breton, and I used to go to the surrealist group meetings, every Tuesday in a café in Place Blanche on Boulevard Clichy in Montmartre. There were all the surrealists who were active in those days. Many had died, others had broken away, but still there were André Breton, Benjamin Péret, Jean-Pierre Duprey; it was a very active group. I always was very drawn to surrealist thought and I still am. I don't think there is a better description of what art is than what Breton offered . . .

Q: Jumping up to the present: You have said that in the past there was neither a market for art nor anyone who lived from art. Now, in comparison, how do you view the situation?

A: I think it has had wonderful transformations. Painters can now live from their work. Of course, this too can be a danger. If it's dangerous not to sell works and be unable to make a living, then it's even more dangerous to sell your work easily, because the standards weaken, and you can become less critical of your own work. For a young painter it is especially dangerous, because one can head off into a completely commercial track. That is, if you know what works will sell, then those are the works that you make, and that's terrible. Art has to be an adventure, after all; painting must be an adventure . . .

Developing a Conscience as a Painter

Alejandro Obregón, as told to Fausto Panesso

———

From Fausto Panesso, *Alejandro Obregón ¡ . . . a la visconversa!*
(Bogota: Gamma, 1989), 9–23.

These are excerpts from a long interview with one of Colombia's leading artists of the mid-twentieth century. He found his style in response to the street violence of 1948 in which the leading presidential candidate was murdered. He reflects here on socially driven painting, and on certain dramatic events of his life such as his brief takeover of the national art school, which lasted just one year.

When I painted the massacres of 1948, I began to include "conscience" in my paintings. I began to take note of the protests that could be made with painting. Never the solutions, because painting cannot solve anything . . . Art can serve for a protest. When I exhibited *La masacre* [*The Massacre*, 1948], the Minister for Governance requested the work's removal from the hall. But it remained on display. I went to the cemetery, and I began to sketch cadavers. I remember a woman's beautiful face that had a bullet wound: nose up, mouth half open, and a gold tooth in her smile. The face was intact, but the skull had no top. I was standing over it, sketching detail by detail, when a hand tapped me on the shoulder. "You are desecrating my daughter." It was her mother. I moved away, quite shaken.

In 1948, we got a crazy idea. Alipio Jaramillo, [Ignacio] Gómez Jaramillo, Julio Abril, Marco Ospina, [Enrique] Grau, and I took over the School of Fine Arts. We collected the signatures of all 150 students who were enrolled. The signatures of 150 people who wanted change. We went to the office of professor [Luis] López de Mesa who was at that time the director of the National University. I remember him looking at us and saying, "With this letter, there is no alternative." Then, with all the scorn of a professor who saw us as little shits, he asked, "Which of you is the youngest?" We looked at each other. I was about six months younger than Grau. Right then and there, he named me director of the School. I unsheathed the dagger and fired everybody. We were driven. We had to throw off the academic rules, because everyone was boxed in . . .

Art is always a symbol. It is the highest form of search for a message through imagery. My painting is about freedom. Freedom is the word that best captures what I have tried to do. I paint what I have seen, what I have not seen, and what I may never see. Painting is born and lives its life between truth and lying.

A work begins as something you are curious about. You start to work, and the curiosity becomes an obsession, and from there, good painting can come. But not for long with just that subject; then you have to say, "Cut!" There is so much to see, and that is because one subject always leads to another, and you evolve. But some subjects become too easy. Then you must kill them. What's attractive about a good painting is that it's difficult, but it looks easy.

Each subject demands its own color. *La violencia* calls for gray tones; it is a funereal theme from the mortuary. In contrast, *El estudiante asesinado* [*The Murdered Student*, 1962] is colorful, almost like a carnival. Bright color can be a requirement for a painter who takes up a theme for an imposing painting . . . In *La violencia* the theme and the color go hand in hand. That work was the midpoint of a three-year period when everything was gray. I began with *Aves cayendo al mar* [*Birds Falling into the Sea*, 1961], which was black and gray. *Los volcanes* [*The Volcanoes*, 1959] is also gray. I painted *La violencia* in a fit of rage, in two days. I could see that I was on the right path so I persevered. It's the immediate reflection that I am talking about. The newspapers, people, the entire environment oppresses you, and you have to register a protest. You have to do your social duty. Once at Princeton University I got one of those questions that pins you to the wall: "Obregón, are you a political painter?" I replied, "No. A painter with a brick in his hand is more dangerous than one with a brush in his hand. As for that story about the pen being mightier than the sword, I don't believe it. It sounds great, but a sword is more dangerous than a pen, any day." What happens is that certain events become the straw that broke the camel's back. I start to paint political themes when I can't take it anymore and I have to let out a protest . . .

When I paint, I feel despair. You always start out to paint the most important work in the history of humanity; you think this about each and every painting, every morning: "This will be the painting!" Then at midday, you look honestly at it and say to yourself, "Well, it won't be the best, but it will be among the best." And then at night, "Oh crap! Just another painting." Nothing is ever what you hope it will be. Painting is a daily dose of disillusionment.

The Necessary Pluralism in Latin American Art

Manuel Felguérez

From *Artes Visuales*, April 1976, 6–7.

Manuel Felguérez resisted the political solutions of the Mexican muralists and carved out his own path. After study in Europe in the 1950s, he returned home to make murals that were abstract and sculptural. This earned him a place among the founders of La Ruptura (The Breakaway), a movement of revolt against previously accepted styles. He wrote this essay after seeing an exhibition of Brazilian folk art at the 1975 São Paulo Biennial, which caused him to reflect on the meaning(s) of the term "Latin American art."

At the most recent São Paulo Biennial, a group of Brazilian artists exhibited work that expressed their formal search through exploration of the popular arts of certain regions of that country. Yet another exhibition of our folkloric art, which is so beloved of our people and protected by our governments.

What is Latin American art?

The art produced before the conquest?

The art created during the three-hundred-year colonial period?

The art of the post-independence era?

Popular art, a product of the backwardness and poverty of large sectors or our population?

Cultured academic art of the nineteenth century?

Could our culture exist without Greece or Rome?

Can we deny the Christian influence on the art of Roman Catholic countries?

Have not the black people on our continent contributed their own sensibility?

Has the cultural imperialism of this century altered our traditions?

Have we not had East Asian influences since the beginning of our civilization?

All of the above means only that we are peoples with a great cultural heritage, and faced with the impossibility of reducing it to one, single product, we must accept that our art is a plural and highly diverse expression.

The creation of any aesthetic object is informed by rhetorical elements that make communication possible. From our rich and varied tradition, anyone who would be a creator must select those rhetorical elements that will enable his work to take its place in the endless chain of art. The result that artists achieve depends on the times in which they live and the selections that they have carried out. Whether they are aware of it or not, artists are shaped by the society, and their work acquires its meanings through it.

For an object to be considered art, it is indispensable that its message be potent, and that it show us some new aspect of reality. What has historically been termed artistic tradition does not include a painting or sculptural work made by just anyone in any manner, because the result of such action is merely that an object exists that did not exist before. This object would of course differ from any that had previously existed. But to be art, it would be further necessary for it to uncover a new aspect of the world that we did not understand before, and that it have sufficient power to influence the viewer's ideology through the simple act of seeing it.

Latin American art can diverge from North American or European art only insofar as its culture varies, and only by that amount. We cannot control this; we can only accept it. If we study the constellation of traditions that nourish our art and that of the United States, we will find that they are similar, but our cultural differences stand out more. I will mention only the best-known example: For geographical reasons, Mexico is the country that has experienced the most North American influence; however, it has not accepted influence from Northern art movements for the last several decades. First was Action Painting, then came Pop Art, Op Art, Super-Realism, conceptual and video art, etc. Not a single significant Mexican artist follows any of those tendencies, and this is not because they lack information about them; nor does it mean that those movements have not affected our sensibilities; it only means that their influence has not dominated us. The experiences of Americans and Europeans have been assimilated so as to yield different artistic results, and the same natural phenomenon has held true in the rest of Latin America.

The artist participates in the society both dialectically and diachronically; creating an art object activates those influences and shows their presence.

This mode of action for trained artists in their environments is very similar across the world. Art does have an international character; the differences that exist between one or more countries do not depend on their rhetorical sources; thus, anyone who does not accept art of the world as part of his own heritage will never realize his potential as an artist. Latin America is not one race, but rather a product of blending. Our culture cannot rely on just one race while ignoring the rest of what we are. Merely being an individual with a different mind and sensibility will inevitably lead one to produce different art objects.

Art is not an individual phenomenon, but rather a collective one without recognizing the fact. This is because the mental structures of a certain generation will cause a group of individuals to seek and to express similar things; thus are born their characteristic styles. Among the many in each generation who seek the same things within one tendency, there are some artists who have the gift of better communication, or of showing more clearly a new aspect of reality; the clarity of their works can influence a change in the ideology of the society, which in turn causes a search for new aesthetic pathways. Art as a social phenomenon implies quantity at its origin and quality as its goal.

The São Paulo Biennial is the proof of all the foregoing. It gives us the opportunity to see how Latin American art, which generally enjoys the same breadth of plural tendencies that exist in the rest of the world, can still produce a range of results. When we see in this Biennial a work inspired by Brazilian folklore, we quickly recognize those origins. But such obviousness is not the true path for art. Art is creation; it discovers new aspects of reality. Therefore, its function is not to show us what we were, or even what we are, but rather to uncover for us what we did not know before, and what we can only know thanks to the existence of art.

PART SIX

Midcentury Architectural Projects

Le Corbusier, the Education Ministry, and Pampulha

Oscar Niemeyer

——◦◦◦——

From *As curvas do tempo: Memórias* (Rio de Janeiro: Revan, 1998), 90–98.

If Latin American modern architecture labored under the shadow of Le Corbusier, certainly Oscar Niemeyer was among the architects who pulled it into the light. Here, in an excerpt from his autobiography, the Brazilian recounts a tense relationship with Le Corbusier. The key to Niemeyer's independence was the project at Pampulha, a landmark in his career. At one point in this excerpt, he accuses Le Corbusier of insisting too much on the primacy of his own vision; Niemeyer is probably guilty of that as well. Fortunately for all of us, this tension led to great buildings.

I had many struggles with Le Corbusier. Only in New York, as we worked on the United Nations building [in the late 1940s], did we actually spend much time together in daily conversations and lunches; only then did I get to know his hopes and anxieties as an architect.

But the first contact I had with him came in 1936 in Rio. Encouraged by Lúcio [Costa] and Gustavo Capanema, ex-Minister of Education, I invited him to give a series of lectures. Le Corbusier, exasperated by the incomprehension of his fellow professionals at home and anxious to demonstrate his talents, turned the invitation into two new projects for Brazil: the headquarters of the Ministry of Education, and the University of Mangueira. At that time, we barely walked around the edges of his architecture. We had all read about his exceptional work and taken it as a sacred scripture, but we were still not in on its details and minutiae, as we soon found out.

And this explains the high-handed disdain with which he departed from the plan that Lúcio developed for the Ministry. Lúcio had proposed a U-shaped building, a solution at variance with the linearity of his usual plans. But in order to shed light on his manner of action and his enthusiasm, I will relate what happened as this project in Rio developed.

Having set aside Lúcio's plan, Le Corbusier created two studies. One was for the ideal site at the edge of the bay; the other was for the site in the city center, which was eventually chosen. The latter was the outline that was developed into a plan by the team that Lúcio organized and that I was a part of.

I had preferred the first study. And, when I saw the designs for the second study heading toward adoption, I became upset and proposed a different idea based on the first study. [Team member] Carlos Leão liked the drawings that I made; he spoke with Lúcio, but I had already discarded them, never thinking they could be approved. Lúcio ordered them dug out, and they were approved.

My plans called for locating Le Corbusier's second design in the center of the downtown lot, with a large lobby open to the plaza on both sides, and with the exhibit halls and auditorium, slightly separate, facing the outside.

But, because my contribution to the plan has been often minimized or exaggerated—as always happens—I will point out that I also suggested other things, such as the elimination of the protrusions in the rear that accommodated the restrooms, the adoption of a central corridor instead of simple circulation, and the exclusion of the lowest panel of the sun visors next to the window sills.

I recall that Jorge Moreira did not like my ideas. He told Lúcio that the project was almost finished and the design concluded. But Lúcio held to his opinion, and my suggestions were accepted.

It is well to remember that it was not my plan that would be built, but rather the second design of Le Corbusier, with its façade shaded by louvers as at ABI [Brazilian press association], and as I had proposed in certain designs and sketches.

We sent the finished design to Le Corbusier along with a photo of a model, and he, not satisfied with merely being considered the architect of record on the project, made his own sketch over the top of our plan. This was later published in a Swiss magazine. But the old master protested too much. Our modifications shown in the photo varied little from his original conception.

We always said that the Ministry of Education project was the work of Le Corbusier. On the cornerstone is engraved: "According to the original sketch of Le Corbusier." Original sketch means the original outline, the basic idea, the architectural invention.

My own architecture began later, at Pampulha. One day Capanema took me to meet Benedito Valadares, governor of Minas Gerais state, who hoped to build a casino there at the "end of the world." And on that occasion I met Juscelino Kubitschek, then a candidate for mayor of [the state capital] Belo Horizonte. I created the designs and showed them to Benedito, but the project took form only later, when JK, now mayor, called on me again.

On the appointed day I returned to Belo Horizonte. JK explained, "I want to create a resort in Pampulha, a more beautiful complex than any in our country. With a casino, nightclub, church, and restaurant. And I would like to see the casino project tomorrow." So I complied, working all night in my room at the Hotel Central. In JK, I had never seen such enthusiasm, such a will to succeed, and such confidence in the undertaking, though many difficulties lay ahead.

The work began. JK followed our progress daily, convinced that this would be an important project for the city. Many times, we rode out in a boat to see the work from a distance, reflected in the surface of the lake. JK could not contain himself: "How beautiful! It will be the most pleasing neighborhood in the world!" But Pampulha gave us many headaches, for JK especially. He struggled to obtain impossible sums of money; he battled against the inertia around him, and against the provincial mindset of his staff.

For me, Pampulha was the beginning of my life as an architect. I began with great enthusiasm! To reach the site, I had to make long car trips over dirt roads, which were sometimes covered with mud. Often I had to stop and ask for assistance. Once a yoke of oxen pulled me out!

The project interested me immensely. This was my chance to overcome the monotony that characterized our contemporary architecture, which had been castrated by an ill-understood functionalism. The dogmas of "form and function" that rose up worked against the plastic freedom that reinforced concrete made possible.

Curves attracted me, the free and sensuous curves that the new techniques encouraged, and that our old Baroque churches used . . . And there Pampulha still sits, in defiance of the naysayers: the small church with its harmonious and varied curves, the casino, the club, and the restaurant. The latter has its curved awning sheltering open-air tables, reminding us that a curve, if well-constructed and supported, can be beautiful, logical, and graceful.

Pampulha interested a lot of people. Lúcio went to see it, and sent me a telegram: "Pampulha is beautiful." And many years later, my colleague [Paulo Mendes] da Rocha wrote to me from Paris: "Pampulha thrilled my entire generation." But the negative criticism kept coming, despite the importance accorded to it in the exhibition *Brazil Builds* [at the Museum of Modern Art in 1943].

I never worried about the criticism. I knew that one day, when people tired of so much monotony, they would begin to want something different. This is what happened when postmodernism arrived, and everyone admired it. Postmodernism was everything that I had been accused of, multiplied by one thousand.

Not even Le Corbusier was on board. I remember him saying once, "Oscar makes baroque buildings, but he does it very well." Years later he contradicted himself: "People say I make baroque architecture. Look at the [curved] awning on my Congress Building at Chandigarh: Not just anyone could do that."

And these statements, which reveal so much, agree with this one by his friend [Amadée] Ozenfant, who wrote in his memoirs: "Le Corbusier for a long time carried out the purist discipline of loyalty to the right angle. When he felt at his back the first breezes of a new Baroque style blowing in from overseas, he seems to have decided to abandon the honesty of the right angle, over which he had a tendency to claim special rights. In the end, the newborn Baroque justifies itself, aided by his immense talent." . . .

It's obvious that my architecture influenced the later projects of Le Corbusier, and this is beginning to be acknowledged by those who write about him.

Landscape Art and Painting

An Interview with Roberto Burle Marx

Ana Rosa de Oliveira

From *Vitruvius*, April 2001,
http://www.vitruvius.com.br/revistas/read/entrevista/02.006/3346.

Here the landscape architect discusses painting and much else besides, showing his endlessly ranging mind. Of particular interest is his acceptance of influence from painters such as Cândido Portinari and Jean Arp; their curving, organic forms influenced his conception of landscape.

Q: If we were to create a timeline for your landscape designs, could we say that initially you had more ecological concerns about valorizing native vegetation and plant environments, and that the more aesthetic drive came later?

A: My earlier gardens did have an ecological focus, but this is relative. For example, I created a roof garden for the Ministry of Education building [in Rio de Janeiro, 1937] with a very abstract design, because at that time I already knew [Jean] Arp. So I don't think we can say that my gardens, even the early ones, had an essentially ecological concern.

Q: You have rarely spoken of your background as an artist. What were the most important moments in your development? What were the most important readings that you did? How did music influence your development?

A: My mother was a musician; she had a very good voice, and was excellent on the piano. She had a certain diabolical, *diabolique*, or divine sensitivity. She loved plants as well. When I began to bring home wild plants that I liked, she never said, "Oh, Roberto, that's dirty"; she said, "What a beautiful thing, I have never seen this before; this species looks like a sacred symbol." Basically, I am not religious, but there are forces that are beyond my explanation. For example, when we enjoy a certain color or a certain moment, for others these may have no importance. It's a mysterious thing . . .

Q: When did you go to Berlin?

A: I was in Europe in 1928 and 1929. I lived for a year in Berlin. Everything that I saw there had great importance in my development: the works of Wagner, the *Pelléas et Mélisande* suite [by Gabriel Fauré], Beethoven's symphonies, [Paul] Hindemith, [Arnold] Schoenberg, Alban Berg.

Q: Beyond the music, you found Brazilian greenery in the Botanical Gardens at Dahlem at that time. Did you make similarly important discoveries among the new styles of painting that were arising in Europe?

A: In Berlin I went to many exhibitions, especially of the German Expressionists. But let me say this: In art, the issues are not confined to the movements in painting; everything that happens in the culture is relevant. For example, when I was going to the Botanical Gardens, I was also going to the opera; there were three opera companies in Berlin at that time. I saw different set designs by some of the best designers. This takes its place alongside music and landscape to form a cultural fabric. Culture is one thing made up of many. I oppose the idea that a landscape designer needs only to understand plants. He also needs to know about Piero della Francesca, and about Miró, Michelangelo, Picasso, Braque, Léger, Karl Hofer, Renoir, and Delaunay. All of those. And I think it is very important in life not to close oneself off in only one field. I also enjoy poetry. And music, such as the work of Béla Bártok. Life consists of knowing how to observe and absorb. Possibly something that may have helped me a lot is that I never lost my curiosity about things. Even at my age I always find something new, such as a color or something else that makes me stop and look.

Q: What about when you returned to Brazil?

A: When I returned, I began going on excursions. I befriended Brazil's best gardeners. Shortly after my return, I got to know [Adolpho] Ducke, a botanist who lived in the Amazon for fifty years. He was originally from Dalmatia, but there is no way that you could say he is not Brazilian. He classified more than five hundred species. We could say that he understood botany marvelously. But he was also a little odd. One day I said to him, "Professor Ducke, I would like to read your books." And he replied, "I will not give you my books, because you are not a botanist and you do not know anything about botany." He was very strict. Well, no, he was not strict; he just said what he thought, and in fact, I was not a botanist . . . As you know, I am to this day still not a botanist, but I am interested in applied botany. It's necessary for my work. I never miss an opportunity to spend time with botanists, just as I always like to hear good music or to read a poem or to talk about the greats of the past. For example, just think about how stunning *Don Quixote* is. I have a German friend who says that if you know the *Iliad*, the *Enneads*, *Don Quixote*, the *Divine Comedy*, and Goethe's *Faust*, then you have a good idea of European literature. Everyone needs to have a good general knowledge of culture, and to obtain this takes a lifetime because there are so many things to learn about . . .

Q: Who were your teachers?

A: The most important one was Leo Putz. He showed the clearest thought and the most culture. [Cândido] Portinari had tremendous technical ability. After working in Pernambuco, I came back to Rio to study with Portinari. I also had others such as Celso Antônio [de Menezes]. He thought he knew more about painting than he actually did . . .

Q: What about architects such as Lúcio Costa?

A: I was very fortunate, because Lúcio lived down the street from my family. I have known him since I was nine years old. If today I am eighty-two, then he is ninety. This shows you how long we have known each other. A lesson in architecture from Lúcio is a lesson from a master . . .

Q: What books were important in your development?

A: I had a friend, the husband of one of the daughters of the composer Alberto Nepomuceno. He brought me a series of books by Le Corbusier: *Vers une architecture*; *Une maison, un palais*; *l'Art décoratif dáujourd'hui*. As I read them, my vision gradually widened. Le Corbusier came here, and he was always an extraordinary figure, with a sharp and clear way of thinking. To choose just one work by him, for example, *Vers une architecture*: In that book he speaks of art with impressive clarity. Later, there were other books, of course. And then, looking at Picasso, at Braque, and remembering what I have seen, all of this along with music, magazines, and exhibitions, all are very important. If we say that we have not been influenced by the work of Picasso, well, of course we have, and I am not afraid to admit influences. If we analyze a work of Picasso, we will see that he has been influenced by all of painting, because he was a genius who could absorb all and still produce work of his own. On that subject, he said a very beautiful thing: "It's better to copy the work of others than it is to copy your own." . . .

Q: Referring to an exhibition of your work at the Museu de Arte de São Paulo in 1974, Geraldo Ferraz came up with the term *Extravasaria* [going beyond] to describe the results that you achieve in your painting. What do you say to that?

A: "Going beyond" is true in the sense that my work does not depend on a fixed formula. Rather, [my painting] finds a way to resist any sense of the routine.

Q: Some critics who analyze your work say that your gardens are like paintings. You initially agreed with that statement but now you do not. Why?

A: To confuse my gardens with paintings is a great error. Each artistic medium has its own means of expression. For example, color in painting is much more fixed and defined than color in a landscape. In a garden, color is defined by the time of day and the light. A square in the darkness is different from one under bright lights.

Q: Can you mention a few projects that you consider the most important?

A: Works that are associated with a city are the most important. The landscape designer is always subordinate to the urban planner. Without understanding a city's needs, and especially without understanding the possible functions of green zones, the landscape designer cannot design any gardens. At Parque Ibirapuera [in São Paulo], I created several visual and aesthetic experiences using pavement and vegetation. At Aterro do Flamengo [in Rio de Janeiro], I experimented with plants that could resist the salt air and the breezes. I assert that without technical knowledge it is impossible to reach a good result. A flower, for example, has symmetry and exemplifies certain principles, such as crystallization. The same happens with gardens. A garden is nature organized by humans, for human use. Discipline often aids in the search for a good result. In the final analysis, an artist is one who finds a way to express himself with intelligence. On the other hand, art for me is a necessity in the search for inner balance. There is, however, one side of art that is as mysterious as life itself. If only we could understand why we have the need to perpetuate ourselves, or indeed why we live.

Integration of the Arts

Carlos Raúl Villanueva

———◦———

From "Síntesis de las artes," *Colección espacio y forma no. 3*
(Caracas: Facultad de Arquitectura y Urbanismo, 1957), 3–11.
Lecture delivered June 27, 1957, Caracas.

*One of the important ways in which mid-twentieth-century Latin American
architecture diverged from modern European building was in the quest to inte-
grate the other arts with architecture. This cause was heresy to Le Corbusier
and gospel to many Latin Americans. The most eloquent advocate for such
unity was Carlos Raúl Villanueva, who exemplified it in guiding the buildings
of the Central University of Venezuela. In this rather eloquent lecture, he sets
forth some historical reasons why the integration should happen, along with
general guidelines for the intersection of the arts. In general, he hoped to drag
modern painters and sculptors out of their "romantic isolation" and into the
public square. About halfway through the lecture he mentions "showing some
pictures," but these are not necessary for us to get the point.*

The arts give testimony to the cultural meanings of every age. In the arts, we
discover the characteristics that mark the specific traits of each period.
Insofar as these traits manifest union of conception or formal harmony, we
will see more clearly the social axis around which humanity and culture
rotate. Moreover, the unity of these human efforts is the basic and necessary
condition for the flowering of an overall integration of the arts. Architecture,
sculpture, painting, and engineering can gather around a common end and
around a collective goal. Such a union of objectives makes possible a visual
synthesis. Architecture today, because of its adherence to fundamental
themes, takes responsibility for first defining the general tone of this synthesis, and sketching from the outset the basic concepts of the structure within
which other visual expressions will take shape.

   Architecture, with the help of engineering, organizes space. Architecture could exist by itself, with its own aesthetic system, isolated and autonomous, without the collaboration of the other arts. This happened in certain Romanesque churches and in the austere, vertical architecture of Mies van der Rohe.

At other times, another type of visual expression dominates. Sometimes sculpture leads the formal evolution and volumetric balancing, and it takes upon itself the principal compositional interest. Such is the case in the architecture of India or in the imposing pre-Columbian monuments, in which a sculptural type of composition takes precedence in architecture. This is to say that, because of the characteristic metaphysics of the cultural and religious focus of those peoples, architecture conceived as a closed, internal space is displaced in favor of a monumental conception of visual arrangement as an external fact. When it is under the leadership of sculptors, architecture is directed more toward the elevation or mystical valorization of a transcendent life beyond humanity, rather than toward the pragmatic recognition of human actions.

At still other times, painting clearly marks out space and content for architecture. In those cases, the theme and the form with which this content is expressed exceed the value of the walls that receive them in importance, vigor, and potent position. These pictorial themes are thus valid "in themselves," independent of the architectural space they inhabit. Moreover, the paintings impress their characteristic seal on the environment. An example of this is the Sistine Chapel of Michelangelo, where pictorial values are evidently superior to the architectonic space and completely indifferent or neutral with respect to them.

When the world of all the visual arts is guided by one concept; when one philosophy leads them; when one vision nurtures its components; then the arts exist on one plane, often in close contact, but they do not fuse together completely. Such total union is not necessary, neither as a goal nor as a consequence of working together. However, the works that flower in such a period, nurtured by allied attitudes, show under close analysis a consistent unity of form.

This is what is meant by "the spirit of the age." It is also a product of the contacts and cultural cross-fertilization that have been more or less frequent according to the greater or lesser facility of communication and transmission within a culture. In the pictures that I will show, we will see clearly the persistence of certain forms that are born in widely separated cultural fields. These show the adaptability of distinct artistic practices, and the highly important influence that technology, with its rigorous focus dictated by function, has exercised on the artistic vision.

There can be times of crisis when the various arts move apart and proceed alone, each on its own path. Although they may take up similar subjects, their languages are distinct and extremely individualized. This happens when it is necessary to rebuild a language, casting aside grammar and syntax that are overused and do not correspond to new human needs. At such moments there may be unity of purpose concentrated on the search for a new elemental vocabulary, starting from zero at times. New roads lead to the elaboration of original, new, and appropriate terms. At those times, the elements that make up the internal structure of each artistic medium need to separate, look within, and perhaps cleanse themselves if necessary, so that after a lengthy analytic period, new foundations can be laid for a more solid construction, to enable the telling of a broader, conclusive, and profound story, where the relationship of form and content can be more explicit and they can bind themselves together more closely. The crisis that developed at the passage from the nineteenth to the twentieth century gave just the occasion for a search to cleanse the language, and can well serve to illustrate the foregoing. In effect, by sharpening the contradictions between the new techniques and the old decorative schemes, between the new social problematic and the ancient forms, humanity in the twentieth century, with eyes focused on the immense possibilities and transformations offered by mechanization, elaborates once again the basic elements of artistic language, strictly separating each medium of artistic expression. Only recently, as this development of language is now concluding, do we announce the possibility and even the necessity of integrating the diverse elements once again.

What are the reasons for this artistic integration, and why is it being proposed by architects, painters, and sculptors as one of the most important ends, and one of the objectives to be reached immediately? Why has the painter approached the architect and asked for the opportunity to work alongside him, in his field? Why does the architect feel the need to call out to the painter so that he will make the architectural surfaces vibrate with color?

As I see it, the reason lies in this: The architect, on the one hand, hopes to deepen the meanings of architecture; he seeks a wider enrichment of architecture's plastic values, through use of color, line, and shape, the traditional painter's instruments, in a more controlled, wise, and attentive usage than has been the case traditionally.

On the other hand, the painter and sculptor have recently come through a personalistic and individualistic phase, now to enter into a new phase that announces human creativity as a vehicle for social cohesion, for expression of human and collective sympathies, and as a mark of responsibility. Whatever their painting and sculpture cease to offer in the way of communication (now that they are freed from an individual, subjective focus) they now try to reincorporate through the rapprochement between art and society in a new relationship that is functional, direct, and necessary. Placing a pictorial or sculptural work in an architectonic context means to show a clear desire to assume social responsibilities. Do we need to repeat that the contemporary artist can no longer create merely for himself, in a personal world whose understanding is circumscribed into a limited number of viewers who float in the sterile social isolation of individual activity? It is precisely as a reaction against this that the artist approaches the architect and offers to collaborate. The artist's call is for his artistic vision to take on new meaning in the social sphere.

This intent to collaborate will not be realized without resolving a range of issues. It is evident that collaboration between artists, with the goal of integration, cannot make an impact without team spirit, solidarity in the task, and companionship. Thus it is necessary that the painters and sculptors have a more or less clear idea of the architect's way of working, of his possibilities as an artist, and of his technical parameters. The painter should understand and utilize the spatial vision that is the architect's territory; by the same token, the architect should take into account the ways of working that are particular to painting and sculpture. Regarding both surfaces and volumes, the architect should respect the artists' modes of creation. There is a substantial difference between an integration of the arts and a program of mere decoration of buildings. In our times, decoration is considered an elaboration of a surface, like a superposition, and as such, it is useless and even perhaps hostile to the architecture. Integration, by contrast, is the product not only of the mutual comprehension between the arts, but also the necessary subordination of their particular expressions. It is the creation of a new being: architectural-sculptural-pictorial, in which we do not notice any split between the different expressive modes. The basic traits of each of these arts should be clearly evident.

Color represents an immense field of opportunity for architects. It can be as potent as the plan and the section as a way of describing a space. As Léger said, color is a natural fact, like fire and water. It was a great scandal, just over a century ago, when the archaeologist [Jakob Ignaz] Hittorff discovered traces of polychromy in one of the façades of a Hellenistic temple in Sicily. The upper portions of ancient Greek temples were painted with pure and bright colors. We also know that the Egyptians painted the reliefs on their walls, with the goal of highlighting and making more visible the parts of the temple that needed accenting. The Romans seem to have been the first to leave their marble and stone materials without polychrome decoration, reserving the brightness of their frescoes for stucco interior walls. In the medieval period as well, many cathedrals show traces of polychromy. Nôtre Dame in Paris had its tympana painted in gold and other bright colors. The sculptures stood out by their black, red, and other shades. In the Renaissance, the interior spaces lost the vibrancy that color can add to the geometric rigor of white surfaces. On the other hand, baroque designers took advantage of all the resources of painting in order to take to the maximum their interest in irregularity and optical illusion. The baroque ceilings with their vertical perspectives in effect abolish the viewer's sense of measurable space. The dense material of the bases and the walls seems to extend up to heaven in sumptuously decorated, enormous masses. Color also has its usefulness as a tool for ordering, balancing, and emphasizing or subordinating volumes and surfaces, or in order to accentuate profiles or affirm spaces. However, using color in this way makes it only one more instrument among others that the architect uses to help establish immediate communication between a building and the person who uses it.

For the architect today, construction materials have their own characters, and they need to be used in accordance with that character, respecting it and valuing it. Therefore most architects use each material according to its inherent qualities, underlining those properties. The artists who work on integration with architecture should also understand and respect the properties of materials, because in this way they will capture the true sense of what we mean by integration.

There is no synthesis without discipline; there is no synthesis without enthusiasm; and there is no synthesis without faith in human values.

It's convenient to remember, along with [art historian] Michel Ragon, that just as lions should not be in the zoo, painting and sculpture should not be confined to museums. The natural environment for animals is in the wild. The natural environment for artworks is in the squares, gardens, public buildings, factories, and airports: all the places where humans perceive other humans as their companions, as their associates, as a helping hand, and as a hope, not as the fading flower of isolation and indifference.

What Is the Social Significance of Modern Architecture in Mexico?

Juan O'Gorman

From "La arquitectura moderna de México: ¿Qué significa socialmente?"
Revista Espacios 15 (1953): 33.

Like many innovators in Latin American modern architecture, Juan O'Gorman had a conflicted relationship with Le Corbusier. He admired Corbusier's designs but resisted the French architect's effort to implant his style seemingly everywhere. Here, the architect of the library of the National Autonomous University of Mexico, that distinctive and highly decorated edifice, attacks the International Style. The principal target is Le Corbusier, who described his design for the Ville Savoye as a "machine for habitation," and his Mexican followers, who were numerous in those days. O'Gorman writes here as a true convert to a regional and realist style that attempts to embody some of the ideals of the muralists.

The Fundamental Difference between Abstractionism and Reality in Architecture

Abstractionist architecture implies an International Style, to use the common term, which is imposed from above and finds regional differences only regarding the structural details of a given building. Regional variations may be caused by a different construction method, or perhaps by climatic differences that necessitate special consideration. Such regionalism may take hold in the arrangement of the floor plan or in façade details such as blinds or shades, etc. But such differences do not affect the essential style of expression. Some examples of such regional accommodation include the student housing at the University of Paris, the Secretariat of the United Nations, the Ministry of Education in Rio de Janeiro, and the science building of the Autonomous University of Mexico. These are four cases of diverse architectural programs that all fall within the International Style, despite their variations in structural makeup made necessary by the variations in climate where they were built.

Realist architecture is diametrically opposed to abstractionist architecture. In realist architecture, the style is not imposed; rather, it arises in each region following the necessity for expression, which is born from below in a natural process of creation, yielding an architecture as collective expression. In realist architecture, the different styles indicate different social conditions and physical differences in the environment; this naturally produces different forms of expression of national or regional character. Regionalism in abstractionist architecture of the so-called International Style is a technical regionalism, which has no impact on the form of expression imposed from above. Regionalism in realist architecture is a distinctive characteristic and it comes about naturally, adapting the forms of expression to the environment.

I propose in what follows, though briefly and incompletely, to explain why abstractionist architecture of the modern type dominates Mexico today. I hope thereby to answer the objections that have been raised against a realist and Mexican type of architecture.

In the first place, it is necessary to analyze the phenomenon of functionalism, because it is the immediate predecessor of current modern architecture.

At the outset, functionalism presupposed that architecture had ceased being an art form and had dissolved itself into engineering. It pretended equally that architecture had left behind its period of empirical knowledge and moved on to the phase of scientific knowledge. Thus its only goal was to provide housing for people in the least costly and most effective manner possible.

Later, functionalism pretended to be a mode of universal expression of the needs of humanity, and thereby to generate some aesthetic emotion. This mechanistic reasoning obeyed an idealistic attitude in the face of the resistance that academic architects across the world lodged against functionalism; this resistance led functionalism to become like an article of faith, a dogma that art could be produced even by machines. This theory had first been broached in France by the Dadaists and the various schools of abstract art in Paris, and the functionalist architects adapted themselves to this.

In reality, this conception of machine-based art, or of technology as a medium for producing an artwork, is a mechanical, idealist, and even religious belief, and it must be taken on faith. Functionalism as an aesthetic position is idealistic because it takes on the character of worship of technology, or a mystical idea of technology.

Colonial or semicolonial countries such as Mexico are fertile ground for the exaggerated development of the mechanistic thesis, because the lack of technology and machinery in those countries makes the acquisition of such means seem very important in the struggle for national economic liberation. At the same time, the idea of veneration and respect for the countries that do have those techniques and machines is implicit in this attitude. For that reason, these countries dominate the ones that lack them. This attitude springs both from the hope for liberation from an inferior economic situation, and from veneration and respect for the countries that dominate them economically.

But architecture is not a machine. Rather, it is a space, a situation, and a place constructed by humanity. Within architecture and around it, human individual and collective life develops. Architecture's assimilation of the machine could not survive, and functionalism as aesthetic expression is finally a denial of aesthetic expression.

Architecture strives constantly to inhabit its social space, both interior and exterior, in a way that answers the need for pleasure in the contemplation of form and color, and for promoting the feeling of well-being in lived spaces. Functionalism could never resolve this problem because human beings need, in addition to their mechanical requirements, sources of pleasure that affirm life and improve health. Thus, the functionalist aesthetic theories were created in the hope of securing and justifying the unjustifiable, and to create belief in the artistic efficiency of the machine-based productions of the School of Paris. Thus it was when an elegant woman from the highest Parisian society presented herself at a reception with a brooch that consisted of a functional hinge bought for ten cents at the store on the corner. Thus it was declared that the functional water heaters and English toilets were marvels of modern sculpture and unconscious products of automatic art-making. It is easy to understand why these theories have not succeeded, and have become no more than sophisticated expressions of fashion, *très amusant de l'esprit francais* [the very entertaining spirit of the French], despite the fact that many intellectuals took them seriously and believed that in this we had discovered the essence of aesthetic emotion.

This critical position could not remain standing, and it gave birth to another theory that is, as an aesthetic concept, the antithesis of functionalism, and precipitated a deeper critical problem in its turn. This theory was born in Paris in the school of painting called Purism, which was led by Le Corbusier, [Pierre] Jeanneret, and [Amédée] Ozenfant. This school intended to achieve what functionalism did not. This abstractionist theory presupposes that by inverting the values of functionalism, one can elevate mechanistic elements as an expressive form, and make of those elements a new modern art.

Functionalism supposed that aesthetic expression could be the inherent result of the mechanical solution of the problem of composition by the logical application of the means of construction. This "new" abstractionist theory supposes that the mechanical media can be the elements that produce aesthetic emotion. In the case of functionalism, the form becomes a consequence of the mechanical function, with the aesthetic theory of the abstractionist school in Paris, under which the mechanical form is taken as a medium of expression and presents itself as functional, but is not. This school pretends to find aesthetic expression through the decorative use of the elements of functionalism, and of the industrial and manufacturing buildings (whose reason for being is usefulness), in order to produce artistic and spatial effects. In this manner they hope to satisfy on the one hand the practical needs, and on the other, the aesthetic needs of architecture. This has been termed the surpassing of functionalism; I will call it the formalization of functionalism with function, which consists of the transitory idea of using elements invented for practical reasons as tools for producing an aesthetic response.

This is the thesis that supports the modern architecture of Mexico today. Its practice leads to an architecture that speaks a common language, but is completely useless, as it is neither the creation of the human imagination nor the synthesis of the practical functions of the engineering of a building. It ends up being the materialization of a contradiction in terms, a clear reflection of the opposing and irreducibly antithetical terms by the regime that has imposed this architecture, and it shows the double incapacity of the dominant classes within this regime: incapacity to produce imaginative or realist architecture, and inability to resolve efficiently our immediate and urgent housing problems in an even purely utilitarian way.

The architecture that has been called modern in our time imitates foreign models in an academic way. With very few exceptions, all the architects of Mexico, from the oldest to the youngest, including students in the universities, have a concept formed from a foundation of clichés of what modern architecture should be. Everyone believes with blind faith in the so-called

International Style and in the abilities of this abstract and academic architecture to produce an aesthetic response.

Therefore, it is necessary to figure out what this modern architecture represents for Mexico. Clearly, the phenomenon can be studied from various points of view, including social conditions and environmental factors.

I propose to examine it from the point of view of the social conditions that seem decisive in this case. From this point of view, one can say that any architectural phenomenon is the reflection of the social conditions of the place where it is made. This does not exclude human action in the process of transformation, which acts on the social superstructure in order to direct, speed up, or slow down this process. I repeat, all art expressions need to be understood as reflections of the social conditions that produce them, either as symptoms of health when they reflect conditions in a state of development and change, or as symptoms of pathology or sickness when they reflect social states in the process of decomposition because they fail to improve conditions for human life.

What does abstractionist architecture represent in the panorama of world culture? It represents the denial of realism, which is the same as saying the denial of interest in the majority of the population, and with this, it has become the reflection of the state of impotence on the part of the social classes who have conceived of this type of art. This is an art unable to defend the interests of its own social class, for it leaves the common masses completely indifferent, and they regard it as alien and strange.

Abstractionist art can only be acceptable for those who have no way of realizing an art with the ability to move people, and it contents itself with being the refined and intellectualized expression of pseudointellectuals who are removed from the actual workers in the countries where abstractionist art is produced.

This abstractionist art has absolutely no social human basis, and it is realized only as the intellectualization of conditions that do not resolve in any way our collective needs.

Architecture of abstractionist content in the so-called International Style has attempted, through its apparently functional appearance, to demagogically appear to be socially useful, obtaining by these means the injection of its antipopular aesthetic contents. But it has not achieved this and will not do so, for this same demagogical fact reveals actively through this architecture of international "style" only that it is the reflection of an international class without culture. It represents the international capitalist interests, which are bankrupt in the face of the socialism soon to come, socialism being the only means of achieving the immediate improvement in the lives of all productive workers in society.

In Mexico this architecture, which has been called the modern architecture of our age, is the denial of all that is Mexican; its dominant characteristic is that it imitates what is foreign. This imitative condition hides itself when it is presented as representative of Mexico in the process of industrialization, but it is only possible to understand this architecture as the reflection of the interests of a class for whom the industrialization of Mexico means alliance with the interests of international capitalism. If the class that is industrializing Mexico was the one that struggled against those interests for its independence, it would express that condition, and that of all the people of Mexico who dream of economic national liberation, with a modern architecture that has a Mexican character and style. If realist architecture has failed in its intent to realize itself as a modern Mexican architecture, this is in part because the dominant classes have also failed in their attempts at liberating our national economy, only to realize themselves as the dominant Mexican independent class. But it is precisely this architecture's imitative and neo-academic condition that expresses the servile condition that this class has imposed on our economy.

This architecture of a colonial condition in our country, as an artistic expression, represents only this inept social class, which needs and finds overseas the resources to maintain its dominance in Mexico. It is a dependent and colonial capitalist class, and Mexico's modern architecture is the undisguised expression of this dependence. The only people who can be proud of this style are those who are either proud of their colonial dependency, or those whose situation of privilege blinds them to reality.

In closing, I will repeat what Diego Rivera has already said. In Mexico, from the colonial days up to the present, there have always been two currents of art production: One is our own Mexican style, which is the work of the people and is called popular art. This current is Mexican and realist in the sense that it comes from below as a necessary, natural, normal, and logical form whose goal is the expression of the Mexican people's hopes and dreams as they struggle for their freedom. This current includes artists of genius such as José Guadalupe Posada, José María Velasco, José Clemente Orozco, Diego Rivera, and many others who have lived and felt and expressed through their original work the dreams of the productive masses of Mexico.

The other current imitates what is foreign and represents colonial submission to the interests of the class that has lived off of the work of the Mexican people while scorning them. This art current has always been imposed from above by the dominant classes that adore whatever is not Mexican. This class is overripe and without character; it sees in foreign things the salvation of its economic status, and it apishly imitates the models of architecture that come to Mexico in elegant magazines from New York or Paris.

Clearly, our abstractionist architecture of the so-called International Style is nothing but one more expression of the second current of art production, symptomatic of the decomposition of a negative world that lacks the least capacity for improving the life conditions of the majority of humanity.

Emotional Architecture?

Matías Goeritz

From *Revista Arquitectura ENA*, May 1960, 17–22.

Here, one of Mexico's most distinctive artists explains his excursion into hybridizing sculpture and architecture in the El Eco Experimental Museum and the towers of Satellite City. Basic to his conception is that architecture must meet emotional needs; he saw the functionalism of the International Style as a failure in this regard. His explorations touched on issues of form in space years before they began to interest North American artists of the minimal movement.

The idea of an emotional architecture occurred to me when I got an invitation from Daniel Mont to build, on a centrally located Mexico City plot, "anything I wanted." This was in 1952, during the heyday of functionalism.

I had never faced a similar problem. Being a painter and a sculptor, I had not taken much interest in the logical functions of a building. But always, when speaking of architecture, I bore in mind the profound impression that great works that united all of the arts had made on me. The tremendous impact of these works, whatever their style or artistic concept, seemed to me to be the most sublime that I have ever known, and I was not bothered by questions of where the boundaries between architecture, sculpture, painting, and even poetry began or ended.

Now, finding myself confronted with the task of erecting a building, I decided to create an Experimental Museum that would begin its activities (or rather its experiments) with the design of its own building. This would be an example of architecture whose function was, in large measure, emotional.

At that time, I wrote the following as a polemical manifesto: "Art in general, naturally including architecture, is a reflection of the spiritual state of humanity in its time. The impression exists that modern architects, individualized and intellectual, sometimes go too far in emphasizing the rational side of architecture, perhaps because they have lost close contact with the community. The result is that people in the twentieth century feel oppressed by so much 'functionalism,' so much logic and utility, in modern architecture. We look for a solution; but neither an external aestheticism understood as formalism, nor organic regionalism, nor any dogmatic confusionism has truly confronted the roots of the problem, which is that humanity in our time—as either creator or viewer—aspires to something more than just a tidy, pleasant, and adequate house. Humanity demands—or will have to demand someday—spiritual elevation from architecture with its modern means and materials. Simply put: feeling, as was embodied in their times by the architecture of the pyramids, the ancient Greek temple, the Romanesque or Gothic cathedral, and including the Baroque palace. Only upon finding true feeling in architecture will humanity again consider it an art form. Beginning with the conviction that our times are marked by deep spiritual questioning, the Experimental Museum wants only to become an expression of these, aspiring—not consciously, but almost automatically—to the integration of the arts, with the goal of communicating for modern people a maximum of feeling."

With that idea in mind, I built the controversial Museo Experimental El Eco in 1952–53, which later became a house of worship, then a restaurant, and finally a nightclub. With just a few alterations and remodelings, the same building could have also served perfectly well as a furniture store, an automobile showroom, or even the home studio of an architect. I am informed that very little remains of that building. The nightclub owners, under the refined guidance of the owner of the lot, have succeeded in destroying or ruining all of my hopes.

Of course, that work was never more than an experiment, nor did I intend it to be more. There were no ninety-degree angles in the entire plan of the building. Some of the walls were thin on one end and thicker on the other. I consistently created an unexpected and at times imperceptible asymmetry, similar to that which one would find in any human face, any tree, or any living being. On the other hand, the building had neither gentle curves nor sharp apexes. The building was created on site and without exact plans. Bricklayer, painter, sculptor, and architect were all practically the same person.

It seems that my work on El Eco had a decisive influence on my other sculptural work in general. I began to see spatial problems with new eyes. I took an interest in volumes of monumental size. I dreamed of building an immense cathedral or pyramid for our times, as a gigantic prayer.

Thanks to my great friend, the architect Luis Barragán, I received four years later, in 1957, another commission even more daring. It was to create the gateway to a new city, which then existed only as plans. On seeing the empty landscape, I thought of vertical columns, such as the towers of San Gimignano [in north central Italy] or the skyscrapers of Manhattan. And thanks to the help and collaboration of Luis Barragán and architect Mario Pani, planners of the new Satellite City, there they are: five triangular towers from thirty-seven to fifty-seven meters high, three white, one yellow, and one orange.

They are not as high as I had at first hoped they could be. There are also just five instead of seven, because the plaza was different and smaller than I would have liked. And the color of one of the towers was recently changed. But here I finally attempted to create a monumental work whose only function would be the arousal of emotion.

The architects insist that the towers are only a large sculptural work, and they are correct. But what does it matter? For me they are painting, sculpture, and emotional architecture. I would have liked to carve small flutes out of the corners, so that travelers passing on the freeway would hear a strange song caused by the whistling of the winds; this would have made the towers music as well. Although for the majority of people the towers probably signify only a giant advertisement, for me, an absurd Romantic in a faithless century, they have been and are a visible prayer.

PART SEVEN

Geometric, Optical, and Kinetic Art

Statements on *Colorhythms* and Sculpture

Alejandro Otero

From *Alejandro Otero*
(Caracas: Museo de Arte Contemporáneo de Caracas, 1985), n.p.

Three brief artist's statements from 1984 and 1985 narrate the journey that Otero made from the flat surface of the painted Colorhythms *to his wind-activated outdoor metal sculpture. He was influenced by his compatriot Carlos Raúl Villanueva, whose theories about the integration of architecture and sculpture lay at the back of his mind. The italics and parentheses are retained from the original.*

The *Colorhythms* arose out of a brief but intense flirtation with architecture: a proposal for a venue of synthesis and integration of the arts. The specifications called for a clear-cut space defined by rigorous artistic elements in mutual, active, and lively relationships, except that it never went beyond a written, or virtual, plan. But there was one result: The *Colorhythms* broke out of their plane; they *created* the architectural space, and they embraced it. (The project was a planned contribution to a new way of understanding the suggestions for integration of the arts; the architects themselves failed at this, not Villanueva.)

Local circumstances forced me to go to France in 1960, when I was in the midst of creating the *Colorhythms*. Practical reasons (the necessary team, the costs and complications of completing the panels, spatial and climatic conditions) and conceptual reasons (I felt that they were coming too easily, that they were perhaps too rigid and intellectual, and not expressive enough) led me to interrupt the series in 1960. "I am a creator," I said to myself, "and soon I will find the ends and the means to continue working." And thus it happened, but via a radically different path. The creative currents then active in France influenced my course, especially the movement known as

New Realism. These works were created out of *junk*, alien to all constructive rigor, in which *direct expressiveness* was posed as the problem in itself.

Summary of the spatial notions that typify our times: In the beginning was the virtual space of painting. Next, the habitable space of architecture. Finally came the real, perceptible, and practical space of my sculptures. Architecture, following the proposals for integration of the arts that Villanueva set forth, was the launching pad for this adventure. It made me feel the specific dimensions of a habitable area from an expressive point of view, and their relationship with the scope and precise situation of the elements that come together to define it. In this sense, my sculptures are essentially architecture. But they deny architecture by becoming useless machines or games for the imagination. When they move, they both create and elaborate the space they contain; they contradict sculpture as well, and become notions (or metaphorical allusions), concepts, and ideas.

Chance, Reality, and Perception

Jesús Rafael Soto

———

From "Statements by Kinetic Artists," *Studio International*,
February 1967, 60.

Here, a leading Venezuelan abstract artist explains his use of simple materials to create aesthetic situations. His conception of relationships as the basis for creative exploration goes against the "specific object" of classic North American minimalist theory. Note also his openness to influence from the abstract music of the fugue.

My works are classical, without confusion or mystification. I work with very simple elements. These elements in themselves are unimportant. A piece of wire, a few lines—what are they? More important will be the relationships which they bring into being.

A piece of wire against a *moiré* background of narrow parallel lines becomes broken up. Its form is "dematerialized." It undergoes a transformation, a metamorphosis. You cannot say which is wire and which is ground. I hang yellow rods in front of the same background, and black spots appear on the yellow. Where has the color come from?

This has to do with reality, with perception. We are forced to question our perceptions, which seem so reliable. When Duchamp set a two-dimensional disc spinning and it looked solid, he was doing the same thing. He made us question our perceptions.

The Impressionists, Cézanne, the Cubists and Mondrian broke up form into light and color. They liberated these elements.

I am not interested in connections between things, but only with their relationships. I am not interested in the connection of one color with another or one line with another. Relationships are more than connections.

There need be no logical connection between the elements in my work. Two themes in a Bach fugue have no logical connection. The work is essentially a relationship. Not between two elements in the picture, but between the principle which governs the picture—for example, the dematerialization—and a general law of the universe which conditions everything. You may call these relationships chance relationships: they cannot be foreseen. They happen by chance, by the laws of chance. It may seem strange to talk of laws of chance, but chance occurrences do not come about independently of laws. It is just that the laws are very hard to discover. That is why we call them laws of chance. It is my aim to discover these laws.

Reflections on Color

Carlos Cruz-Diez

From *Reflections on Color* (Caracas: Fabri Art, 1989), 36–37.

Here the artist describes what can happen when color is separated from its usual descriptive or expressive function. It becomes an element in flux, as interactions among colors in the artist's work set off optical events in the eye and mind of the viewer. These ideas form the basis of Cruz-Diez's long series of works titled Fisicromía, *or* Physichromy. *He later took these explorations into three dimensions by illuminating spaces with colored light.*

After graduating from the School of Fine Arts in Caracas, I thought that the work of an artist was essentially to express himself in order to make a sort of great chronicle of that unknown and magical world called Latin America. This was also an affirmation to confront cultural dependence. This resulted in painting that was aesthetically conventional, and an ambiguity between political events and the timelessness of art.

In 1954 I started having the same thoughts that, in principle, all artists have at one point in their lives when they begin to doubt the validity and transcendence of their own painting. At that time I structured a conceptual platform which so far has allowed me to do my work based on a nontraditional perspective of color.

Study and constant experimentation revealed that conceptually, the element of color in painting had not changed throughout time, as had happened with drawing, chiaroscuro, perspective and composition. The same concept has prevailed since ancient times: first you draw a form and then you color it, as if color were something added to form. Only the impressionists, the pointillists, the fauvists and the expressionists assumed different attitudes toward the chromatic phenomenon, while some Constructivist and abstract artists insisted once again on the "form-color" relationship.

Based on this analysis I started to research methodically what artists had done and written about color throughout time. I also made contact with the world of physics, chemistry, the physiology of vision, and optics. I searched for what philosophers and humanists had thought about the phenomenon of color perception. I did all this aided by my knowledge of image multiplication, color photography, photomechanics and the different systems for printing on paper. I concluded that the perception of the chromatic phenomenon is unstable, that it is constantly evolving, that it is subject to many circumstances and that this characteristic had never been put to use by artists.

For example, the impressionists were never able to overcome the contradictions underlying their experiences. They wanted to be more genuine than the academicians by reconstructing the ephemeral quality of light on the static support of the canvas; but in the time it took to observe the model, prepare the color mixture on the palette, and return to the canvas, the situation and the color relationships had changed. This is why their attitude towards the model was the same as the academicians': that is, an artificial and static reconstruction of a changing reality.

This evidence and all my previous experiences with color helped me create a support structure that would allow me to materialize and demonstrate the changing condition of the chromatic experience. The solution I found to the eternal **binomial form-color** was to divide the form, transforming the colored plane into a succession of color parallels placed vertically, which I called **chromatic event modules**. This structure allowed me to prove that *color is constantly in the making*, that it happens in time.

GRAV Manifesto

Transforming the Current Situation in Plastic Art

Julio Le Parc

————◦————

From an exhibition brochure, Maison des Beaux-Arts,
Paris, October 25, 1961.

This is one of the most radical manifestos of any postwar art group. It proposes to do away with many of the conventions of art creation and reception. The principal author was the Argentine artist Julio Le Parc, who carried out its terms in low-tech, relatively simple creations that often included motion and viewer activation.

The Visual Arts Research Group [GRAV] invites you to demystify the artistic experience, and to join our effort to clarify the situation as we set out new foundations for appreciation.

The Visual Arts Research Group is made up of painters who focus their efforts on the continuous investigation and visual realization of basic facts, in order to tear the visual arts loose from their conventions.

The Visual Arts Research Group believes it useful to give its viewpoint, although it is not final, and it invites companion analyses and further confrontations.

General Propositions:

1. The Artist-Society Relationship

This relationship is presently based on:

The unique and isolated artist
The cult of personality
The myth of creation
Overly esteemed conceptions of aesthetics and anti-aesthetics
Creation for the elite

Production of unique works
Dependency on the art market

Proposals to transform this relationship:

Eliminate all mysticism from the conception and realization of the
work, reducing them to a simple human act
Seek new means of contact with the public and with created works
Do away with the category "work of art" and its myths
Develop new modes of appreciation
Create works that can be copied and multiplied
Seek new means of creation beyond painting and sculpture
Liberate the public from inhibitions and deformed appreciation brought
about by traditional aestheticism, creating new artist-society
situations

2. The Work-Eye Relationship

This relationship is currently based on:

The eye as intermediary
Extravisual proposals (subjective or rational)
Dependence on the eye at a certain cultural and aesthetic level

Proposals to transform this relationship:

To eradicate completely the intrinsic values of the stable and recognizable
form, such as:
Forms that idealize nature (classical art)
Forms that represent nature (naturalistic art)
Forms that synthesize nature (cubist art)
Geometricized forms (abstract constructivist art)
Rationalized forms (concrete art)
Free forms (informal abstract art, tachism)
To eliminate the arbitrary relationship between forms (relations of
dimension, placement, color, meaning, depth, etc.)
To displace the usual function of the eye (recognition through the form
and its relationships) toward a new visual situation based on periph-
eral vision and instability
To create an interval for appreciation based on the relationship between
the eye and the work, transforming the habitual sense of time.

3. Traditional Plastic Values

These values are currently expressed through the work of art that is

  unique
  stable
  definitive
  subjective
  obedient to aesthetic or antiaesthetic laws

Proposals to transform these values:

  Limit the work to a strictly visual situation
  Establish a more precise relationship between the work and the eye
  Anonymity and homogeneity of the forms and the relations between them
  Emphasize visual instability and the moment of perception
  Seek the work that is nondefinitive while also precise and deliberate
  Displace interest toward new and variable visual situations based on
     constants originating in the eye-work relationship
  Note the existence of indeterminate phenomena in the structure and
     visual reality of the work and, from there, conceive new possibilities
     that will open new fields of investigation.

PART EIGHT

Neoconcrete Art in Brazil

Neo-Concrete Manifesto

Ferreira Gullar

———

From *Jornal do Brasil*, Suplemento Dominical, March 22, 1959, 1.

This is one of the more exciting, and also difficult, artistic statements. It reasserts the primacy of firsthand, sensory experience in art appreciation. In the interest of elevating bodily sensations, it opposes rationalism and calculation of any kind, especially theories of concrete art. Previous movements, such as neoplasticism, suprematism, and constructivism, it says, have hinted at the primal sensory meanings that neoconcrete art emphasizes, but they have been derailed by an overly rational type of art criticism that emphasizes form over sensation. The neoconcrete artists, here in the voice of the poet Ferreira Gullar, call us back to a fresh and spontaneous sensory encounter with art.

The term "neoconcrete" indicates taking a position regarding nonfigurative "geometric" art (neoplasticism, constructivism, suprematism, [Bauhaus-oriented] School of Ulm), particularly in regard to concrete art, which has been taken to a dangerously exaggerated rationalism. Working in painting, sculpture, printmaking, and literature, the artists participating in this first Neoconcrete exhibition find themselves, in light of their experiences, needing to revise certain theoretical positions adopted up to now regarding concrete art, because none of those positions satisfactorily explains the expressive possibilities that their experiences have opened.

Born, with Cubism, out of a reaction against the Impressionist dissolving of the pictorial language, it was natural that so-called geometric art take a position diametrically opposed to the suggestive and technically easy paths of painting at that time. The new discoveries in physics and engineering, opening an ample perspective for objective thought, inspired among the partisans of that revolution an ever-growing tendency toward rationalization of the principles and processes of painting. A mechanistic notion of composition invaded the language of the painters and sculptors, creating, in turn, equally extreme reactions of a retrograde character, such as magical realism, or an irrational character, such as dada and surrealism. There is no doubt that, behind the theories that consecrated the objectivity of science and the precision of mathematics, the true artists—such as, for example, [Piet] Mondrian or [Antoine] Pevsner—built their works by going toe to toe with expression, and often overcame the limits imposed by the theory. But the work of these artists has up to now been interpreted based on theories that the works themselves denied.

We propose here a new interpretation of neoplasticism, constructivism, and the other allied movements, based on their mastery of expression and giving prevalence to the works over the theories. If we attempt to understand the works of Mondrian according to his theories, we will be obliged to choose between them. Either we profess that the total integration of art with daily life seems possible, and we see in Mondrian's work the first steps in that direction, or the possibility of integration seems to grow more remote and his works show his frustration. Either the horizontal and vertical are the fundamental rhythms of the universe, and the works of Mondrian apply this principle, or the principle is invalid and his works are shown to be based on an illusion. But the truth is that the work of Mondrian is there, fertile and alive, above and beyond these theoretical contradictions. Nothing is gained by seeing Mondrian as a destroyer of the surface, of the plane and the line, if we do not pay attention to the new spaces that that destruction built.

The same could be said of [Georges] Vantongerloo or Pevsner. It matters little which mathematical equations underlie a sculpture or painting by Vantongerloo, because only the direct perceptual experience of the work lends any "meaning" to its rhythms or colors. Whether Pevsner began with descriptive geometric forms or not is an uninteresting question in view of the new space that his sculptures brought to birth, and of the cosmic-organic expression that his shapes reveal. It may be of some specific cultural interest to determine the proximity between art objects and scientific instruments, and between the artist's intuition and the objective thought of the physicist or engineer. But from a point of view of aesthetics, the work begins to be interesting insofar as it transcends these external approximations: [It is interesting only] for the universe of existential meanings that it at some point establishes or reveals.

Because [Kazimir] Malevich recognized [in the manifesto of Suprematism] the primacy of "pure feeling in art," he rescued his theoretical definitions of rationalism and mechanism, and gave his paintings a transcendental dimension that today guarantees their notable contemporaneity. But Malevich paid dearly for his courageous opposition to both figural art and machine-based abstraction; he has been considered up to now by certain rationalist theoreticians as only a naïve soul who did not well understand the new pictorial world. In reality, Malevich had already expressed his impatience within so-called geometric painting, and also a will to transcend both the rational and the sensory, which shows itself in an irrepressible way.

Neoconcrete art, born of the need to express the complex reality of modern humanity in the structural language of the new art, denies validity to scientific and positivist attitudes to art, and raises again the issue of expression, incorporating the new "verbal" dimensions created by nonfigurative constructive art. Rationalism takes from art all its autonomy and attempts to substitute irrelevant qualities brought from notions of scientific objectivity. Thus the concepts of form, space, time, and structure—which in the language of art criticism are linked with existential, affective, and emotional meanings—are confused with a theoretical application, which tries to turn them into science. In truth, spouting the preconceptions that today's philosophy renounces (Maurice Merleau-Ponty, Ernst Cassirer, Susanne Langer)—and which crumble in all fields of endeavor, beginning with modern biology, which surpasses the Pavlovian mechanistic science—the concrete rationalists still see humans as machines among machines and attempt to circumscribe artistic expression within this theoretical reality.

We think of the work of art neither as machine nor as object, but as a quasi-body; that is, a being whose reality is not exhausted in the external relationships among its elements. The work is a being that, while breakable into parts for analysis, can be fully understood only through direct, phenomenological experience. We affirm that the work of art transcends any material mechanisms on which it may be based. We do this not for any external reason: It surpasses materialism by transcending those mechanical relationships (which Gestalt theory objectifies) and by creating in itself a tacit meaning (as Merleau-Ponty says) that emerges from it as if for the first time. If we had to find something comparable to the work of art, we would say that there is nothing, either in machines or things taken objectively. But perhaps there is, as Langer and [Vladimir] Weidle claim, in living organisms. But even this comparison does not suffice to express the specific reality of the aesthetic organism.

Because the work of art cannot be limited to merely occupying objective space—it already transcends that by founding a new meaning—the objective notions of time, space, form, structure, color, etc. are all insufficient, either for understanding the work of art, or for taking account of its so-called reality. The difficulty of terminological precision in describing a world that does not give itself to notions has led art critics to the indiscriminate use of words that deny the complexity of the created work. The influence of technology and science has been so strong that today, roles are reversed and certain artists, confused by this terminology, are tempted to make art based on these objective notions and apply them to their creative process. Inevitably, the artists who work this way barely illustrate even those a priori notions. This is because they are limited by a method that already prescribes beforehand the results of their work. Fleeing from spontaneous and intuitive creation, they think of themselves as an objective body in an objective space. Concrete rationalist artists only invite a reaction of stimulus and response from the viewer. They speak to the eye only as an instrument, not as a human mode of taking in the world and giving oneself to it. They speak to the eye-machine and not to the eye-body.

Because the work of art transcends the mechanistic space, notions of cause and effect lose all validity. And the notions of time, space, form, and color are so integrated in the work—by the very fact that they did not exist before the work existed—that it would be impossible to speak of these in analytical terms . . . [The work of art] is always making itself present, always restating the impulse that created it and where it originated. If that description brings us back to the primary and full experience of the real, it is because neoconcrete art intends nothing less than to reassert that experience. Neoconcrete art founds a new expressive space . . .

The participants in this first neoconcrete exhibition do not constitute a "group." They are not united by dogmatic principles. The evident affinity that their investigations in various fields share has brought them together and unites them here. The commitment that they undertake binds each to his own experience first, and they will remain together as long as those affinities last.

Beasts [*Bichos*]

Lygia Clark

―――――

From a diary entry, 1960. Associação Cultural O Mundo de Lygia Clark, Rio de Janeiro.

Lygia Clark took the idea of viewer-activated art in a fruitful direction with her series of tabletop-sized, hinged metal sculptures. Because these works are all completely asymmetrical and complex in construction, viewers can interact with them but cannot put them into any shape that they desire; the hinges and flat shapes resist certain configurations and predispose the Bichos to others. Here the artist discusses the ramifications of interacting with one.

This is the name that I gave to my works from this period, because of their fundamentally organic character. Beyond that, the hinge that joins the planes reminds me of a spinal column.

The disposition of the metal flanges determines the positions of the Beast, which seem at first limitless. When I am asked how many movements the Beast is capable of, I reply, "I don't know, and you don't know, but it knows."

The Beast has no wrong side.

Each Beast is an organic entity that reveals itself completely within its interior space of expression. It has affinities with snails and conchs. It is a living organism, an essentially active work. Between it and you is established total existential integration. In the relationship that is established between you and the Beast, there is no passivity, for you or for it. A type of one-on-one interaction develops between the two living beings.

A real dialogue is established in which the Beast has its own well-defined answers to the stimulation of the viewer. This relationship between man and Beast, previously metaphorical, becomes real.

The Beast has its own set of movements, which react to the stimulation of the viewer. It is not made up of static and isolated forms that can be manipulated at will and indefinitely, as in a game; on the contrary, its parts are functionally related, like those of a true organism, and its movements of parts are interdependent.

The relationship between you and the Beast consists of two types of motions. The first, done by you, is purely external. The second, by the Beast, is produced dynamically by the Beast's own expressivity. The first motion (of yours) has nothing to do with the Beast, because it did not initiate it. In compensation, the conjugation of your gesture by the immediate response of the Beast creates a new relationship, and this is possible thanks to the movements that the Beast knows how to make. It is the Beast's own life.

My Experiences with Dance

Hélio Oiticica

———※———

"A dança na minha experiência," notebook entries. Projeto Hélio Oiticia,
Rio de Janeiro.

These hand-scrawled notes, with their run-on sentences and idiosyncratic punctuation, express a crucial concept for neoconcrete art: the potential transformation of a viewer into a participant. Oiticica sought to empower viewers through bodily engagement and action. Specifically, his experience with samba dancing led directly to the creation of his series Parangolés *[Capes], fabrics of various textures and shapes stitched together for viewers to wear while dancing. Probably he realized the goals of this text most fully earlier in 1965, when he invited residents of the hillside favela of Mangueira to wear his capes while dancing at the Museu de Arte Moderna in Rio. The quote marks and parentheses are retained from the original.*

November 12, 1965

First of all, as I feel my work is susceptible to excessive intellectualism, I think it necessary to clarify my interest in dance and rhythm, in particular the samba. I see this interest as a vital necessity of dis-intellectualization, of shunning intellectual inhibitions and as a necessity of free expression. This was my first step in a reexamination of myth, and a new foundation for my art. Therefore, for me, dance is an indispensable experience of the greatest vitality, especially as a vanquisher of preconceptions, stereotypes, etc. As we will soon see, I had already experienced some of this in my art with the *Parangolé*, and everything related to it, for *Parangolé* influenced and affected my other bodies of work, such as the *Nuclei*, the *Penetrables*, and the *Bolides*. Not only that, it was the beginning of an important social experience, the end of which I do not yet know.

Dance is the search for the direct expressive act *par excellence*. It is the opposite of ballet, which is excessively intellectualized by the insertion of "choreography" that seeks transcendence through the act. However, a "diony-siac" dance, which is born in the inner rhythms of the collective, is external-ized as a characteristic of tribes, nations, etc. In dance, improvisation rules over organized choreography; the freer the improvisation, the better. There is a type of immersion in the rhythm, a vital and complete identification of ges-ture and act with rhythm, and a fluidity in which the intellect remains obscured by a mythic internal force that is both individual and collective (though in truth the two cannot be separated). The images of dance are mobile, quick, and inapprehensible. They are the opposite of the static icons charac-teristic of other visual arts. In reality, dance and rhythm are themselves plastic acts in their essential, raw state. Dance sets us on the path to immanence.

This immersion in rhythm is both an art and a pure creative act. It is the creation of an act in itself, of a continuity; it is also a creator of images, as are all acts of creative expression. Thus for me, dance was like a new discovery of images, a continuous creation of images, and it consistently affected the visual expression of my work.

The overturning of social preconceptions, and of barriers that separate groups, classes, etc., may be inevitable and essential in the realization of such a vital experience. In dance I found a connection between collective and individual expression, which was an important step toward the rejection of abstract ideas of social class status, and toward the comprehension of a total-ity. The bourgeois conditioning to which I was subjected from my birth was undone as if by magic, though the process had already begun before I was even aware of it. The disequilibrium that I see in this social dislocation, the complete discrediting of the structures that rule our lives in society (espe-cially the Brazilian one) was inevitably laden with problems which renewed themselves every day. Arising from this process of discrediting the social class system, the dynamic of the social structure revealed itself to me in all its crudity, in the most immediate expression. Not that I condone its exis-tence, but for me it became abstract and artificial, as if I had suddenly seen a map from a higher plane, or a system from outside.

The naturally occurring marginalization of artists is relevant for me. This position implies a total lack of social place, at the same time as the discovery of my "individual" place as a man in the world, and as a "social being" in the total sense, not as one included within a determined layer of the "elite," not even the artistic elite, which exists on the margins. (I am speaking of true artists and not of the "habitués" of the art world.) No, the process here is deeper; it is a process in society as a whole, in daily life, in the objective mode

of being, and in the subjective life. It would be the will for an integral position, social in the most noble sense, both free and total. What is of interest to
me is the "total act of being" that I feel in myself—not partial acts, but a "total
act of living" that is irreversible and unbalanced, undertaken in the interests
of balance for the self.

The old position regarding the work of art is abolished. This is true even in
works that do not demand participation from the viewer, because what they
propose is not transcendent contemplation but rather a "being" in the world.
Dance likewise does not propose such a "flight" from this immanent world,
but rather reveals it in all its plenitude. What was for Nietzsche "Dionysiac
drunkenness" is in truth an "expressive lucidity of the immanence of the act,"
an act that cannot be characterized by any one of its parts, but only by totality
in itself. It is a total expression of the self. Is this not the cornerstone of art?
The *Parangolé*, for example, when it demands participation through dance, is
only an adaptation of the dance to a structure, and vice versa of a structure to
the dance—and this is simply another version of the "total act of the self." The
gesture and the rhythm take on new forms, determined by the demands of
the structure of the *Parangolé*, since this dance is the beginning of the structural participation. It does not deal with determining levels of evaluation for
one or another expression, because the one (pure dance) and the other (dance
with *Parangolé*) are both total expressions.

What is conventionally called interpretation has also evolved radically in
our times. Interpretation is not merely repeating a creation (a song, for example), but rather giving it a new expression according to the interpreter. Today,
interpreters can take on such expressive importance that they may overpower
the song or whatever else they interpret. This is not about an individual's
celebrity status, although this exists as well, but of a real expressive valorization of the self. In the past, celebrity status immortalized certain persons
because of their interpretations of famous works (in opera or theater, for
example). Today the problem is different: even if the works interpreted are not
masterpieces, genuine musicians (in the field of popular music, for example),
reach a high level of interpretive expression. Nat King Cole, for example,
creates through his singing what one could call a "vocal expressive structure,"
independent of the quality of the music he interprets. The song becomes a
creation that is his, not as a simple interpreter but rather as a highly expressive
"vocalist." And an actress such as Marilyn Monroe, for example, by her mere
interpretive presence, possessed above all else a creative quality, that is, a
"structure of expression." Her presence in certain mediocre films gives those

films uncommon interest, because of her actions as interpreter. What is of interest here is that the vocalizations of Nat and the interpretive actions of Marilyn stand above the quality of the music or text interpreted . . .

April 10, 1966 (continuation)

On one hand, the experience of dance (the samba) gave me an exact idea of what a creation by bodily act might involve, which is continuous transformability. On the other hand, it showed me what I call the "being" of things, that is, the static expression of objects, an expressive immanence. In the case of dance this is the immanence of an expressive bodily act in constant transformation . . . This is the key to what I call "environmental art": It is eternally mobile and transformable, and structures itself by the act of the spectator; and the static thing is also transformable after its fashion, depending on the environment in which it participates as a structure.

An environment is needed for creating these works. The proper concept of "exhibition" in the traditional sense already must evolve, because to "exhibit" such pieces would be of questionable interest. I affirm instead the creation of structured spaces, free for both creative participation and intervention by the viewer. A pavilion of the sort that they use these days for industrial expositions would be ideal for such purposes (and much more interesting than anemic little art exhibitions!). It would be an opportunity for a true and effective experience with the people, playing, in the sense of participating creatively, and a far cry from the shows for the elite that are so much in fashion today. This experience should include objects ranging from the established fact to the "beings" that architecturally structure the pathways or spaces for movement, to the "transformable facts" that demand some sort of inventive participation by the viewer (dressing, or unfolding, or dancing), up to the "facts for doing." The latter means to give the raw material to each person to construct or make what he or she wishes, for the motivation and the stimulus are born from the fact that the people are "there for something."

The execution of this plan is complicated, demanding a lot of rigorous planning by a team; that much is clear. The issues to be explored are many and varied. (In another part I will explain what I consider as the structural categories of my new conception of an environmental art.) It can and should include collaboration by a range of artists with different ideas, all focused on the general idea of a "total participatory creation," which would include developing all the works created by the viewers, or rather, the participants.

PART NINE

Postwar Figuration and Versions of Pop

The Cactus Curtain

José Luis Cuevas

———

From *Evergreen Review*, Winter 1959, 111–20.

José Luis Cuevas here rebels against the domination of the muralist movement in Mexico. Cuevas opposed the mural style in various ways: favoring cosmopolitan or literary themes over nationalistic ones, drawing over fresco, personal over public art. Here he details some of the opposition that he faced in the art world of the time. The title of the essay refers to the Iron Curtain that once separated Communist from non-Communist countries in Europe.

I do not pretend to be a leader of the young, and I am not trying to recruit an army of rebels to storm the Palace of Fine Arts. I will limit myself to stating what I firmly believe to be the convictions of other members of my generation both in the fine arts and in other intellectual fields. If what I have to say is of any use to young artists, either now or later, I will feel that I have paid a debt. But even if what I suggest is not followed in the future, even if most of my generation chooses to conform and to stick in the same rut, I will still feel that my own conscience is clear, for I will know that I have stated publicly my refusal to conform with the harmful situation that exists in our cultural life.

I am not equipped to deal with other fields. Permit me to restrict myself to my own, but this time I propose to use the narrative form, in order to express my ideas more coherently.

Juan was fifteen years old. His father was a plumber, or a cobbler, or perhaps a minor official, one of those who, for a ten peso bribe, will settle within the legal period what would otherwise take months. Juan was born with a talent that occurs very often among the population of the Republic of Mexico. This talent, this rich and ancient legacy, was not that of taking bribes, an infection poisoning the blood of the whole country, but of creating another, unknown world, the world of art.

Juan stood out in grade school because of his excellent drawings. A school inspector saw them and told his teacher to encourage him. This continued until one day, Juan was given a prize and entered art school. Let us pretend it was La Esmeralda, to make the fable more realistic. Juan completed all of his classes with the same competence he had shown in grade school. His professors praised him, his fellow students looked up to him, and he graduated from the school with diploma in hand. Thus far all had gone well. Mexico is a great nation, with opportunities for everyone. Even the sons of bribe-takers, or of plumbers or cobblers, have the chance and the right to study art. We live in a grand democratic country. *¡Viva México!* There is only one insignificant shadow across the happy progress of our narrative, and that is the fact that Juan's father, as a plumber or bribe taker, felt cheated: He considered his son a good-for-nothing, and he was sure those drawings of naked women were the result of unspeakable secret vices. Juan's father was of the people, and it is for him and those like him that walls have been painted in Mexico for thirty years, in fresco or in other more rapid techniques. But all of the techniques have been useless. Juan's father and his next-door neighbor and his brother and everyone else of his class have never seen a single mural. Or if they have, they have agreed with the janitor of the building that it is terrible. Others of the same class have gone even further in their appreciation, scratching the murals with knives, writing dirty words on them, smearing them with tar, etc.

Juan blamed his father for not understanding in all those thirty years that an artist's duty is to paint for the people. At least, so says an all-powerful majority in the country. Juan had no idea what to do with his diploma or the pictures he painted in school. He could not hang them at home because his mother had decorated the living-room with portraits of [popular actors] Jorge Negrete and Pedro Infante, both of them set off with black crepe and artificial flowers. As for Juan's father, he had adorned his wardrobe with refreshing pictures of [actress] La Peluffo, and on his share of the wall there was a lovely blonde advertising Coca-Cola (which also, of course, refreshes) and a portrait of Ratón Macías, whom he, as a good Mexican, considered the greatest boxer in the world. There was no place in that house of the people for Juan to hang his works. One day, feeling an urgent desire to smoke, he went to the comer store and offered a drawing to the storekeeper, a man of the people, in exchange for a pack of cigarettes. The man laughed, naturally, and refused. At home there was never any mention of the artists who are supposed to be the apostles of the people. The talk was about the latest amorous adventures of [actress] María Félix and the latest sensational crime. There was never any reference whatsoever to the art that is supposed to be of and for the people.

They had taught Juan at La Esmeralda to draw simplified figures—smooth, undulant, curvilinear, with large hands and feet—and to use special effects such as foreshortening, so that certain intellectuals would say that he produced "strong" works, of profound popular origin. They were not two-dimensional works. They tried to achieve three-dimensionality by an almost automatic method of drawing, a strict, uniform intensity of line. With such a formula, all is solved: it works equally well for portraying a man with a bandana, an Indian woman selling flowers in the market, a worker in the oil fields, or one of those proletarian mother-and-child scenes which have been turned out for over thirty years without there having intervened, for the good of Mexican art, a single Malthusian or neo-Malthusian to hinder such an empty repetition of maternity.

Juan had not had access to books on the art of other countries either in school or in the public library, much less in the Palace of Fine Arts. Nor were there any museums in which he could see foreign art of the present or the past. When there was an exhibit of some artist who was not Mexican or who refused to follow the style he had been taught to believe was the only one, Juan's friends told him it was not worth seeing, because it pertained to an exhausted, degenerate culture, to inferior races that have nothing like the grandeur and purity of the Mexican race, which is the only one in the world that has complete command of the truth. On one occasion a friend told him about a certain Hitler, who pronounced the same things about a blond race that talked from the esophagus. But Hitler was wrong: if he had known the Mexican race with its dark skin, straight blue-black hair, almond eyes and labial speech, he would have changed his doctrine. The superior race was in Tenochtitlán [Mexico City] and environs, and it was the indisputable possessor of absolute truth.

But one day in a bookstore on the Alameda, Juan saw an art magazine containing things very different from his own work. Some of them were unintelligible to him, and others struck him as absurd, but all of them fascinated him. "So there are artists in other countries too," he said to himself, "not just here in Mexico." He went back to the bookstore several times, and began to see meaning in what had at first been mere puzzles. The absurdities revealed a logic of their own; everything took on order and shape in his mind. After a number of these visits he no longer felt any desire to continue working in the style he had been taught. The new ideas had begun to intrude among the local themes he was treating, and his work was being dominated, and vitalized, by other concepts.

Juan needed support for his new work, because he had lived till then on what his proletarian father brought home after taking bribes at the office. One friend suggested the salon of the Plástica Nacional as a solution; another advised him to join a national association; both solutions offered him a certain breathing-space. He decided on the former, and to carry it out he had to see an abbot-like functionary in the Palace of Fine Arts. We shall call him Víctor for convenience, although his last name may or may not have been Reyes. His friend took him to see this amiable clerk, but first he warned him not to bring any of the capitalist bourgeois works he had recently turned out under the influence of decadent foreign magazines. Juan insisted, but his friend was so upset that he finally compromised and brought both his earlier and later things.

Víctor "Reyes" gave him a questionnaire asking whether the artist belonged to the Mexican school, and then asked to see his portfolio. Juan began to show him his drawings and sketches in chronological order. when he arrived at the new things, Víctor asked dryly, "Will you please explain these monstrosities that look as though they had been taken from the waiting-room of a Wall Street bank?" Juan was distressed. The clerk, with his abbot-like nature, had to follow the dictates of the clerical tribunal to which he belonged, there in that dazzling palace whose glass curtain was made by Tiffany. Juan knew he would lose everything if his application were rejected, because his father would make him become an apprentice bribe-taker. "My friend," Juan stammered, "these things are here by sheer mistake. They belong to a foreign acquaintance of mine, a would-be painter who asked me to keep them for him. Excuse me, Víctor my friend . . ."

This was the proper treatment, and Juan entered the salon of the Plástica Nacional. Later, following the advice of another friend, he joined a national association, where both his errors and good judgment would be protected as long as he followed the line traced previously by who knows what comrade. There were conquests to be realized both in the salon and the association, and new demands to be made: "Give us more walls to decorate for the people!" Juan's two friends told him that this was the newest and clearest demand of the courageous young men who paint in Mexico, but he had read in a history of Mexican painting that it had been the hue and cry for almost forty years. However, it was convenient for him to follow the majority. Perhaps he would receive a fat commission. When the others shook their clenched fists, he did too.

Now that he was protected by official and semiofficial institutions, Juan began to make progress; he had genuine talent, even though he could not use it as he wished. He began to sell his drawings and paintings to tourists in search of souvenirs of their trip. He knew they were stale and lifeless, but the tourists did not care about their execution as long as they had local color, as long as their themes were Mexican. In this matter, his artist friends and his foreign customers were in complete agreement.

Juan sold his work so regularly that he could afford to marry. He observed that when he dressed his wife in a Tehuantepec costume or one of those other colorful folk-costumes that Columba Domínguez wears in her pictures, his clients paid better prices. After a while she hardly took off her disguises even to sleep, because a buyer might wake them up in the early morning after a night on the town.

Juan accepted all types of commissions in order to maintain his success. He always wore overalls, like a working-man, and *huaraches* [sandals], and a big mustache like Zapata's. His style featured massive, corpulent figures, but if a commission for a mural specified lean, cadaverous figures, he painted them, knowing that the compromise meant a few more pesos in his bank account and increased prestige among his friends in the association.

He was quite willing to let his career be furthered by the dithyrambic criticism of the champions of nationalism in Mexican art. He knew that Van Gogh was a Post-Impressionist, and that Giacometti was an elderly Swiss sculptor (almost seventy) of the School of Paris, who occasionally painted. But when a critic named J. C., the dean or president or who-knows-what of Mexican critics said that "Van Gogh was a fauve," or announced with angelic innocence that Giacometti was "a young French painter," Juan kept still. If he had protested, he would have been condemned to silence and neglect. If he had corrected one of those baroque art critics—for instance, J. C., whose Mongolism is one of the puzzles of our cultural life—he would have been ostracized forever by the frustrated painters who cannot finish a canvas themselves and therefore obtain a weekly column in the press, in order to babble about an art of the people, i.e., the father and mother of Juan the contented conqueror.

He also had to give evidence of his nationalism during café conversations, and agree with his friends' opinions. Therefore he had to maintain that the acting of that witty illiterate, Cantínflas, was equal to or even superior to

Chaplin's pure, intellectual genius. He had to assert that a monument to vulgarity like [composer and pianist] Agustín Lara should be included in supposedly-serious anthologies of Mexican poetry. He had to maintain to the point of nausea that Rufino Tamayo was a traitor, rejecting both his good work and his bad with the very same arguments, and dismissing him without further analysis as corrupted by Paris. If that merchant of housemaids' tears named Fernando Soler said that his neo-realistic films were better than the Italians', Juan agreed. He even agreed that the schoolboy pornography of [the amateur theatrical group] Poesía en Voz Alta was a praiseworthy effort. He repeated formulas, watch-words, and dogmas, and felt strong. Tequila is the best drink in the whole world. "There is no other country like Mexico." ("*Como México no hay dos.*") The rest of the universe ought to eat enchiladas. He felt strong and secure, and he lost his desire to progress, to change, to grow. He followed the "only possible" direction for the arts, He retreated once and for all behind the cactus curtain. *¡Viva México!* End of story.

Juan is a fictional character, but he is based on the actual people who swarm around our national culture. They stifle and terrify it, while those who ought to fight back are too apathetic or too frightened to speak up. I must admit, of course, that Juan's story has a happy ending, exactly like those in Hollywood's blissful dream-world. But it is also the happy ending of modern Mexican art, and although it is definitely happy, it is just as definitely an ending. I reject the idea that a culture should achieve a certain end and then halt there, and that is why I have rebelled.

My mistake—if I may speak of myself—has been to oppose the set pattern I have outlined in this story. When Víctor Reyes gave me a questionnaire that asked if I belonged to the Mexican School, I answered with a sacrilegious question. When I was requested to paint a series of murals in which I would have to subordinate (that is, falsify) my pessimistic view of life in favor of an optimistic vision, I turned the job down, even though it was in other ways a tempting offer. I have not wanted to become a Juan; on the contrary, I have fought against the Juans all my life. Against vulgarity and mediocrity. Against superficiality and conformity. Against the standardized opinions that are parroted over and over again, without interruption, from the opening of an exhibit to the discussion afterwards at the café. I protest against this crude, limited, provincial, nationalistic Mexico of the Juans, but thus far I have been answered only with personal attacks, even though my own attacks have always been aimed at works of art and the theories behind them, never at personalities.

I want to repeat that I do not consider myself to be either a pioneer or a reformer. I have tried to work within an accepted artistic tradition, and to bring to it something of my own, something that would carry it forward, however little that something might be. If what I am trying to do is not appreciated in my own country, if I am to receive personal insults instead of serious criticism, perhaps I should look for a different way of explaining my efforts. Perhaps I should consider the cactus curtain an impregnable fortress. But I believe we can progress only by refusing to conform, and I believe I have the right as a citizen and an artist, to rebel against conformity. That is my unpardonable sin.

I should also admit that the Mexico I have attacked is not the only one. There is another Mexico, one that I deeply respect and admire: the Mexico of Orozco, Alfonso Reyes, Silvestre Revueltas, Antonio Caso, Carlos Chávez, Francisco Goitia, Tamayo, Octavio Paz, Octavio Barreda, Carlos Pellicer, Manuel Bravo, Nacho López. I am proud there is a publishing project in Mexico like the Fondo de Cultura Económica, and a rostrum like *México en la Cultura* for the expression of nonconformist opinions. I am delighted when I hear praise for *Los Olvidados* and *Raíces* in other countries, although both films were box-office failures at home. It is this other Mexico that encourages me to protest because it is the true, universal Mexico, open to the whole world without losing its own essential characteristics.

There is a younger generation in Mexico with ideals similar to those I have been discussing. I wish to associate myself with it. I am not setting myself up as an arbiter, and I am not seeking disciples. I approve of many different tendencies and directions, of many roads in art . . . but only when they are free and meaningful extensions of life itself. What I want in my country's art are broad highways leading out to the rest of the world, rather than narrow trails connecting one adobe village with another.

By way of conclusion, I would like to offer two brief parables. The first concerns a Tibetan mission that asked for American economic aid some twenty years ago. In the name of the Dalai Lama it requested only the most essential foods and materials, because nothing that represented modern progress could enter the sacred gates of Lhasa. No wheels, no electricity, no machinery of any kind. Nothing that would threaten the control of the theocracy over its ignorant subjects. The second derives from the same country. Around the middle of the last century a very respectable gentleman suggested to the government of the United States that it should close down its Patent Office. Why? Because everything that was necessary had already been invented.

A Conversation about Alberto Gironella

Moderated by Rita Eder

———

From Rita Eder, *Gironella*
(Mexico City: UNAM, Instituto de Investigaciones Estéticas, 1981), 27–36.

Here, the founders of a gallery share reminiscences of the Mexico City art scene in the 1950s. In those days, Alberto Gironella and José Luis Cuevas seemed poised to lead Mexican art in new directions, away from the dominant muralist style. The founders recount some successes and controversies, especially regarding opposition from David Siqueiros. Participants in this discussion include the Russian-born Mexican painter Vlady (Vladimir Kibalchich Russakov); Horacio López Suárez, a professor of literature at the National Autonomous University of Mexico; José Bartolí, a Spanish painter active in Mexico after 1939; and writer and critic José de la Colina.

Vlady: One day Alberto came over to see me and my wife, and he announced the goal of opening a gallery with [painter Enrique] Climent in the garage of his family home . . . It seemed like a good idea, but just at that moment I met up with Héctor Xavier ("The Totonac from Veracruz," we called him), who also brought up the idea of opening a gallery. Héctor told me about a Dominican who had changed his apartment into a gallery, with each artist exhibiting in one room. They had opened it to circumvent the existing galleries in Mexico City, which were few in number, monopolized by nationalism, and very conventional. Inés Amor and Lola Álvarez Bravo had galleries of this type; they were very sectarian, very communist, and very nationalistic. It was the worst of all communisms, the darkest night of the century still.

I told my wife about Héctor Xavier's idea, and I also spoke with Enrique Echeverría, a friend of ours who had just received a grant to travel to Spain and paint there. In those days he was very interested in the project, though he left very soon. We began to search for a location. First we found an apartment, but later we found a house. The rent was beyond our means, so we resolved to each take one room [for a studio] and leave the living room for the gallery. We called it Galería Prisse.

López Suárez: The name Prisse came up by chance. While the painters were moving in, a Swedish fellow came by, met everyone, and talked with them about painting. Soon a cat walked in, and when the Swede saw it he called out to it, saying "Prisse, prisse." Before he left he bought a painting from each of the artists. That is when Alberto suggested the name Prisse for the new gallery, without even knowing what it meant, in honor of this Swedish collector, our first client and supporter. My job was to send out letters to all of our potential buyers. I went to the gallery in my spare moments, and we still met every Saturday at Alberto's house. The basic idea was to create an art center where all the other painters of talent who had something to say—that is, those not allied with the "Mexican School"—could exhibit for free. Prisse was founded with absolutely no profit motive.

Bartolí: In 1952, Prisse became a gathering place for a new generation of painters who opposed the legend of the Three Great Ones, who had both made and broken the world of painting. Of course, by then Orozco had already passed away, but there remained Rivera and of course Siqueiros, who devoted himself to attacking us. It was basically a political matter. Siqueiros accused us of being abstract artists when in reality there was a wide gulf between us and abstraction. Siqueiros made chaos out of nothing, and that chaos was possible in part because of the small scope of the Mexican cultural world. The same was true in the political realm, which was also of narrow dimensions. Prisse was a nucleus that attracted people from a younger generation who felt the urge to go beyond muralism and the machinations of those cliques that considered themselves Marxist, even though they never read Marx and did not know who he was. Our group around Prisse confronted the nationalists with clear and intelligent opposition, and they never forgave us for that.

Siqueiros started out by alleging that Prisse was only a nest of page-boys from Paris. He also called us the whores of Paris, without realizing that he himself was surrounded with people who dreamed, pined, and yearned for Paris. It was not only Siqueiros but the aura surrounding the Three Great Ones. [Rufino] Tamayo also lined up against the Great Ones, but his ideas also kept him from agreeing with our generation. Still, he never became our enemy, and he visited us many times . . .

We staged Cuevas's first exhibition in Mexico. It was principally Vlady and Alberto who in reality discovered him; Cuevas will never say this, but it is true. Cuevas met them in Alberto's studio along with one other person; perhaps it was Anita Brenner. Vlady came to us and said, "Would you like to see some drawings by a guy who resembles [composer Franz] Schubert?" We went over, and saw that they were very good. Some were influenced by American illustrations, but the best were drawings that he had made in an insane asylum where his psychiatrist brother worked, and who helped him to gain entry. Alberto and Vlady agreed that it would be a good idea to exhibit them. Vlady took charge, and spent over a month gathering Cuevas's drawings. We made a catalog, and a mathematics professor, another refugee from Spain, helped me to hang the works. Alberto also showed for the first time in Prisse. I especially remember his painting *La condesa de Uta*.

Vlady: Alberto based this painting on a famous photograph that he had of [the medieval stone sculpture] *The Countess of Uta*, which he had fallen in love with. His painting shows serenity and elegance. He made it on a stiffened canvas with very warm colors: pinks, soft rose, greys, and silvery tones. And it came out well, because Alberto puts something into everything that he touches, and he knows how to look, which is difficult in a country with neither tradition nor museums.

De la Colina: With *La condesa de Uta* Gironella began a new phase of his development: to create art in response to art, introducing disturbing or critical elements into an interpretation of an existing work. He took a photograph of the famous sculpture, and translated it into pictorial language, as if quoting from [poet] Juan Ramón Jiménez: "With your stone, I will smash you on your crown of stone." [Art critic] Antonio Rodríguez, who wanted to be a Raquel Tibol [art historian] wearing pants—that is, a political dictator of the arts—thought he had uncovered a crime, so he shouted, "Plagiarist, plagiarist!" He could not understand that Alberto had used that sculpture for subject matter, just as one uses an apple or a building. He had translated something from sculpture into the technique of painting. How could this be plagiarism? If he had made another sculpture, copying it just as it was, then yes, Alberto would have committed plagiarism. But the aesthetic commissars, those who believed in socialist realism and other Stalinist concepts, missed the point. Those beasts were now confronted with painters who did not want to march to the rhythm that "the Colonel" [Siqueiros] was beating.

Bartolí: In Prisse there were many other exhibitions. We showed Vlady, Echeverría, Héctor Xavier, and several others along with myself. But what was interesting about Prisse was that it gave an opportunity to young painters who were not in line with the old teachings of the Three Great Ones and their somewhat shoddy patriotism . . . Not only painters, but also poets came to the gallery. It was an open forum . . .

Among the artists and intellectuals who frequented Prisse, there was little political awareness. Very few of us had that, so we may have appeared like elitists, or even like dandies. Of course, this happens with every movement that tries to break with the norms of any community. This cannot and should not be avoided, though, because soon enough the ideas will be clarified. In crises of consciousness, those who identify with elitism will move away from that position as soon as they discover that an elitist consciousness can play no role in a group that has well-developed ideas.

De la Colina: The attitude of that generation, in defending aesthetic freedom, took a political position by rejecting politics. They rejected the artistic nationalism that had informed the rhetoric of the [PRI, or Party of the Institutionalized Revolution, the leading political party]. With Cuevas, this rejection took on a special virulence in confronting Siqueiros and his slogan, "There's no pathway except our way." But Gironella also rejected Siqueiros, as he states in his autobiography. Siqueros condemned any personal expression of feeling in art, which he said amounted to "selling out to North American imperialists." And his choirmasters, Rodríguez and Tibol, also criticized and attacked these so-called uncommitted painters. (The word "commitment" was widely used in those heady days.) Cuevas arose as the chief opponent to Siqueiros, in one corner of the ring. It's curious that Siqueiros could thus impugn Cuevas, for Siqueiros himself painted in a personally vain style for his whole life, even making bombastic self-portraits. Alberto also answered Siqueiros, but in a more subtle and even literary way, which attracted less attention, but still hit the target in the right spot: his dictatorial ego . . .

Bartolí: Prisse ended [in late 1953] because at a certain point it became an absolute disaster economically. We went for up to six months without paying the rent. The curious thing is that Siqueiros accused us of working for the CIA, as if the gallery were a CIA front. This was also said by others who thereby did a lot of damage to Mexican culture without realizing it . . .

Vlady: Gironella's mature artistic development got a new boost with the start of a new gallery that took up, in some respects, where Prisse left off. In 1954 we opened Galería Proteo, which had the goal, like the previous space, of supporting new modes of art not connected to the "Mexican School." The goal was to unite both young and established artists in order to advance the struggle for contemporary art. And critics such as Margarita Nelken, [Jorge] Crespo de la Serna, and Ceferino Palencia supported those painters.

The So-Called "New Figuration" of Argentina

Luis Felipe Noé

—————

From a lecture at the University of Texas at Austin, October 1989.

The intellectual leader of the Nueva Figuración group here recounts its found-ing and early life. Like many artists, he worries about the name that the critics use to describe the group. But this commentary, recollected many years after the facts it recounts, also vividly reconstructs the Buenos Aires art world of the time. The seemingly untrammeled expressive freedom of this group made them the most notorious, as well as the most radical, of the moment. Their combina-tion of expressive intensity and commentary on their contemporary culture also foreshadowed by almost twenty years the neo-Expressionist movement in Europe. This text originally included many quotes from other sources, which I have deleted in an effort to preserve Noé's voice.

I will attempt to tell the story of the group Nueva Figuración as I personally lived it, beginning with my first solo exhibition. It was the fifth of October, 1959, in the Galería Witcomb in Buenos Aires that my friendship began with three of the four people who are the main characters of the story.

That day, I arrived deliberately late and nervous at the gallery, because I greatly feared a terrible disappointment in the love affair that I had always had with the art of painting. At the doorway, I ran into the artist who had taught me in his private studio in 1951 and 1952: Horacio Butler, one of the best-known Argentine painters, who had himself studied in Paris with Othon Friesz and André Lhote. I will always remember what he said to me at that moment: "I arrived early at this show, fearing that I would not like it, so that I could leave without having to tell you my opinion about it. But I have been waiting for you for more than a half hour to tell you that I have learned a great lesson: Doing the exact opposite of what I taught you has led you to excellent results." At that moment I was twenty-six years of age, with half a law degree and a job as a journalist. Three years before, I had recklessly taken up the task of art criticism in the daily *El mundo*, and I had just begun a job as a copy editor of political news for *La prensa*. My paintings were dark, shiny, and thick, with sudden flashes of light, sometimes glowing reds against blue backgrounds; the imagery was more or less fantasy-based. In that same year, 1959, Buenos Aires had witnessed the first two exhibitions of the Informalists, and one month after my show, the City Modern Art Museum had staged a large exhibition of that group, showing its roots in Spanish and French painting.

The organizer and the soul of the Informalists, Alberto Greco, whose mixed-media black paintings contained paint splashes and smelled of dank old buildings, approached me at the opening that day and expressed enthusiasm for my work. He introduced me to the other Informalists. If my painting did indeed include splashes and drips like theirs, it also had a structure in the form of allusions to the human figure. Thus I departed from Informalism, though my style was linked to it. There are still critics and historians who say that I began as an Informalist, but I regard this as an error.

At that opening I also met Rómulo Macció and Jorge de la Vega. Macció, two years my senior, had already had three solo exhibitions, and I had reviewed the first of them in 1956. A graphic designer and self-taught painter, he was already among our young rising stars. Initially, his career was linked with the abstract surrealists of the Boa group, which was part of the international surrealist association Phases. Their characteristic trait was psychic automatic drawing, but Macció was already searching for new formal means to include the figure. A few months prior to my show, he had held in the same gallery an exhibition of paintings which showed both notable influence from de Kooning and also a great vitality. Our common interest in approaching the figure in a new way drew us together . . .

I already knew de la Vega, because he had been a friend of my sister during their studies at the Faculty of Architecture. I had admired his work in earlier years for his ability to paint like Modigliani, though he was only three years older than me. He approached me at the opening to say that he was interested in the path that my paintings suggested, and that he had been painting geometric canvases and was searching for a way out of that. The son of a Sunday painter, de la Vega had learned art in the architecture school. Perhaps this led him to geometric painting, but his work was based more on feeling than on rigor, with a sense of line that seemed related to textile weaving . . .

By 1959, abstract painting in Argentina had become elegant, refined, and sensitive, preoccupied more with quality than with adventure. Painters in general in those days were divided into two irreconcilable camps, the abstract artists and the figuratives. The former represented the new sensibility, but the latter regarded them as mere decorators. If the Informalists were devoted to the sensitive construction of abstract paintings, then de la Vega, Macció, and I felt that a synthesis of the two camps was possible, starting from the Informalist position. From that day, our complicity was sealed. Soon de la Vega showed me new darker and more textured paintings, based on his previous work, but executed with free, lyrical gestures.

At that moment, my father was in the process of closing down a hat-making factory that my grandfather had created in the late nineteenth century. It was located in the San Telmo district, next door to the house where my grandparents lived. This factory, with its industrial-era machines that might have gladdened the hearts of André Breton and Max Ernst, lay unused. My father offered me the building as a studio, and soon Greco and Macció asked to share its ample spaces . . .

In 1960 Macció, de la Vega, and I began to conceive of the idea of creating a movement which would upset all the presuppositions of both the abstract and the figurative artists. Macció introduced me to Ernesto Deira, a lawyer who had studied painting with Leopoldo Presas and Leopoldo Torres Agüero. Deira was a strong figurative painter influenced by Goya, especially by the Black Paintings, but with much freer brushwork. He was a highly cultured person with a very defiant spirit, and soon he was filled with enthusiasm for our idea. We began to form a movement which would synthesize both abstraction and figuration, transcending the struggle between the modern Montagues and Capulets [the warring clans of Shakespeare's *Romeo and Juliet*]. With a freer artistic language, we would form a relationship with our own times and its crises, hoping to achieve an art of our own but without nationalist or folkloric elements. We were inspired by Spanish Informalism and by North American action painting, but more by their vanguard positions than by their actual styles.

As we began to work, we began to sense that another duality of the day would have to be breached: the opposition between nationally based art and international contemporary art. We felt, as I later wrote in my book *Anti-Aesthetic*, that the supposed opposition between the international vanguard and locally based nationalistic art was absurd because it was impossible. They operate on different levels, the vanguard in relation to time and the nationalist in relation to space; but in reality, the artist is always embedded in a certain time and place.

After about a year and a half of work, while I still practiced as a journalist, in May 1961 I opened my fourth solo exhibition, at Galería Bonino, a show titled *Serie Federal* [*The Federal Series*]. I was inspired by a particularly violent period of Argentine history, the early nineteenth century, a time when the Federalists and the Unitarians struggled for power. I made heavy use of the red of blood, of passion, and of the Federalist flag in those works, in a gestural style that directly addressed that historical theme. In the catalog to the show, I wrote, "I want painting to take up a cause against all conventions, even vanguard ones, which might stand in the way of the full development of its expressive force. The only worthwhile effort is one born of risk."

The year 1961 also marked our first group exhibition. Because we preferred to create a movement beyond the four original founders, we invited other artists whom we thought might work in a manner parallel to ours. Thus we invited Greco to join, but he refused because he regarded figurative painting as a step backward . . . [In the end] only two artists accepted our invitation: Sameer Makarius and Carolina Muchnik. The former was born in Egypt and had studied in Germany and Hungary. Though quite active as an abstract artist, he was then better known as a photographer. He did not limit himself to capturing reality, but he worked on the raw film, creating what he called projectograms. With this method he drew imaginary figures directly onto film which took on great energy and force when developed and enlarged. His series titled *Temas Bíblicos* [*Biblical Themes*] was the basis for our invitation. Carolina Muchnik at that time painted imagery from tiny brushstrokes that seemed to both create and destroy themselves at the same time.

Also in 1961, de la Vega staged his first neofigurative exhibition at Galería Lirolay. He created freely brushed images in which line and color interacted energetically over empty white spaces. Deira's art, in contrast, showed black backgrounds with masses of people floating above, painted in vigorous strokes. Macció's canvases were highly contrasted, with anguished human forms showing some of the impact of a publicity poster over their white grounds. Yet they were executed with great formal sensitivity; he used a palette knife loaded with various colors. My works fell within the style of the *Federal Series* but without the historical themes.

Our first group exhibition was called *Otra Figuración* [*Other Figuration*]. We had no clear idea of how to name the show, and "New Figuration" was not coined until the 1962 essay by [French critic] Michel Ragon. We had thought of that name for our show, but rejected it. I had proposed the para-doxical "Abstract-Figuration," but we finally went along with Macció's pro-posal of *Other Figuration*, which was inspired by *Un Art Autre* [*Other Art*], the name that [French critic] Michel Tapié had given to European informal-ism. Perhaps the term *Figuración Libre* [*Free Figuration*] that French painters in the 1980s used would have been the best, because it described our goals and methods . . .

What is important to remember is that we did not use the term *Nueva Figuración* ourselves, nor did we ever title any of our shows that way; we staged just one exhibition with the title *Otra Figuración*. After 1962 when we realized that we were not really a movement but rather a group composed of four artists, we exhibited together with just our four names: Deira, Macció, Noé, and de la Vega, in alphabetical order. But as soon as the term *Nueva Figuración* was coined in Paris, critics began to use the term to describe our work and that of others who came along a similar pathway later . . .

Our first show was widely recognized as novel, and it made a big impres-sion, though it was almost universally praised. The same had happened with my exhibition of the *Federal Series*. This fact led me to say to Jorge de la Vega that if everyone liked my painting, then I must not be showing them any-thing new, and I must be on the wrong path. De la Vega responded that he was tempted to shatter the rigid structure of the frame, and liberate his forms into real space. It would hardly be a surprise if the Madí group, even though they painted geometrically, were somehow on his mind. What is certain is that he and I spoke a great deal about this during our voyage to Europe by ship [in late 1961]. One of the first exhibitions that we saw [in Paris] was *Figuration Autre*. Soon Macció and Deira arrived as well. We had each secured various grants for the journey, except for de la Vega, who traveled with his own funds earned as a drafter in an architectural office.

While taking our trip, we left behind a cultural environment in Buenos Aires that was speeding up in an interesting way. Shortly after our depar-ture, Greco showed his series *Las monjas* [*The Nuns*]. [Antonio] Berni, one of the most important Argentine painters, who had since the 1930s been creating neorealist paintings with large figures in quite solid compositions, staged an important exhibition that showed a radical new direction for him. He called it *Juanito Laguna*, and there he exhibited very large works showing a new manner of making socially conscious painting. Inspired by the theme of the poor districts (similar to the *favelas* of Brazil) and having a child as protagonist, he had intelligently expanded upon the discoveries of the

Informalists who worked with almost any material. Berni used flattened tin cans to perfectly reflect a world made from castoffs. And his manner of working seemed to fit with the logic of neofiguration. At the same time [Kenneth] Kemble and others presented the exhibition *Arte destructivo* [using broken items salvaged from garbage dumps].

On the ship I had said to de la Vega, "Up to now, I have worked with the idea of composing by joining figures together, but that seems invalid in a world of contrasts and tensions. I need to think about creating relationships from opposition; it makes no sense to paint a *Last Supper* in a climate of unity in which Christ, the apostles, Judas, the objects on the table, and the consecrated bread and wine are all painted in the same way with the same atmosphere." Shortly after our arrival at the apartment that we shared in Issy-les-Molineaux near Paris, I created a work in response to this challenge which I titled *Mambo*. It was a diptych in which I painted a woman's head in black and white, which dissolved into the background. Just below, for the other half, I turned the canvas backward and nailed onto the support a silhouette painted in bright colors which continued the head above. Naturally, the stretcher frames were visible in the lower half. This was the beginning of my theory of the "shattered vision" and the rupture of the unity of the work of art.

De la Vega supported what I had done, and he began to shatter his stretcher frames and wrap the canvas casually around them. I remember especially a *Bruja* [*Witch*] that he created at that time. We continually urged each other onward, and this encouraged us more than the art environment of Paris, which we found rather mediocre and decadent. I remember saying to Jorge, "We came here thinking that Paris was the center of the art world, only to find that the center is in New York." This was a time when the French art world was deeply divided between those who ignored this fact and those who recognized it. In any case, Paris did help us to shed any sort of solemnity that we felt about the act of painting. We noticed with pleasure that Mondrian, for example, left traces of masking tape on some of his compositions, which meant that he was not as obsessively fixated as our geometric painters were. The risks that we had spoken of before had to be transcended. We felt the need to shatter all kinds of conventions.

Macció and Deira took a studio in Fontenay-aux-Roses, another suburb of Paris. They were more respectful of painting for its own sake, and viewed our experiments with skepticism. If de la Vega and I were more interested in rupturing pictorial structures, they were preoccupied with freeing the gesture. We thought more about artistic issues, while they were interested in painting, but we all agreed on creating content-filled works that cast aside conventions.

We returned to Buenos Aires after a little less than a year. I was the last to arrive; the other three met me at the dock with the news that we had a studio where we could all work together, the same one where Deira had worked before. This moment marked the real foundation of the group, but already in Europe we agreed that we would stage a show of the four of us shortly after our arrival. At that time artists had formed various groups, but we were the only ones who worked all at the same place with the same goals. We commented on each other's works and strived for new experiences. I remember Deira creating a work holding the brushes behind his back, and de la Vega taking on a new problem with each new canvas.

As soon as we arrived, Alfredo Bonino, who had galleries under his own name in New York, Rio de Janeiro, and Buenos Aires, offered us an exhibition in the latter gallery [for October 1962]. That show created so much talk and scandal that he enthusiastically invited us to stage a new show for the next month, which we made even more outrageous. Many critics who had earlier praised us now severely criticized us, with three exceptions: Aldo Pellegrini, Hugo Parpagnoli, and Jorge Romero Brest. Pellegrini wrote: "They have broken all of the conventions that tie down Argentine artists, such as good taste, effort, of painting as a gestural activity, but above all the belief in the sacred mission of art, the source of many mystifications." That exhibition defined our particular interpretation of New Figuration. (Though I believe that an adequate term has yet to be found. I ask myself, could it be "Free Figuration"?) Jorge Romero Brest, director of the Museo Nacional de Bellas Artes, invited us to stage a large exhibition there the following year.

At the same time as the show at Bonino, we had a show called Esto [This] at another gallery; this consisted of drawings on the subject of the reality that we found in Argentina on our return. The government of President [Arturo] Frondizi had fallen, and two military factions were fighting each other in the streets of Buenos Aires. This sensation of social breakage led me to create the next year a series of works that reflected this through their shattered structure. Thus it was that I created works such as Introducción a la esperanza [Introduction to Hope], which depicted a multitude of people holding up signs. But the multitude was painted on one canvas in black and white as the signs they held up were other attached canvases, painted in color. I also painted a completely political work on the theme of the fire in the Jockey Club, an event that happened in 1955 during the regime of [Juan] Perón.

The year 1963 was fundamental for us. We worked with great abandon, to total exhaustion . . . In that same year the di Tella Institute organized two prize competitions, one national and one international, as they had done every year since 1960. The jury, composed of Romero Brest, Jacques Lassaigne [curator of the Paris Museum of Modern Art], and Willem Sandberg, director of the Stedelijk Museum in Amsterdam, awarded Macció the international prize and me the national prize. The prize was a travel grant to a destination of our choice, so I decided for New York, while Macció preferred to take his chances in Europe.

Against the wishes of Deira and myself, and to some extent those of de la Vega, the group began to fade . . .

DOCUMENT 46

Marta Minujín against the Easel

———

From *Confirmado*, October 7, 1965, 64.

Here, a rather defiant artist confronts a skeptical reporter. This interview took place at the competitive exhibition of the International Prize of the Di Tella Foundation, which was awarded every year in Buenos Aires by an international jury. Building on the innovations of Nueva Figuración, Marta Minujín entered in 1965 with El batacazo *[The Long Shot], an environment that included sculpted figures posed to simulate weightless space travel, caged flies and rabbits, flashing neon silhouettes of soccer players and astronauts, and a playground slide that ended on an effigy of a movie goddess. She explains why this is the most appropriate art for the moment.*

Q: What is this?

A: It is a visual event. Something that I have done so everyone can collaborate with me on its permanent realization. Viewers are on the same plane of creation with me. There is no dichotomy between us, but rather a unity: dynamic, ever-changing, hallucinatory, infinite.

Q: Do you think you have achieved this?

A: I consider it the only open path. Easel painting is definitely dead. And buried. These times are not for the contemplation of static objects.

Q: Do the viewers agree with you? Because people still hang paintings in their homes, and they still go to exhibitions of easel painting.

A: That is a different problem. But with *El batacazo* the only relevant responses are the ones that actually arise. The work acts on viewers in a compelling way. It obliges them to wake up and live, to directly face the unexpected, the surprising, and circumstances unconnected to reality. All of which should loosen their moorings, weaken their inhibitions, and let them act in full freedom.

Q: They may even have some fun as well.

A: That would not be the ideal outcome, but why not? To enjoy oneself is in any case a vital act. But what really results from the viewer's participation is a freeing of imagination. Most people's imaginations have gone to sleep.

Q: And so *El batacazo* is a wake-up call?

A: Practically, yes. This part is easy to understand: Entering the environment of *El batacazo* elicits a shocked reaction. Later, remembering it without going back to it, the experience can be enriched with new elements.

Q: So it is important to not return to *El batacazo* so that its effect can be felt? Will returning to it spoil the experience?

A: No, it won't be spoiled. But the transformed memory of the experience is more important than the fact of the experience itself. This is the basis of the viewer's participation, and that's why the work needs to be destroyed [at the end of the show].

Q: Why do you think that this type of work, and not some other, best defines our times?

A: I maintain that a painting, as traditionally conceived, is a static fact. People today are too agitated by the vertiginous events around them, which happen at jet-speed and intensity; they can't stop for a moment. It's undeniable that an easel painting can neither transmit nor document the changes that happen minute by minute. We need a special dynamic, which I seek and find in my work.

Q: But the viewers are not reacting in the way you describe. Some laugh; some become angry.

A: They are not prepared to encounter this visual fact because it violates their presuppositions.

Q: This means that your goals of integration, of communication, of participation, fail from the outset. If viewers are not prepared to grasp the purpose of the work, then the purpose loses its essence.

A: It is neither lost nor altered, though it could be postponed. It's undeniable that whatever their attitudes, viewers' participation is assured, and that is what justifies and affirms the goal of the work of art.

Q: Is that why you call *El batacazo* a work of art?

A: Of course, but it is a different type of art; it is a vital art. The work does not reside in the objects and mechanisms that I have put in place, but rather in the moment that the viewer lives while inside it. The work's unfolding is in that awareness, not in the forms, which we might relegate to the status of accessories.

Q: A soccer match might also be a vital art form.

A: Precisely. And I hope that my works are experienced like a soccer match or an auto race, not contemplated intellectually in search of intellectual pleasure. I would prefer to set up my works in the street, not in an exhibit hall.

Q: But they are in an exhibit hall. How have you accepted this?

A: I have not completely accepted it, but I still cannot escape certain inevitable conditions.

Q: Conditions such as the nearness of easel paintings? Because the winner of the International Di Tella Prize is James Rosenquist, a painter.

A: I have entered the prize competition. But I don't want to judge my colleagues.

Furniture and Bad Taste

An Interview with Beatriz González

Katherine Chacón

———◦———

From Beatriz González, *Retrospectiva*
(Caracas: Museo de Bellas Artes, 1994), 13–15.

This interview with one of Colombia's more audacious artists touches on the important questions of taste and medium. Her pathway to popular culture can be usefully contrasted with the route of North American pop artists. Like them, she began to work from popular imagery, although she claims to have been unaware of Roy Lichtenstein at the time. Soon after, she began to paint her imagery onto used furniture, an important evolutionary step. Here, she discusses how it happened.

Q: You had great success [in 1965] with [the painting] *The Suicides of Sisga*, which was based on a press photo. But before that, you had created *The Turkish Girl*, also from a photo. Why this change from sources in the history of art to more or less common photographic images?

A: After I did the series based on Vermeer, I had a horrible moment in which it seemed that I was becoming an abstract artist, so I resolved to work instead with images of children. At the outset, I made some drawings that mixed a strong influence from [Fernando] Botero of 1964 with my recent interest in pastel. (My sister had brought me from Europe a large box of pastels that had three levels, which I enjoyed very much.) My treatment of the bodies of the children in pastel was very much like Botero, but the faces were influenced by some photos of Lyndon B. Johnson and Richard Nixon that had been published in *Life* magazine. Then I decided to take my own photos. At my nephew's first communion, I photographed a Middle Eastern child; she wore a velvet dress with many bangles, and she was seated on a metal chair. It was a delicious moment because I was choosing the model and taking the photo myself, rather than cutting pictures from a newspaper. Later, when I introduced changes to the photos, they led to works such as *The Child Montage*. Those were important canvases, each more cropped than the last, but they ended up boring me. I liked *The Turkish Girl* and *The Child Montage*, but the rest of them seemed to show a purely aestheticist attitude that I did not find convincing. I began to think that I was acting just like one of those many women who paint. My colors were pretty; I knew I had a good palette, skill, and good brushwork, but the works had no feeling and I again began to feel lost.

During this period, the faces were my biggest problem. I noticed that the girls were coming out like Botero, so I began to slim down the volumes, and move toward flatter bodies, like bad paper cutouts. I hoped to reduce the volume to flatness. But a face can't be reduced to flatness because it becomes an oval shape with lines and points, like a drawing. One day I opened the newspaper and saw the photo of the youths of Sisga who had committed suicide. The story was that a gardener went crazy and told his girlfriend that the world is so full of sin that it's better to stop living; so they decided to throw themselves into the freezing waters of the lake at Sisga, shortly after having their photo made with a bunch of flowers in their joined hands. Although it was a rather beautiful and romantic story, my interest focused on the picture reproduced in the press: Those flat faces had just the look that I was seeking. The photo that impressed me the most was not the original, published in *El espectador*, but rather the one that appeared in [the magazine] *El tiempo* from *El espectador*. Because it was a re-publication, the image had flattened out even more, become grayish, and lost all contrast. I immediately painted over a girl that I was working on, with free strokes, and over the top of that I painted *The Suicides*. But it bothered me that the earlier painting was still beneath them, so I created another version, which is now in the Museo de Arte Moderno La Tertulia, in Cali. But I was still not pleased with the work, so I remade it again; that version is now in the Museo Nacional [in Bogotá]. In the latter work, I especially like how the hands and flowers came out.

That work gave everyone a lot to talk about, and not all of the talk was pleasant. [Arts patron and administrator] Inocente Palacios liked the work a lot, and gave it a prize at the Eighteenth National Salon of Artists. He saw me as related to the pop art of Lichtenstein, but Lichtenstein had never crossed my mind. Our education at the university ended with

Pollock and abstract expressionism, and I got to know those works on a trip to New York guided by [art critic] Marta Traba in 1961. Pop art was still unknown here, and I did not even know who Lichtenstein was, but I was completely sure that I had found the right path for my art.

Q: Next, you began to work with cheap color prints.

A: Yes, and I began to seek new themes for my work. I received a good critical education from my mother. She was a critic herself, and she often showed us things in bad taste in a humorous and satirical way, though she herself soon began to varnish leather stools in bright oranges and greens. So I began to build on my visual education, wondering why I was so drawn to work with such a bright palette. In search of conclusions, I found chromolithographs, those color plates that the publisher in Cali sold that reproduced European paintings in bright posters. I filled many tubes with those, and I began to work, certain that I had found my path.

Q: OK, so you used those posters because they had a formal relationship to what you were seeking. But in both the photo of the suicides—whose story seemed beautiful and dramatic but also represented an act so full of sentimentalism that it is tacky—and in the color posters, we might see a tendency toward kitsch or bad taste. Didn't those particular themes influence your choices?

A: I think they did. Once I found the suicides, I knew that I had reached a good place, and it was related to the concept of taste. Not that it was good or bad taste, but that the people themselves chose those subjects, because they used them to decorate their homes. I think at that point that I veered toward sociology, because at the root, more than a merely visual search, I wanted to reflect on the question of taste, partly because I have always been put off by excessive refinement. At that time, [art critic] Germán Rubiano wrote an article claiming that I had sacrificed all that is formal, pictorial, and well-schooled. His interpretation was correct: I denied certain pictorial qualities in favor of visual effects and a coherent investigation.

Q: Is this why you moved away from oil paint, and began to experiment with enamel?

A: When I created *Ríonegro, Santander* [with oils in 1967], I took a lot of pleasure in the wet brush and the thick stroke. After searching for what was flat and perfect, there I was painting thickly. I both enjoyed this and worried about it. Later [in 1968], I painted the feet of the woman in *Underdevelopment 70* deliberately dirty, without the bright color that I had used earlier, and I began to think that I was doing something unhealthy, because I was getting too much pleasure out of making things that lacked subtlety. On reflection, I noticed that I was contradicting or attacking the notion of the refined provincial girl who goes to the capital to test her talents. Those two works showed me that oil is not the appropriate medium, because it already implies refinement and elegance. I renounced oils and moved on to enamel. Near my house there was a parking lot that had an image of Simón Bolívar painted in an oval shape. I went to see a man who made billboards and asked him to make me two ovals. I painted Bolívar and [Francisco de Paula] Santander on them and I entered them in the Nineteenth National Salon of Artists. I got both a prize and the biggest scandal of the year, and that's when I understood that enamel and brilliant colors correspond to popular taste.

Q: Is that where the idea for your first objects came from?

A: First came the beds, which had a lot to do with my mother's inclination toward things made in bad taste. I saw metal beds in the stores and I said to myself, "Someday I have to buy one of those." When I finally bought one, I went home and noticed that it was the same size as a [1970] painting that I had made called *Almost-Still Life*. I attached the painting to the bed, and that was the beginning of the objects. I sent that and two other similar works to the São Paulo Biennial in 1971, but some people told me that I was participating in the Biennial before my time. I wondered if they were suggesting that my work was still immature, but I told myself that they were saying it because my type of art was not yet in style. Referring to it, Marta Traba coined the term "marginal painting" in an article that she wrote about me. When I arrived in São Paulo, the newspapers were all saying that my work was the most likely to get a prize. The public reaction to my pieces of metal furniture was impressive, because in Brazil those colors have a lot of impact. Although I did not win any prizes, the press took notice of my work; it was an important moment.

Q: When [curator] Fabiana López and I were discussing the arrangement of your work [for exhibition], we asked ourselves if you thought in sculptural terms. But I know that you don't, because your work is based on painting, and it grows out of a type of painting that works on the connotative possibilities of imagery. There has been much debate about this question.

A: That discussion irritates me, because my works were always paintings, never sculptures. When I make them I am never posing questions of volume and space. For me, a painting is a painting: that is, a flat area that forms are painted on. The furniture is like the frame. Like the altar-frames of the colonial period, which were huge. I think of the object as the frame.

Q: Except that in those cases the frame influences the meaning of the painting, enriching the connotative play. I understand the objects as the results of a process by which you deeply internalized the visual devices of the painting and how to perceive it.

A: There has always been this discussion, but only recently have I been able to accept that my work has a sculptural element. I was even selected for an exhibition of Colombian sculpture in New York [in 1993]. In the past, I would not have allowed this, but one softens over time . . .

Painting Violence

An Interview with Fernando Botero

Valeria Shapira

From *La Nación Revista*, June 25, 2006.

In the late twentieth century, Colombian figurative painter Fernando Botero suddenly created a long series of works that depicted the violence in his country, a novel subject for him. This was followed in 2005 by a series devoted to the torture of prisoners by American reservists at Abu Ghraib prison during the Iraq war. This interview, done while the artist was working in a studio in Italy, takes up the question of the role of politics in art.

Q: You have always spoken of art as a matter linked with pleasure. How do you adjust this concept, in view of the works you have painted about the violence in your country?

A: Art should give pleasure. Most of the masterworks of painting take up more or less pleasurable themes. But there have been a few artists devoted to more dramatic subjects, among them Matthias Grünewald and Hans Baldung. Usually, these vivid subjects form a special class in an artist's production, as occurred with Goya in his painting *The Third of May, 1808*. So I believe that it is possible to adjust, to change from a dramatic theme to one that is pleasurable, as long as the artist is true to his style and the result produces aesthetic pleasure . . . I oppose art that becomes a witness to its times as a weapon in a struggle. But in view of the magnitude of the drama that Colombia faces, the moment came when I felt the moral obligation to leave a testimony about an irrational time in our history.

Q: In some earlier works of yours from the 1960s, the theme of violence was also present, and in the 1970s you made some paintings on the general theme of warfare. Why did you wait so long to make this series of works about the violence in your own country?

A: Because I now have sufficient maturity to make them; the same is true of the series on the tortures in Iraq.

Q: As a young man you worked at a newspaper and had a lot of contact with journalists. To what extent does the daily news influence you as you begin a work? The series [about Iraq] that you mentioned, about [the tortures at] Abu Ghraib, seems to have come from indignation that the published pictures of those horrors aroused in you.

A: My youthful experiences as an illustrator at a newspaper were not important. Like everyone else, I read the newspapers, and the news affects me. Obviously, the news of the tortures at Abu Ghraib made my blood boil. Because a country such as the United States, which presents itself as an exemplar of compassion and defense of human rights, has no right to do what it did.

Q: When you work on those themes, do you hope that they have some effect in the political sphere?

A: At the moment that it is created, art has no effect. But later, when the newspapers have stopped reporting on certain things and most people have forgotten them, art still exists as a sort of permanent accusation. That is its power. If we do not remember the bombardment of Guernica, we still remember the painting of it by Pablo Picasso.

Q: Your style is unmistakable. To what extent can the subject that you take up influence your style, when it is already so well-established?

A: The subject generally is the reason for making a painting, but at the same time it is part of the pleasure of art. When you look at an impressionist work, you want to be there, inside the painting. And when you look at *Las meninas* [by Diego Velázquez], what sweetness you find there, in that family scene! So the subject is important in the work.

Q: You are a Latin American artist. Can art have its own identity in this part of the world, now that everything seems to be going global?

A: Unfortunately, there is no Latin American art as there should be. Globalization has been with us for a while.

Q: Are you still a nomadic artist?

A: I rest by changing my studio and my country. I became accustomed to these changes, which have much to do with my work.

Q: In what sense?

A: The months that I spend here in Pietrasanta are devoted to my work in sculpture. Just now I am creating some sculptures that I have had in mind for some time. This is a magical place, with the best foundries. It's also the place of marble, where you can forget that painting even exists.

PART TEN

Political Conceptualism, 1960s–1970s

Insertions into Ideological Circuits

Cildo Meireles

———⊕———

From *Cildo Meireles* (Rio de Janeiro: Funarte, 1981), n.p.

One of the most distinctive forms of Latin American conceptual art was born when Cildo Meireles inscribed subversive and provocative statements onto banknotes and returnable Coca-Cola bottles, and then set them loose anonymously into the marketplace of military-ruled Brazil. These Insertions into Ideological Circuits, *as he called them, raised potent aesthetic issues regarding authorship, public, and political content. Here, he describes the genesis of his thought.*

I remember that in 1968, 1969, and 1970, we knew that we were beginning to touch on interesting subjects. So we stopped working with metaphorical representations of situations, and began working with situations themselves, in reality. Moreover, the type of work we were doing had a transitory nature, and this became another characteristic. It was a type of work that finally dispensed with the cult of the pure art object; things existed according to the reactions that they could provoke in society. This was exactly what we had in mind: to work with the idea of the public. At that time, we risked a lot on this work, as we intended to reach a wide and undefined number of people: that thing called the public. Today, however, there is the danger of creating a work while knowing exactly who will find it interesting, and why. The notion of the public, a broad and inclusive notion, has been substituted and deformed into the notion of the consumer, that sector of the public that has spending power.

In reality, *Insertions into Ideological Circuits* was born from the need to create a system or a language for the circulation and exchange of information that did not depend on any type of centralized control, a system essentially opposed to that of the press, radio, and television. The latter are typical examples of media that reach an immense audience, but within their system of circulation there is always a certain type of control and determined check-points along the way. In other words, the right of insertion is exercised by an elite that has access to the development of the system, sophisticated technology, and large sums of money and/or power.

Insertions into Ideological Circuits was born as two projects: The *Coca-Cola Project* and the *Banknote Project*. The work began with a text that I wrote in April 1970, which read in part: 1. In society there are various methods and mechanisms of circulation (circuits). 2. These circuits are obviously linked to the ideology of the producers, but at the same time they can passively receive insertions into their circulation. 3. This occurs as often as people trigger them.

The *Insertions* also arose from our observations of two more or less common practices: the traffic in chain letters (those cards that you receive, copy, and send to others) and the messages in bottles that you throw into the ocean. These practices imply a notion of a circulating medium, a notion crystallizing most clearly in the case of paper money and, metaphorically, in returnable containers such as soft-drink bottles.

From my point of view, the important factor in this project was isolating and defining the concept of the circuit. And this concept determined the dialectical charge of the work, while interfering with all of the effort contained in the essence of the process (or medium). In other words, the [Coca-Cola] bottle always brings an ideology along. Thus, the initial idea was the discovery of the natural circuit, which exists and on which it is possible to create a real work. In reality, the character of the "insertion" in the circuit always has the character of subversive information.

This insertion capitalizes on the sophistication of the medium, as it provides an amplification of equality of access to mass communications, that is, in providing a neutralization of the original ideological propaganda (from either industry or the state), which is always anaesthetizing us. It is an opposition between awareness (insertion) and anaesthesia (circuit), considering awareness as a function of art and anaesthesia a function of industry. Because any industrial circuit is naturally both broad and alienating.

Of course, art has a social function and should have the means to be intensely engaged, showing greater density of awareness in relation to the society from which it emerges. The role of industry is the exact opposite of this. As it exists today, the power of industry is based on the greatest possible coefficient of alienation. Thus, my notes on the *Insertions* specifically place art in opposition to industry.

Transactions in the visual arts are often based on either the mystique of the work itself (the wrapping: canvas, etc.) or on the mystique of the creator (Salvador Dalí or Andy Warhol, for example). Or it comes from the mystique of the market (the property game: exchange value). But in reality, none of these aspects should become primary. As soon as distinctions of one type or another arise, next comes the distinction between who can and cannot make a work of art. As I thought about it, the *Insertions* exist only insofar as they were not the work of one person. That is, the work exists only to the extent that other people use it. Another proposal is the idea of the need for anonymity. The question of anonymity involves the question of authorship. You would not work anymore through objects, because the object can become a practice, or a thing over which you do not have any type of proprietary control. And you would try to raise other issues: first, attempting to reach more people, insofar as you do not need to go after the information, because the information comes after you; and as a result you would have the right conditions to explode the notion of a sacred space . . .

Regarding the museum, the gallery, and the canvas, they are all sacred spaces for representation, and they all become a sort of Bermuda Triangle: anything, or any idea that you place in them, is necessarily neutralized. I think that people have tried to prioritize a commitment to the public, not with the buyer or the art market, but with the audience itself sitting out there in the seats. This indefinite face is the most important part of the structure. [My goals are:] To work with this marvelous possibility that the visual arts offer, and to create with each new idea a new language for expressing it. To work also with the possibility of transgression at the level of reality. That is, to create works that do not merely exist in a conventional, consecrated, or sacred space. Works that do not merely take place on the level of a canvas, or a surface, or a representation. To work no longer with the metaphor of gunpowder, but to work with the gunpowder itself.

Seventeen Questions regarding Art

Horacio Zabala

———◆———

From leaflet, Centro de Arte y Comunicación (Buenos Aires), 1972.

This statement by an Argentine conceptual artist reflects two important debates that roiled the Buenos Aires art world in the late 1960s and early 1970s: "How political should art be?" and "What is art, after all?" Although these questions arose during a time of aesthetic and political upheaval, they are probably relevant for any period.

1. What polarities define our era?
2. Is one of them the world of abundance and the underdeveloped world?
3. Are conditions of development in some countries dependent on conditions of underdevelopment in others?
4. Is the world of abundance and extravagance also a center of cultural diffusion?
5. Does art have a function in this?
6. Is art autonomous?
7. Does art lack relevance in the face of reality?
8. Does art express the contradictions and transformations of the culture?
9. Is art rooted in the cultural and productive bases of the community?
10. Is art a pastime?
11. Is art reactionary and outside time?
12. What is the relationship between art and politics?
13. Can art generate useful questions and answers?
14. Can art offer a synthesis of conflicting input?
15. Can art offer a maximum of possibilities with a minimum of resources?
16. Is it possible to create a code of visual meaning that could be understood by everyone?
17. Is it correct to say that any artistic idea, even before it is realized, has lost all revolutionary meaning?

The No Manifesto of Tribu No

Cecilia Vicuña

———◉———

From *Spit Temple: The Selected Performances of Cecilia Vicuña*
(New York: Ugly Duckling Press, 2012), 58. Translation by Rosa Alcalá.

Prior to the onset of the Chilean military dictatorship in 1973, an interdisciplinary avant-garde was already active. One such group was the Tribu No, or No Tribe, organized in Santiago in 1967 by poet and sculptor Cecilia Vicuña. This group's street actions encouraged noncompliance with social norms before such gestures became highly suspect and subject to censorship under the military government. Most of the artists named in this poetically written manifesto practiced spontaneous or fantasy-based creativity. The group's name also means tribuno, *or* tribune, *an orator who speaks out for the interests of the common people.*

Charlie Parker's no-movement, that is what we are in the warm and unsettled night of the South. As long as life persists in our individual, yet united, experiences, nothing will bother us.

We manifest no desire and no characteristic. We offer no manifesto to avoid being pigeonholed, and we are not afraid to pigeonhole ourselves—that would be as likely as suddenly becoming Polynesia's most daring parachutists.

We upset order with our exacerbated immobility. The no-movement is Charlie Parker's, John Coltrane's, Nicolás of Cusa's, Martínez de Pasqualis's, Rimbaud's, Philoxenes's, and, most of all, André Breton's and [Friedrich] Hölderlin's. In reality, we do not want to become demonstrators, since it would make the experience predominantly public.

We undermine reality from within; that is why we are subversive and loving. Furthermore, we are so minor and unknown that we delight in our freedom.

Tribu No's campaigns are not highly clandestine, and the only visible results for those of us who live-not the no-movement are our stupid works.

We hope to turn solitude into the world's new idol.

                                ha ha

We say no-thing. After speaking centuries of IT, IT remains a secret.

Our macabre intent is to leave humans naked, without preconceived notions, without conventional attachments-attire.

Have no fear. Our works will take years to manifest. We are not playing around.

The interior of the seed is soft.

IT is known only by living IT. Whatever IT is.

IT is yet to be discovered.

Statements on Crosses and Feminism

Lotty Rosenfeld

———❦———

Submitted by the artist.

Here the creator of One Mile of Crosses in the Pavement *discusses its influences, intentions, and possible meanings. This work, one of the better-known conceptual interventions by a Latin American artist, was first executed in Santiago in 1979; the work was the product of a search for art that could seem subversive and yet escape the censorship of the military government. She later re-created it at several politically charged locations, including Checkpoint Charlie on the Cold War border between East and West Berlin; in the tunnel that passes under the Andes between Chile and Argentina; and in front of the White House on Pennsylvania Avenue.*

On the Influence of Joseph Beuys and Wolf Vostell on Her Practice

The meager information that we were able to obtain during the dictatorship about art outside Chile, and particularly about Beuys and Vostell, came from Nelly Richard, who in 1977 offered a seminar entitled "Today's Art. Information. Interrogation" at the Instituto Chileno-Norteamericano de Cultura. In the same year, Ronald Kay brought a group of graphic works and documentations of happenings to Chile to exhibit in a gallery, an unusually advanced event for those times. Without doubt, both of these contributed to the radical turn that my art practice took. I was already in a state of questioning and searching for new means of production, especially on the themes of occupation of public space and how various aspects of daily life could be aesthetically fertile ground. Then, in 1981, Diamela Eltit and I visited Vostell in Berlin and we spoke with Beuys on the telephone. I learned from both of them about their works, and my admiration for them also grew. I wanted my [later] participation in Documenta XII [in 2007] to take the form of an intimate salute to Beuys alongside his row of trees.

On Possible Meanings of the Crosses in Street Interventions

I understand the dashed lines in the road as a metaphor for everything that is imposed in the name of order, narrowing our habits and training our minds. My intervention in the road was a gesture of defiance which says "No" to any predetermined course which seeks to "order" individual persons in the hope of making people politically docile and economically productive. Though this art action originated in a dictatorship, it can be valid beyond that time and place. These dashed lines exist in nearly all the paved streets in the world, which has given me the opportunity to extend my work beyond my own country and its borders. By introducing a small crisis in the sub-system of community ordering, the work invites viewers to rethink their dependence on such codes.

On Signing the Crosses, and on Working Solo or with Help

At the end of the first set of crosses, I signed and dated the pavement in chalk; the purpose was to mark or signal the beginning of a work that had no end. And as I was also a member of CADA [Actions of Art Collective], I joined in the theoretical reflections during the time of that group's existence. With the passage of time—thirty-five years have gone by—I no longer have the same physical ability to carry out my long interventions myself. Moreover, since 1979 I have begun using an adhesive tape that requires two people in order to stick it onto the pavement. But these modifications do not change in the least the meanings of the actions.

On the Location of the First Set of Crosses

That street where I made my first action was and still is part of what we would call the upper-income district. In 1979, that area was far less populated and had less auto traffic. Today, as is natural after so many years, there are more lanes for traffic, tall buildings, businesses, etc.

On the Availability of Equipment and Materials during the Dictatorship

During the dictatorship, there was a great spirit of solidarity among those of us who struggled against it and staged resistance on the various fronts. This allowed us to realize our public interventions at little or no cost. In either individual work or collective work with other members of CADA, the most expensive tools for our actions were video cameras and editing equipment. But fortunately, we also obtained all of this without cost.

On the Relationship between an Action and Its Video Documentation

In order to go beyond the temporal limits of the art actions, I had to find a way to prolong or multiply them. Video is the device for prolonging the action and documenting it, and also for replaying it. Video and photography in my work are parts of the "production" of my work, and they take part in its creation. In this way, video is advantageous because it is a portable support which contributes to making sense of the art work. Videos and photographs must be understood as autonomous works because they are conceived in a certain time and place outside of what they record, but this recording gathers meaning, dimension, and heft in the present, in its continual actualization. Thus, a video of an art action is the constant presence of that art action, its activation as a work, and its critical reference point. And in a certain way, its urgency. More recently, using digital video allows me to undertake new aesthetic operations, to adopt new technologies that amplify the circulation and build alternative political spaces. To create zones of cultural resistance is what I have always been interested in. Using digital media allows a wider democratization of the image.

On the Influence of Her Early Printmaking Work on Later Actions

Probably it had little or no impact. I rather think that the dictatorship and my political activism were the principal influences on my later art. In 1977, my work was in a transition period. Chile was in a military dictatorship, and very few dissident initiatives could be expressed openly, and in that context it became necessary for me to rethink my role as an artist.

On the Question of Feminism

I am most interested in working on social, aesthetic, and political subjects, in considering my materials and connecting them, or possibly transforming them, in an effort to undermine rigid categories. While I do believe it to be important to view art through the lens of gender (as a political matter), I ask myself if critics or official criticism ever read the work of men as masculine. I think that addressing gender is very important as a response to discrimination, but paradoxically it is also a form of reduction and perhaps even exclusion.

In my work, the act that corrupts the order of symbols and perverts their structure is the act of a woman. But a long tradition has marginalized the work of women in the production of meaning and has nullified their participation in the world of symbols. Starting from the art world, I have acted as a woman, taking the initiative in recasting this sector of social practice, becoming an investigator of the rupture of the symbolic order. In the context of our basically patriarchal social structure, I have confronted the foreseeable limitations, hindrances, and obstacles, and I believe that at times my work has overcome these obstacles. In a world controlled by the art dealers, curators, and galleries, the situation of a Chilean woman artist is doubly or even triply oppressed. But the main task is to make yourself heard, since visibility is controlled by interests I cannot compete with; not because my work lacks visual power, but because visibility in the national and international circuits is granted by the machinery of propaganda.

Can Art Change the World?

An Interview with Alfredo Jaar

Cristián Warnken

———

From *Una belleza nueva*, Televisión Nacional, Santiago, Chile, October 2008.

Television reporter Cristián Warnken has interviewed a great many well-known Chileans over his long career; here, he takes on the postmodern political artist Alfredo Jaar. The questions are direct and penetrating, and the artist responds with equal clarity. From a lengthy session, I have excerpted parts dealing with Jaar's views on political art, and his early projects under the military dictatorship.

Q: The poet Vicente Huidobro has written [in *Ver y palpar*, 1941], "We must make the leap from the heart out to the world. / We must create a piece of the infinite for every person." How do we make this leap today, from the heart to the world? Can art still accomplish this today? Can art make that jump?

A: It's a difficult leap, very difficult. It is at bottom an act of faith, not only for the artist, but it also demands faith on the part of the viewer. Because we live in difficult times, and we face a difficult reality, which I have always found impossible to represent. But I have always thought that rather than representing reality, we artists create a new reality. And thus, this leap into the world, this world into which we send our works, is also a new reality. There is a void, a gaping void, between the so-called real world and the world that the artist invents. And that gap is what I am interested in exploring. That void. Often one gets lost in the leap and ends up landing nowhere; I see that as a challenge.

Q: You could say that after all of our crises, and after modernism itself, that art has landed in a sort of cynicism, or even despair. Once artists thought that they could change humanity, that they could change the world, and they said so. But today, art seems to be a product that is confined to galleries, and functions only in closed circuits, and only for certain people. Art has lost its power and its vigor, and anyone who wants to recover that power is attempting something that has already been done, or a task that has already proven futile or impossible. How do you feel as an artist in the face of this state of art in the twenty-first century?

A: I love how you put that, because, look: I am not afraid to be sincere, and I am not afraid to be naïve. I always say it straight out: "I don't like the state of the world, and I want to change it. You may laugh, but at least try to understand what I mean by that, and what can be done." You have to declare your intention up front, to give the viewer a chance to accept your act of faith. Viewers may then accept that you want to change the world, and they will thus enter the game.

Q: Can art still change the world, or change people?

A: I believe that it can. I believe that art creates models. Art does not concretely and immediately change the world. But it can indeed create models of thought and life, and these models can be shared with an audience. This audience that enters into the new model which you offer them, perhaps they will pick up something from it that they can apply in their own lives. That is, if viewers enter into the space that you have created, and you succeed in moving them, arousing their feelings, or stimulating their minds, you will have affected a small change, and this small change can become significant in the decisions that people make after seeing the work.

Q: So perhaps one sort of art needs to die so that another can be born? I remember a phrase of Joseph Beuys, who said in one of his exhibitions, "A person must be born, because he does not yet exist. And art needs to be born, because it does not yet exist."

A: I basically believe that when viewers enter a gallery with one of my installations, I am asking that they change a little, mentally or physically. So that when they enter one of my installations, they must adapt to the physical and spatial conditions of the work, and it will affect them. It does not always happen—maybe it almost never happens—but basically that is what I try to do. The viewer should leave one of my works a changed person.

Q: The viewer's reaction is almost a physical response, not just a mental one. What is this physical response? Classical writers called it catharsis. Do you relate to that?

A: It has something of that. In my works, there is a desperate attempt to
    involve viewers; to involve them physically, emotionally, and intellectu-
    ally, because I have always believed that art is communication. And this
    communication, following the exact definition of the term, demands a
    response. To put it simply: If there is no response, then there is no com-
    munication, and there is no art. So the plan of my works always includes
    elements of a strategy for communication. I establish points of entry for
    viewers, whatever the cultural baggage they may carry into the new
    space that I have created, so that they can enter. And in that entering
    there can occur a change: physical, mental, emotional, intellectual. In
    my works, this physical and mental involvement is essential; without it,
    my work cannot function.

Q: I imagine that today it's difficult to achieve this change in viewers, or in
    us, because we exist in the society of the spectacle. We are all basically
    mere spectators, consumers of images. We long ago ceased being either
    witnesses or participants in reality. Do you in any way try to subvert or
    attack the society of the spectacle?

A: Absolutely. I often cite Guy Debord [author of *The Society of the
    Spectacle*, 1967], which I regard as a fundamental book. He predicted
    the world that we live in today, and maybe even beyond today. The way
    our culture has developed is probably causing him to turn over in his
    grave, because the truth is that we have a society in which the spectacle
    rules. The mass-media landscape that surrounds us, that informs and
    forms us, and even teaches us, is the society of the spectacle. And it's
    difficult to penetrate that. But art can create tiny openings, cracks in the
    spectacle that surrounds us. These openings may be only skin-deep, on
    the surface. A work of art is a success when the crack is wide enough for
    someone to jump through. And there they may discover, below the sur-
    face of the spectacle, a world or reality that they have not visited before.
    This is difficult to achieve.

Q: That reminds me of what a French poet once said—René Char, a poet of
    the anti-Nazi resistance, who was a hardy survivor, and hid out in his
    native town. But he did not take refuge in the small world of literature
    and art; he compared poetry to a rose that grows up through the cracks.
    He offered his poems as an art of resistance. Does being an artist today
    mean resisting?

A: Yes it does. I am fascinated by the fact that so many students today make
    the decision to study art. It's very surprising. While the society of the

spectacle and the society of consumerism calls out to them, and the society almost forces them toward careers in economics, sciences, and "sensible" careers, it seems extraordinary that despite all of those influences in the surrounding culture, young people decide that they want to be artists. And even the fact of that decision is an act of resistance, even before they actually become artists. Because they had to resist family pressures and pressures from the culture. All of those forces tell them, "You must succeed, and live a life in which economic practicalities take center stage, because one needs a certain amount of money to board this train that we are all riding." And therefore, when they decide to take such a radically different path, that is a sign that the younger generation believes that art and culture still count for something.

Q: It's a faith that we have lost. Let's talk about when you were a young man, when you made that leap, when you made your first works: You asked people if they were happy. I am looking at a picture of one of your early works, a billboard, in the midst of all the advertising, which reads simply, "Are you happy?" This was in the early 1980s . . . How did you get to that point?

A: Well before that, my father wanted to be a doctor, but for economic reasons he couldn't. So he wanted his children to be doctors. We were five brothers, and two became doctors, but I escaped. As a child I did want to be a doctor, because family pressures are strong. When I began to show manual skills, no one said that I should be a pianist or an artist, they said that I should be a surgeon. In those days my Spanish was still not very good, because I had only recently arrived in Chile [from Martinique], so I could not qualify for medicine. Mathematics was easier. So I got into the architecture school. And I was very afraid of failure, because of all this family pressure to be a physician. But within three months [of entering architecture school], I discovered a wonderful world and felt like the happiest person on the planet.

Q: What did you discover?

A: I discovered a new world of thought, of creativity, a magic world that I had no idea existed. I always say that everything I learned about art, I learned from architecture. This gave me a certain advantage, because the type of art that I make arises out of my architecture studies and not from art studies, which I never had.

Q: As an artist, and as an architect, you are solving problems. How is the creative process different for architects and artists?

A: Just yesterday, I got together with some architect friends. I simply told them, "I'm doing exactly what you do. The first part of my process is identical to yours." We both analyze prospective sites carefully, trying to find their particular essence, and not just in physical terms. We are not speaking just in terms of light, scale, and circulation, because a space is much more than that. We have to analyze the aura of a space: its sociology, its political quality, its cultural temper. We consider all of these elements as we focus on a space. And once we have understood this essence—a term that arises from an architect's studio, where I first apprenticed—we propose something. And the proposal in my case will be freer than that of my compatriots, because they are architects and have to build something. I do not work under those constraints, so I can propose something to be made that is more reckless. And it will produce an effect that differs radically from that of architecture. But at the outset, my method is very much based on that of the architect . . .

Q: Let's come back to your billboard project, where you placed signs alongside the road and also in the city, asking people if they were happy.

A: I did that between 1979 and 1981. I was applying some methods of architects, which means to work with a theme and to develop it by stages. I was like an architect, working and producing. We should remember that this was in the depths of the dictatorship, very difficult times, and censorship was in place. But even worse than the official censorship was the self-censorship that fear can bring about. I wanted to explore the question of how far one could go in the face of that fear and self-censorship. We were in a situation in which each one of us would set our own limits: I want to go this far, or that far. Chile was at that time deeply polarized, and we argued about many things, but in my idealistic, poetic, utopian state of mind I wanted to speak of basic, essential things (just as architects do). And the theme of happiness occurred to me. It was such a logical and essential subject in a country where we all suffered so much. In those days I was reading the *Studies on Laughter* [by Henri Bergson]. I had been reading it more or less as therapy, in those times when no one laughed. So I developed this project called *Studies on Happiness*, after the *Studies on Laughter*. I developed it step by step, first by doing surveys in the streets; I thought they could not touch me for doing this. My naïveté was almost ridiculous. But I have never been afraid of being ridiculous, so I did it. To carry out my survey, I gave each respondent a mint as I asked the question, "Are you happy?" I asked them to place the little mint in one bag or another to vote. If they did not want to vote, they could keep the mint and eat it. And many people did not want to vote, because they were too afraid. They saw that a friend of mine was photographing me from a distance, so they hurried away eating the mint . . .

I have always found it difficult to create art, very difficult. I see an empty room, a blank sheet, an empty canvas, and I really don't know where to begin. And communication, too, is difficult, when many of the world's problems arise from a lack of communication. So I am interested in communicating. What I try to do, to aid communication, is to edit in order to arrive at just one idea. I deeply believe in the power of the solitary idea. The error that many young artists commit when starting out is that they try to say too many things. You look at a work, and you see thirty-seven messages in it! It's impossible to communicate that way. Thus I edit, edit, and edit, in order to arrive at the essence of what I want to say, and to be unafraid of simplicity. To be simple is not the same as being simplistic. And because I work with themes that have some scope and complexity, I welcome simple ideas.

The Catherwood Project

Leandro Katz

———•———

From *Leandro Katz: Two Projects, A Decade* (New York: Museo del Barrio, 1996), n.p.

The artist here describes the background and goals of a project in which he rephotographed Central American sites visited by explorers in the nineteenth century. The sort of quotation that this work embodies was typical of postcolonial art in the 1990s, but this essay shows that Katz developed a sort of admiration for the way in which the explorer-artist Frederick Catherwood worked to rid himself of cultural biases in the framing and depiction of the Maya monuments.

One hundred and fifty years ago, John L. Stephens and Frederick Catherwood undertook a series of expeditions into the Maya area of Yucatán, Chiapas, Guatemala, and Honduras, uncovering ancient monuments that rivaled the famous ruins of Egypt. Stephens and Catherwood were the first English-speaking travelers to explore the regions originally settled by the Maya.

John L. Stephens (1805–1852) practiced law in New York before he took up his work as a writer and antiquarian. Because of ill health, he began traveling in the Near East, Greece, and Egypt, and his first essays concern the ruins and artifacts of ancient civilizations there. On a visit to London, he met Catherwood, whose drawings of digs in Egypt and famous map of Jerusalem he had already admired.

Frederick Catherwood (1799–1854) was an Englishman who had been trained as an architect but whose real talent lay in his ability to render views of ancient monuments with great accuracy and insight. With the aid of a camera lucida—an optical device that preceded the invention of photography—he developed a technique of drawing that he used while documenting Robert Hay's expeditions in Egypt, drawings which became a marvel of the period.

The first collaboration of Stephens and Catherwood, *Incidents of Travel in Central America, Chiapas, and Yucatan*, was published in 1841 and ran to

12 editions in its first year. In 1843, they brought out *Incidents of Travel in Yucatan*, the result of a subsequent trip to that part of Mexico. Both of these books are composed of detailed descriptions of their extensive findings and many steel engravings made from Catherwood's drawings, so excellent that even today they are frequently referred to as perfectly accurate records of the objects they document. In 1844, Catherwood published his *Views of Ancient Monuments in Central America, Chiapas, and Yucatan*, a book of 25 color lithographs, reprinted in Mexico in 1978.

My appreciation of the drawings of Frederick Catherwood and the paradoxical elements that appear when these drawings are observed next to the restored monuments became a main area of concern in my work. During the summer of 1984, I had the opportunity to work in the Yucatan area, photographing the Maya sites drawn by Catherwood from the same vantage points that he used when making his camera lucida drawings. In this way, I started to compile the elements of a work-in-progress called *The Catherwood Project*, a visual reconstruction of Stephens and Catherwood's expeditions. I continued this project in the summers of 1985 and 1986, covering other sites in Yucatán and the Chiapas region in Mexico. During December and January of 1987/88, I completed the itineraries of the two expeditions, photographing the sites of Quiriguá in Guatemala, and Copán in Honduras.

My intention when starting *The Catherwood Project*, which resulted in nearly 4,000 black-and-white photographs and 1,800 color, was not only to reappropriate these images from the colonial period, but also to visually verify the results of archaeological restorations, the passage of time, and the changes in the environment. In this "truth effect" process, issues having to do with colonialist/neocolonialist representation became more central, particularly during the last section of the project.

Three different approaches are used to produce the works in this project:

- The first approach attempts to adopt as closely as possible the same points of view used by Catherwood, which at times included lower or elevated perspectives. Each print in this method juxtaposes a reproduction of Catherwood's published engraving side by side with my final photograph.
- The second approach incorporates a view of my hand holding Catherwood's published engraving in front of the documented monument, making the comparison the subject of a single photograph.

- The third approach obviates the visual evidence of Catherwood's point of view and it follows his vision of the site directly and without visual quotation. At this stage, although the original structure is still being followed, the conceptual rigor of the project becomes more abstract.

In the process of covering the itinerary of the two expeditions, I became aware of Catherwood's struggle to depart from his Eurocentric style. It has been well documented that previous explorers could only manage to document the sites by merely reproducing the style and the vision of the Romantic period. The line in their drawings was wrong, their final results a fiction. In Catherwood's work, because of his Piranesi School training, or perhaps due to the aid of the camera lucida, the artist managed to enter the mind of the Maya architects, challenging his own Western hegemony.

During January of 1993 I completed my work with the monuments and their documentations by Catherwood, emphasizing the issue of architectural rendering, of which Catherwood's work presents an extraordinary example. While Catherwood's vantage point became the main reflexive aspect of my approach to the work produced in the first phase of the project, it became clear upon its completion that I should work further on the architectural aspect of the monuments.

Stephens describes Catherwood as standing on top of a crudely made scaffolding or standing in mud, veiled with a net and with gloves on to protect his hands from mosquitoes, having great difficulty in depicting the designs on the Maya monuments because they were so complex and their subjects so entirely new and unintelligible. Catherwood rendered these sculptures and buildings—so different from anything he had seen before—with such skill and open-mindedness that his drawings are still useful today. He did not see in them vestiges of other cultures; he saw them as something new. And as much as his works manifest a clinical, profound accuracy, they also reveal moments of slippage and subjectivity, the result of malaria seizures perhaps, or of working in difficult locations to later reconstruct the views from sketches and memory. All these contradictions make his work even more fascinating.

Since Catherwood had platforms and scaffolding built for his vantage points, I went back to a few of the sites in the Puuc Hills of Yucatán with equipment that allowed me to get very close to architectural details and adopt a parallax-free perspective. I also concentrated on working in very dark internal chambers using a portable lighting technique that I had developed in the later part of the project in Honduras. The Institutes of History and Anthropology in Mexico, Guatemala, and Honduras had previously facilitated the work on the sites, and since *The Catherwood Project* had already received serious recognition, access to the ruins during night hours was facilitated. This allowed me to control the light needed to record specific details in Maya architecture, and to use an "open flash" technique, lighting huge monuments in sections with a single flash unit.

PART ELEVEN

Trends of the 1970s and Early 1980s

In the City of Angels, Chameleons, and Phantoms

Asco, a Case Study of Chicano Art in Urban Tones
(or, Asco Was a Four-Member Word)

Harry Gamboa Jr.

———————

From *Chicano Art: Resistance and Affirmation, 1965–1985*, ed. Richard Griswold
del Castillo, Teresa McKenna, and Yvonne Yarbro-Bejarano
(Los Angeles: Wight Art Gallery, University of California, 1991), 121–25.

Here, one of the founders tells of the genesis of Asco, an important performance art group based in Los Angeles. Their response to ethnic discrimination colors their art and thought more than is generally the case with contemporary art groups across Latin America. Their artmaking was deeply integrated with protest, and Asco combined elements of dissent with both conceptual and performance art.

In the 1960s there was no oasis in the urban desert. The still lifes were painted among the still dead. No one cried over spilled paint. Children finger painted/ pointed as their older brothers and sisters danced in the shadows of global atrocities. Napalm bombs were no match for the palms that line the streets of L.A. Blank-faced mobs surfed on heat waves that crashed onto concrete shores. Police clubs kept the beat to a repressive rumba. Love beads got lost among the hate mail. Many could not float upstream on the dry bed of the L.A. River.

In East L.A., the cryptic stylized graffiti made it difficult for insiders and outsiders to read the writing on the walls. The "Mexican American" population was undergoing a metamorphosis that would transform is psychological and political character from that of a stoic oppressed minority to that of an active self-affirming Chicano culture. Although negative stereotypes abounded in the minds and media of the dominant culture, the disproportionate number of Chicano youths in military body bags, unemployment lines, [and] penal institutions, and on the streets suggested that other forces influenced their fate. The reality of fatalistic passivity was incompatible with the absurd demands of a rapidly changing society that threatened to erase those peoples who would not blend into oblivion in the mythic American melting pot.

In 1968, five Los Angeles public high schools (Roosevelt, Lincoln, Wilson, Belmont, and Garfield) were shut down for one week by the successful mass student demonstrations known as the East L.A. blowouts or walkouts. National media and law-enforcement attention was focused on the events and the individuals who dared to challenge the status quo and inferior segregated educational institutions for economically disadvantaged Chicano youth.[1] The walkouts served as a catalyst for organizing community based political groups and for widening their activities to address the social, political, and economic concerns of the Chicano community.[2] As the major political and news events of the era were explosively unfolding, James A. Garfield High School functioned as a major breeder reactor for urban Chicano culture. Although Garfield High was noted for its excessively high dropout rate, the administration was inclined to deal with education as a punitive measure enforced by corporal punishment, locked security gates, high fences, a stern dress code, and harsh expulsion policies.[3] With over 3,000 predominantly Chicano students faced with unequal opportunities at home and probable over-representation in the fields of death in Vietnam, the high school gained mounting notoriety as a trendsetter of Chicano fashion, etiquette, violence, and slang. The competing adaptations of aesthetic standards, codes of loyalty, and levels of assimilation were popularized by the highly visible car clubs and games. However, the majority of students were unaffiliated youth. The Jetters were an informal category of students who were interested primarily in countering the established norms with their sardonic attitudes, parties, and excessive concern for fashion.[4]

During the 1960s through the early 1970s members of the inspirational Thee Midnighters, the acclaimed Los Lobos, and the infamous Asco attended Garfield High: David Hidalgo, César Rosas, Conrad Lozano, Francisco González, Patssi Valdez, Willy Herrón, Gronk, Diane Gamboa, and Harry Gamboa Jr. Two other artists, Mundo Meza and Cyclona, as well as the performer Humberto Sandoval also attended Garfield High during that period. The mutual awareness of the musicians and artists in the midst of social and political change allowed them to convey their shared experience through personal and group expressions of music or art. Although Los Lobos and

Asco did not become formal groups until the 1970s, the individuals and their artistic interests influenced the quality and direction of life on the high school campus.

On August 29, 1970, the largest antiwar protest demonstration to occur in East L.A. brought a highly publicized Chicano community together for a massive display of unity. The Chicano Moratorium, as it came to be known, was the target of a well-orchestrated plan for disruption by the Los Angeles Police Department, the Los Angeles County Sheriff's Department, and other police agencies.[5] The demonstration ended violently when riot-equipped police attacked members of the community who had gathered to hear public speakers at Laguna Park near the boundary between the city and county of Los Angeles. The excessive police brutality sparked a major riot along Whittier Boulevard in East L.A., during which buildings, cars, and buses were burned and several individuals were killed, including the prominent *Los Angeles Times* journalist Rubén Salazar. Salazar's death at the hands of the L.A. County Sheriff's deputy Wilson served to publicize widely the seething conflict between the Chicano community and the police.[6] As the police onslaught at the park intensified, Francisca Flores, publisher of *Regeneración*, a Chicano political and literary journal, encountered Harry Gamboa. As they ran from the clouds of tear gas and swinging clubs of the police, she handed him a copy of her journal and then disappeared into the havoc of the surging crowd.

During the late 1960s, Gamboa assisted Francisca Flores with her newsletter, *Carta editorial*, and worked on propagandistic newspapers such as *Chicano Student News* and *La Raza*. *Regeneración* covered a complex spectrum of interests that included creative writing, represented by Frank Sifuentes, and graphic art work by Ben Luna.[7] Excited by the possibility of disseminating the work of writers and artists who closely reflected the urban Chicano experience of his generation, Gamboa became editor of volume 2, issues 1 through 5.

Willie Herrón and Patssi Valdez had been working together on various art projects since high school. Gronk was rumored to be living in a tent or on the roof of the gymnasium of East Los Angeles College. Gronk's work had appeared in an issue of *Con Safos*, a political-humorist magazine. Valdez had worked with Gronk, Meza, and Cyclona on various spontaneous public art actions in East L.A. that had dealt with issues of gender diffusion. Gronk, Meza, and Cyclona would oftentimes dress in long, flowing velvet robes layered with satin, silk, and lace clothing, and promenade, arms interlocked, to a quick-paced goose step, shoving pedestrians out of their way along a crowded section of Whittier Boulevard. However, the mandatory draft law, moving with even more momentum than they, swooped down on Herrón and Gronk. After a protracted struggle, the two artists obtained legal alternatives to active combat duty.

In 1971, Gronk's head was shaved by the U.S. Army after he had painted the interior mural *Cyclona* at the Equal Opportunity Program offices at Cal State [University], Los Angeles. The mural was whitewashed soon after its completion. In 1972, Herrón shaved his eyebrows and painted the exterior mural *The Wall That Cracked Open*.

Gamboa individually approached Valdez, Herrón, and Gronk, and invited them to work on *Regeneración*. They all agreed to donate their talents and were soon at work on their first issue. The four artists worked long nocturnal hours, for weeks at a time, to create original pen-and-ink drawings for the publication. Herrón provided studio space in the garage behind his mother's house (his popular mural, violent gang police activity, and Eva's Liquor Store were only a few yards away). They discovered that they shared many experiences, enjoyed a common sense of dark humor, and were intensely committed to personal expression. At times, the nights of work gave way to group discussions of their collective influences. Occasionally the conversations were highly focused, but mostly the dialogue flowed in and out of a hundred subjects: drop drills, Guadalupe tattoos, smeared lipstick, no privacy, off ramps, foreignness, disagreements, blind curves, comics, pinkeye, jump starts, Dick and Jane, no heat, stray bullets, Spam, alleys, fake genuflections, riot squads, photo booths, cucarachas, bongos, dunce caps, low riders, Molotov cocktails, the twist, lard, dead ends, grinding without music, Che, pompadours, 24-hour daydreams, Daffy Duck, hostile crowbars, bumble-bees, bubble asses, tunnel vision, Peter Lorre, bruising pinches, *Alarma*, cliques, spiked heels, racist TV, La Llorona, hit-and-run insults, flat puppies, pachuco fairy tales, English only, false eyelashes, last dimes, black spray paint, Mr. Machine, Beatle boots, ditching parties, zero chance, lizard faces, unholy water, no air conditioning, dancing curls, psycho-cholos, quicksand, outcast treatment, La Cruda, tacit extortion, doomed love affairs, mariachis, false invitations, blistering belts, hero assassinations, Heckle and Jeckle, white bread, laughing in public, melted crayons, official low expectations, transparent lampshades, bitter *pan dulce*, search and seizure, cheap funerals, fire ants, suspicious stares, rude service, black widow hairdos, jalapeños, hiding in fear, brown skies, missing cuff links, lysergic acid diethylamide,

Migra maggots, shattered glass, Dolores del Río, barbed wire, chorizo sin huevo, hip-hugger bell-bottoms, flaming monks, drunken wild teens, stained blades, cold burritos, baby trigger fingers, El Cucui, vinyl upholstery, barrio barriers, and rip-off artists.

The drawings by Gronk were broodingly implicit with dream-sexual connotations. Herrón's work was technically astute with disturbing hallucinatory illusions. Valdez created graphic images of pain and death. Gamboa drew distorted faces that glared deeply into their own psychological dilemmas. The artists dealt with the emotions of repulsion, elation, and rejection and with unconscious visual charges stemming from personal perspectives that allowed them to view the world at a distinctly different slant. After several intense months of drawing and eclectic conversation, they decided to manifest their ideas in the public arena of the streets.

On December 24, 1971, Herrón, Gronk, and Gamboa arrived unannounced on the corner of Eastern Avenue and Whittier Boulevard. Herrón was the representation of Christ/Death, dressed in a white robe that bore a brightly colored Sacred Heart, which he painted in acrylic. His face had been transformed by makeup into a stylized calavera [skull]. Gronk personified Pontius Pilate (aka: Popcorn): he wore a green bowler hat, flaunted an excessively large beige fur purse, and carried a bag of unbuttered popcorn. Gamboa assumed the role of a zombie altar boy and wore an animal skull headpiece to ward off unsolicited communion. The three had constructed a 15-foot-long crucifix out of corrugated cardboard boxes that they had found and defaced with brown, orange, and gold spray-painted squiggles. They performed *Stations of the Cross* as an alternate ritual of resistance to belief systems that glorified useless deaths.[8] Herrón bore the cross, and Gronk and Gamboa accompanied him in silent procession along Whittier Boulevard, which was packed with last-minute shoppers, cruisers, and police. The immediate reaction of the audience was primarily confusion laced with verbal hostility. The various stations were located along a mile-long stretch of the boulevard. The final station was located at the U.S. Marine Recruiting Station at the Goodrich Boulevard intersection. They placed the cross at its entrance and observed a five-minute silent vigil that ended when Gronk blessed the site with handfuls of scattered popcorn. The remnants of the ritual were left in place as they quickly vanished from the scene.

At the onset of 1972, rumors of a bizarre religious sect in East L.A. began to surface. The community had been subjected to a barrage of misinformation and had witnessed the falsified reportage of events that had taken place in East L.A. during the years of political upheaval. *Stations of the Cross* had left a reverberating impression of spiritual doubt and doubtful spirituality. *Regeneración* was published in February and became immediately enmeshed in the controversy that surrounded this active group and its nontraditional forms of expression. The "politically correct" members of the Chicano movement (including students, academicians, political organizers, and artists) were intolerant of the visual imagery presented in the publication. Their strongly traditionalist sentiment was expressed on numerous occasions by individuals who said that Herrón, Gronk, Valdez, and Gamboa had left them with the sensation of *asco* (nausea).[9]

Muralism began to flourish on the walls of East L.A. The majority of these murals incorporated pre-Columbian motifs, gang symbolism, abstract graphics, or politically didactic imagery. Most of the murals were amateurishly executed, but several were contextually and aesthetically effective. Herrón was one of the first to incorporate existing and new graffiti into the composition of his murals.[10] Although the mural movement began to bring positive publicity to a community that until then had only been maligned or neglected by the mass media, the four young artists experimented with other forms that expanded the parameters of Chicano art.

The lessons taught by the anti-Chicano propaganda of commercial television and mainstream journalism were not lost on the artists. The manipulation of imagery, the repetition of so-called facts, the saturation of negative images and opinions over time, the vacuum of objective information, and the distillation of lies had been a cumulative, socially damaging process through which the established educational and media systems affected the Chicano population. Although they lacked financial resources, the artists were intent on countering the negative stereotypes that had plagued the public image and private psyche of contemporary Chicanos. They were concerned about the efforts of traditionalists to replace old stereotypes with new ones.

In November 1972, Herrón, Gronk, and Gamboa exhibited mixed-media works at the Mechicano Art Center in East L.A. Even with minimal promotion, the exhibition drew a crowd of nearly two hundred. Herrón's large mixed-media paintings, Gronk's humorous drawings, and Gamboa's somber assemblages touched on a wide spectrum of socio-aesthetic concerns including violence and street life. The expressive and surreal quality of the works jarred the sensibilities of the primarily traditionalist audience. Although some supported them, a few socially influential individuals insisted that the works were not Chicano. Others echoed the term *asco.*

On December 24, 1972, Valdez, Herrón, Gronk, and Gamboa returned to Whittier Boulevard, intent on transforming muralism from a static to a performance medium. Valdez was the Virgin of Guadalupe in Black, dressed in a black crepe gown, a black and silver cardboard aura, and an aluminum calavera on the back of her head. Gronk was an Xmas Tree, embellished with three inverted lime green chiffon dresses, many red glass bulbs, and a five-pointed star painted in acrylic on his face. Herrón was a multifaceted mural that had become bored with its environment and left. Gamboa documented the event on black-and-white and color slides as well as Super-8 film with the intent of using such imagery to reach a conceptually different audience from those who had experienced the performance directly.[11] *Walking Mural* followed the same severely beaten path along the boulevard as *Stations of the Cross* a year earlier. Several individuals, converted in passing, joined their silent walk through the crowds.

In the final week of 1972, Gronk, Herrón, and Gamboa spray-painted their signatures onto all the entrances to the Los Angeles County Museum of Art (LACMA) in reaction to the negative response of a museum curator to their query about the possibility of including Chicano art in museum exhibitions. The artists momentarily transformed the museum itself into the first conceptual work of Chicano art to be exhibited at LACMA. Gamboa and Valdez returned to the site the following day and documented the work in photographs. The signatures were completely whitewashed later that night.[12]

In 1973, the four artists adopted Asco as the name of their art-performance group.

Notes

1. US Congress, Senate, Committee on the Judiciary, Subcommittee to Investigate the Administration of the Internal Security Act, *Hearings on the Extent of Subversion in the "New Left."* Testimony of Robert J. Thomas, 91st Congress, Second Session, January 20, 1970, pt. 1, 23, and centerfold list of "Individuals Officially Connected."

2. Elaine Woo, "'60s Blowouts," *Los Angeles Times*, March 7, 1988, Metro Section, 1.

3. Harry Gamboa Jr., "Reflections on One School in East L.A.," *L.A. Weekly*, February 6–12, 1987, 18.

4. Harry Gamboa Jr., "Jetter's Jinx," *Playbill*, Los Angeles Theatre Center, October 3–6, 1985, 1.

5. Rodolfo Acuña, *Occupied America: A History of Chicanos*, 3rd ed. (New York: Harper & Row, 1988), 346.

6. Advisory Committee to the US Commission on Civil Rights, *Report on Police–Community Relations in East Los Angeles, California* (Los Angeles, CA: The Committee, 1970), 16–18.

7. *Regeneración* 1, no. 9 (1979): 1–16.

8. Museum of Contemporary Art, Los Angeles, *Summer 1985* (Los Angeles, CA: Museum of Contemporary Art, 1985), n.p.

9. Constanza Montana, "From Barrio to Big-Time," *Wall Street Journal*, October 17, 1986, 24.

10. Jerry Romotsky and Sally Romotsky, "Placas and Murals," *Arts in Society* 2, no. 1 (1974): 286–99.

11. Dana Friis-Hansen, *L.A. Hot and Cool* (Cambridge, MA: MIT List Visual Arts Center, 1987), 13.

12. Nancy Drew, "L.A.'s Space Age," in *LACE: 10 Years Documented* (Los Angeles, CA: Los Angeles Contemporary Exhibitions, 1987), 9.

Art and Politics of the Poster

An Interview with Rupert García

—————

From *The Fifth Sun: Contemporary and Traditional Chicano & Latino Art*,
ed. Ralph Maradiaga (Berkeley, CA: University Art Museum, 1977), 27–30.

Rupert García is one of the leading Chicano poster artists. This interview was conducted in 1977, near the height of the Chicano art movement. Noteworthy is the continuity that he shows with Mexican popular art traditions, dating back to Posada and earlier. In response to a query from the current book's editor about the applicability of his comments today, the artist said that this interview reflected its time and context. While he might wish to change a few modifiers, the essence and spirit of the interview still stood as valid for him.

Q: Is there a Renaissance in Chicano Poster Art?

A: There is a Renaissance in the historical understanding of Chicano culture. For example, we have a history of poster art by our Mexican relatives that goes back to at least the nineteenth century (not to mention the poster art of Spain); the poster work of the 1910 Revolution, and the posters produced since the 1930s by the Taller de Gráfica Popular. Like the Chicano mural movement, our poster art must be seen both in its immediate and in its historical dimensions. This approach to understanding Chicano posters and murals also applies to other aspects of our culture, heritage, and history of struggle.

Q: Are there distinctive qualities that distinguish the Chicano poster from other posters?

A: Yes. It can be identified in several ways: (1) the use of language—Spanish, Pocho (a combination of English and Spanish) and Calo (usually identified with Pachucos). The use of Maya (language of the Mayans) and Nahuatl (usually identified as the language of the Aztecs) is also used by Chicano poster makers. Any one of these languages or any combination of these languages as text in a poster would clearly identify it as being

Raza/Chicano. (2) The images often used by Chicanos are unique to them because of their particular history. We use the calavera, the corazón, jalapeños, the Pachuco, the farmworker, low-riders, pintos-pintas, Virgen de Guadalupe, nopales; we make references to the indigenous peoples of Mexico and the Southwest, colonized Mexico, and Mexico since independence from Spain; we use images relating to our history in this country since US imperialism provoked the Mexican-American War (1846–1848) and stole half of Mexico (which the Mexican government illegally acquired from Spain, which the Spanish government had stolen from the Native American peoples—that area which is known as the Southwest of the US of A). (3) The use of color by the Chicano is unique. (4) The humor depicted in much of our work, humor as defined by us, is distinctive in Chicano art. These are only a few examples that go into making Chicano Art, Chicano Art.

The question of the existence or non-existence of Chicano art stems from two contradicting sources. On one hand, Chicanos, like other oppressed people, are involved in a struggle against centuries of domination, and the Chicano artist has been working within this militant context. This means that Chicano artists have an adversary in the protectors of "official bourgeois culture." These people and the millions who identify with them find Chicano or any other Third World cultural assertion threatening. The questioning of our art is ultimately directed at our existence—for a people have never existed without an Art which is identifiable to them. So, what is being asked is "do you exist?" This challenge that our art makes threatens the very oppressive, inhuman, degrading social fabric under which my people have suffered since the making of the Chicano—that fabric woven with racist threads of capitalism, white male domination and Anglo-European cultural values.

Q: Would you say that the way a Chicano poster artist approaches making a poster is both personal and public?

A: Yes. Chicano poster artists, as well as Chicano creators in general, do feel a tight responsibility between themselves as artists and their people. Whereas I believe Anglo artists, in general, are more alienated from their own people and their own "real" culture than Third World people are. I think we can say that this feeling of responsibility is related to the feeling of an extended family. I don 't mean "extended family" in the negative and stereotypical, narrow way Anglo social scientists have defined it in the Chicano community, but the real sense in which we

Raza know it—a sense of collectiveness and responsibility. When we make poster art, we feel a very close tie with our people, very, very close. I think that's why we try to make such fine posters; it becomes an expression for someone in our family, which indeed is the case.

Q: Is Chicano poster art an "art form" or is it something else, like a commercial commodity?

A: Yes and no. All Chicano poster art is "art." I think in some instances it is "fine art" and in lesser instances it is commercial art. Some of our posters are straight propaganda. To help clarify my answer, I think we have to make the distinction between these different elements in poster art. The propaganda poster requests the viewer to immediately act regarding whatever issue is being expressed in the poster, but a propaganda poster also can be considered "fine art." That is to say, the visual elements of this type of poster—color, shape, etc. and subject matter—sometimes transcend the immediate responses of the viewer. For example, a poster may be created to request that you attend a particular rally or benefit, but once the event has passed, the poster as a visual experience can stand by itself for years; that's why we keep some posters and not others.

Q: Poster art depicts a certain time in history and documents it. Do you think that Chicano poster artists are documenting their history?

A: Yes, and that's a very good question. For Third World people, Chicanos in this case, poster art most certainly documents our history. This is so because the poster and the event being depicted are both part of that event. In some instances, the poster is the only document existing as a record that the event took place. When making a poster, I sometimes become conscious of this and am reminded of my responsibility to be accurate.

Q: Is there a relationship between the Chicano Poster Art and the Chicano Mural Movement?

A: Definitely. We both emerge from the same social context of struggle and similar socio-aesthetics and both are public art. Chicano consciousness of being an oppressed people led us to examine our history from contemporary to pre-Columbian times. In doing this, we became aware of our peoples' historical use of the poster and the mural. We also came to know that both the mural and the poster had been used by our predecessors as a means of announcing events, disseminating information, and recording historical events. In the case of mural painting, we have models like Orozco, Rivera, Siqueiros, and Tamayo, the pulquería muralists, the colonial muralists like [Juan] Cordero, [Rafael] Ximeno y Planes, [Francisco Eduardo] Tresguerras, [Juan] Gerson, and others and the murals of pre-Columbian Americans. The poster tradition of Chicanos goes back to the nineteenth century with Posada, the turn of the century with Orozco and the poster makers of the Revolution—the Taller de Gráfica Popular of the 1930s (which still exists), and the student posters coming out of the 1968 rebellion in Mexico City. The Chicano artists consciously and unconsciously weave back and forth between the mural and the poster because there exists a similar socio-aesthetic relationship between them: Both are public, both are created for flat walls and therefore employ similar visual techniques, so that they might structurally work with and not against the wall's surface (otherwise the viewer would have too much to see), both usually employ representational images in a monumental way. These similar conditions might explain why so many murals and posters have been created by us since the 1960s.

Q: Could you comment on your work—what motivates you to do a poster?

A: Maybe the best way to answer that is to give an example. The one poster that comes to mind is the Angela Davis design I did in 1970. She was in prison at the time on trumped-up charges connecting her to an alleged conspiracy with Jonathan Jackson and his attempts to free the Soledad Brothers, George Jackson, Fleeta Drumgo, and John Clutchette. It was clearly a set-up to discredit her and get her off the street. By doing this, it was hoped that Angela Davis's political work and influence would be checked. I felt that her criticisms concerning oppression and struggle were correct, and that her imprisonment was a way of shutting her up. Being a Chicano, and developing an understanding of the common struggle of Third World and other oppressed peoples, I supported her. I also saw her stance as universal: people have the right to be critical and to fight back when human rights are denied or taken away. One way of showing support for Angela's universal statement of human rights and freedom was for me to respond visually. By this time, I had been making posters for over two years and the poster once again became my medium. What I had to do was to come up with a symbol that would represent Angela Davis and her beliefs. I happened to come across a photograph of her in a newspaper and it seemed to have the quality I wanted. In using this photograph, I was able to show her as a very sensitive black woman—sensitive but serious in her political convictions. I wanted to use an image that would immediately capture the eyes of the passer-by. To do this, I chose a large black shape and a smaller sienna shape to depict hair, shadow and skin texture; peacock blue color was selected for the text. All of the shapes and colors were bold, flat and aggressive; the viewer couldn't help but be "grabbed" into a visual dialogue. With regards to the text, I used Spanish to express international solidarity between Black and Raza peoples, and the solidarity with our struggling comrades in Latin America. Al the time, I recall thinking especially of the Cubans and their struggles.

Q: Would you say that your poster art is "universal"?

A: Anything I do relating to people is universal. If you're making a visual statement about Chicanos, you're making a particular statement about a particular segment of the developing and struggling human family. What I mean is the Chicano expression and struggle is not divorced from other art, people, or universal conflict. Our fight for freedom and human dignity is part of the struggles for freedom in Africa, Latin America, Indo-China, and the Middle East. There is always a relationship between any of my posters, whether they are about Attica or Deportation, Angela Davis or Kent State, The Indochina war or Zapata, Lipton's Tea or Lolita Lebrón. All of these statements are politically interrelated, and because I view myself as a Chicano, I relate and identify with the Third World struggle and people's struggles wherever they exist. It is from this understanding of social relationships that I get my strength and support to continue making the kinds of pictures I do. What is unique about this is not that I am able to make these connections, but the particular way in which I visually realize the relationship. For me, the important question is how I visually express this social dynamic between me and the rest of the world.

Getting to Painting through Theater

An Interview with Guillermo Kuitca

Graciela Speranza

———

Excerpted from *Guillermo Kuitca, obras 1982–1998* (Bogotá: Norma, 1998), 11–23.

Guillermo Kuitca was something of a child prodigy as a painter, holding his first solo exhibition at age thirteen. In his later adolescence he began to doubt the future viability of painting, in part because of the censors during Argentina's military dictatorship but also because of the previous history of Argentine vanguardism in the New Figuration, happening, and conceptual movements. Here, the painter talks of his early days, his frustrations with painting, and how interdisciplinary work in the theater opened a new sense of possibility.

Q: Let's begin with the relationship of your painting with the theater. You said once that there was something important about the classic baroque idea of the world as a stage. But didn't you also attempt to give your painting more breadth by thinking of the canvas as a stage set, which could widen the limits of painting?

A: It's very tempting to think of the theater as a space analogous with painting, above all because projecting it onto painting gives the illusion that the canvas expands and extends itself in a way that is not exclusively visual. But I think I have at times overstated this relationship, because if the theater could indeed have broadened the scope of my work in some way, at the same time it could detract from its most potent referents, which are definitely painterly. Ever since the theater first appeared in my paintings in the form of theater plans, I have tended to think of it as an inspiration, but not all the time. The relationship to the theater arose in part with this idea of the world as a stage, and the same time because I saw very clearly that the limits on painting, and not only on mine, in the beginning of the 1980s, were very large, imposing, and potent. Theater, on the other hand, seemed like an inexhaustible world. In those days, from my somewhat limited viewpoint, I had practically convinced myself that nothing was possible in painting, but everything was possible in theater. I don't know exactly what I meant by saying this, but I remember that this idea was present in my painting. It was as if in my work, just as on a stage, I could do almost anything, but if I limited myself to a purely pictorial mental space, then I could not do anything. Even though, thinking of it in another way, there was not a sudden burst of theater in my paintings, but rather just the demarcation of a scenic space.

Q: What was your first exposure to the theater?

A: A friend of mine, Carlos Ianni, with whom I later collaborated on theatrical works, was working at the Teatro Payró. I used to enjoy going to visit him, and seeing the theater from the other side; now that I think about it, I even liked the ticket racks, and seeing how they rolled up the tickets and stuck them into the perforated seating chart. In those days, Jaime Kogan was the director and taught a course on that subject. I was very young, about sixteen, and they encouraged me to take it. Soon I had to leave the course, but even so, what Kogan said was very interesting to me, and I secretly took some of what he said into my work. I think this was my first real exposure to the theater.

Q: Many have pointed to the importance of Pina Bausch's [modern dance] company to your painting. Did that happen at the same time?

A: My encounter with Pina Bausch, which I myself initiated at a crucial moment for my painting, took place three or four years later. The curious thing is that the first encounter was not with her performances but with photos of her works. It was common during the days of the military government to go to the library of the Goethe Institute or the French Consulate to look through books, magazines, and other things. In the Goethe Institute I once found a book about Pina Bausch that had tremendously intriguing photos. I felt a great identification with those images; I am not sure why. Soon, in 1980, her company appeared at the Teatro San Martín in Buenos Aires. The first program opened with *Café Müller* and it had an enormous impact, a true shock.

Q: What was it that produced the jolt?

A: A complete identification. I am not sure what skepticism means for a nineteen-year-old, but I remember that I was then very skeptical of everything. It seemed to me that all of poetry, literature, and theater were pretentious; I hated the dance, I hated every attempt at emotional expression, and I was irritated at the protest art that arose during the dictatorship. All of the paths that art seemed to be taking were irritating to me. I had not yet traveled to Europe or to the United States; my world was Buenos Aires, and except for the cinema—I often saw classic and contemporary films—the arts all irritated me greatly. But when I saw *Café Müller* I identified with it completely, at a scale of one to one. This was exactly the type of work that I was seeking, and if you asked me what type of artist I wanted to be at that time, I would have said exactly that. Looking back, I now see a certain naïveté in that appreciation, but at that moment I had found a work that had nothing in it of what irritated me about art. The potential that I sensed was enormous, deep, and even aggressive. Aggression in art tempted me quite a lot, and for the first time I sensed that this was what I needed. It was almost by chance that I found it on a stage. What I was searching for appeared there, but it could have come from some other quarter.

Q: I suppose that for someone who had been painting since the age of six, an inspiration of such potency that came from outside painting can be quite liberating. In some ways it freed you from what Harold Bloom called the anxiety of influence.

A: Yes, but at the same time I perceived another anxiety that was not greater than the anxiety of influence. Because, if everything I was hoping for could be found on a stage, then what was I doing painting? For some reason, perhaps mere cowardice, I did not abandon painting, but I suppose that this somewhat childish axiom that I mentioned earlier appeared, "everything can be done in the theater; nothing can be done in painting." I think that in the genealogy of that phrase there are echoes of phrases that had influenced me from an early age, such as, for example, the statement of Isadora Duncan, "I could dance on that chair," or that [Sergei] Eisenstein said that he could make a movie out of *Das Kapital* [by Karl Marx], phrases that I had heard my elders say and that I had taken on board. I had found no corresponding inspiration for my painting, and I suppose that, beginning at that time and for many years thereafter, I had to create the circumstances in my work so that these new experiences could find a place. On the one hand, I would like to think that my painting could change or enter a crisis in response to what happens to me in other spheres, but on the other hand, there is something specific in my work that is independent to such an extent that it does not respond to stimuli from daily life. In any case, beginning right then, my work was shattered into a thousand pieces until I found, three or four years later, a place for my new experiences in about 1980.

Q: That enthusiasm is what took you to Wuppertal [to Pina Bausch's studio].

A: During Pina Bausch's visit to Buenos Aires, I got to know two members of her company, Janusz [Subicz], a Polish dancer, and Nazareth [Panadero], a Spanish ballerina. In December 1980, when I went to Europe, I went to Wuppertal to see them again. The stories of these two dancers seemed to me admirable because they had left everything in order to work with Pina Bausch. Nazareth had probably come from some obscure academy in Barcelona or Madrid, and she was so disillusioned with everything that she preferred to dance in Paris at [the night clubs] Sans Souci or Crazy Horse before deciding on modern dance, which took her to Pina Bausch's company. Janusz was a typical child prodigy, trained at the strictest classical ballet academies of East Europe, but he left it all behind for her company. These stories, even more than the influence of theater itself, seemed very heroic to me because Pina Bausch in some ways demanded of her dancers that they forget all about their training. Moreover, in those days I made my one and only attempt at writing: I wrote a novel imagining their lives because I found something fascinating in them; but even that was just the beginning, because probably most members of that company had similarly interesting stories. My goal then was to get to Wuppertal. I was not very clear about why; maybe even I hoped to get into the company. I arrived in time for the last performance of *Bandoneón*, a work that Pina Bausch had choreographed to tango music after her trip to Buenos Aires. I had traveled for about two days, constantly changing trains, before I arrived at that quite ugly industrial city in the middle of nowhere, so that when I arrived to see *Bandoneón*, at the end of a very long day, I remember seeing Pina Bausch seated out with the audience; she asked me if I would like to sit down but I declined. I just stood there saying to myself, "I can't believe what I am seeing." I just wanted to go and hide. I spent a few days at Janusz and Nazareth's house. One part of the company had gone to Italy to perform *Café Müller*, so I stayed with the rest of them sharing their daily routine in that German city. The company was composed of dancers who had renounced ballet, and I felt like an artist who had renounced painting.

Q: Were you attracted by the idea of an experimental theater group stranded in a provincial city?

A: I probably got the impression that art is not always found in the great centers or in a great city. The most surprising thing about Wuppertal was that the company members were convinced that in that place there was nothing to do except to work. And what impressed me most of all was seeing how this group of artists kept on working in that completely unreceptive environment. The place could not have been more obscure, more middle-class, or more dull, but their creative force was overwhelming. I observed the scandalous reaction, when the audience threw bananas and lettuce at the stage during the performance of *Bandoneón*. That stayed with me. Obviously I saw that it was not necessary to live in a place that accepted you.

Q: Or at least you got the idea that a fluid dialogue between artist and audience is not absolutely necessary.

A: Yes. What I found most interesting was the experience of a creative group lodged in the middle of nowhere. It shouldn't be that way, but it was like being in the Cabaret Voltaire [with the Dadaists in 1916], or like traveling in time to observe a reaction of that sort.

Q: Have you ever been back there?

A: I left promising a quick return. I had agreed with Janusz and Nazareth that we would meet up again in Amsterdam, but that never happened, and I never returned to Wuppertal. From that moment, I began a quest to forget all about it. The experience had been so strong that the work I created on my return from Europe was not a new beginning, looking forward, but rather it sprang from a desire to get something out of my system. The next year, in 1982, I painted the series *Nadie olvida nada* [*Nobody Forgets Anything*], and I staged my first dramatic performance with Carlos Ianni under the same title. That phrase "nobody forgets anything" seems today to be totally linked with the question of the disappearances under the dictatorship or with the movement Nunca Más (Never Again), but this is not quite true. I can accept that things happen in art in ways other than how we think they do, and I accept the version that holds that this series was influenced by the Argentine experiences, by the Malvinas/Falklands War, and by the social context, but when I used that title I did not think about that; I was thinking of my experience in Wuppertal with *Bandoneón*.

Q: What was this first performance work like?

A: It was a kind of collage of texts, including things that Carlos Ianni wrote, along with texts taken from [Juan] Goytisolo, from [José] Lezama Lima, all staged in a series of scenes and images, imitated after various works by Pina Bausch.

Q: Nobody forgets anything, and especially nobody forgets Pina Bausch.

A: My work had its own thread, but her influence was dominating.

Q: What did this new post of theatrical director mean to you?

A: I saw that I could do it. I led a rather large group of maybe twenty-five or twenty-six actors, some of them professionals. Carlos had more experience in theater, but for me it was all fairly new. The next year we made *Besos brujos* [*Bewitching Kisses*], a type of performance for the opening of *Ex-Presiones '83*, the first group exhibition of that kind at the Centro Cultural Recoleta. The performance revolved around an actress who was hit with buckets of water as she named the other artists in the exhibition, surrounded by flamenco dancers. Of the three pieces that we performed, probably the best one was *El mar dulce* [*The Sweet Sea*]. Although it too was influenced by Pina Bausch, it was also deeply in dialog with my painting at the time. The theatrical experiences directly fueled my canvases, beginning with photos that I took of the performances of *El mar dulce*, and I used paintings from the *El mar dulce* series in the performances.

Q: Was your theater work an extension of your search in painting, or did the two endeavors split at some point?

A: I remember that in 1981 I painted very little and I was feeling lost, but other experiences were also in play. During my European trip I saw some important shows, such as *The New Spirit in Painting* at the Royal Academy. This show gave an enormous boost to the medium, which had been completely exiled from the scene. To see new imagery was very important for me at that moment because I had been feeling a certain pressure, not only because from the theatrical side I was hearing that in theater everything was possible and in painting nothing was. But also from the painting side people were saying that nothing more was possible. So the appearance of the Italian trans-avant-garde and the neo-expressionist movements in a certain way recontextualized my work. *The New Spirit in Painting* included not only great painters such as late Picasso, Bacon, and Warhol, but also Clemente, Paladino, Schnabel, Salle, and other very young artists who were only eight to ten years older than I was.

Q: In the midst of such confusion regarding the future of painting, that context empowered you.

A: Only in part, because I did not identify with such an expressionist approach. I saw my work as more speculative and more detached; I did not feel such urgency to paint, and I did not feel that pictorial explosion.

Q: Was there something in *The New Spirit in Painting* that particularly attracted you?

A: I think the work of Francesco Clemente was the most intriguing at that moment. He interested me because he used all kinds of media and his creativity seemed boundless. Clemente himself also appeared in the work in various guises, sometimes humiliated, sometimes rather sick, and this interested me a lot.

Q: Next you went to New York for the first time. I suppose that this too must have had an impact.

A: Only relatively, because I did not know anybody there, and I did not know where the galleries were; I went only to MoMA [the Museum of Modern Art] and the Metropolitan. The final impression that I got of New York was that there was nothing for me there. I was staying in a terrible place, I had no money, I did not know anybody, and I was rather disoriented. It had been a long four-month journey and all I wanted to do was to go back home.

Q: So this was the outcome of your trip to Europe and New York?

A: I returned laden with my experience in Wuppertal, and with the idea that New York was not a place to stay, and after about a year in crisis, I began to paint what is in some ways still my style. If at first glance it's difficult to see the connection between a canvas from 1982 and a work from *La Tablada Suite* [1991–92], for example, I could say that my work really began at that point, and even though the path is not straight it has a certain continuity . . .

Q: In *El mar dulce* from 1984, we see the famous image from *The Battleship Potemkin* [of the baby carriage bouncing down the steps], which later reappears in your work. Why this particular choice?

A: The baby carriage [from the Odessa Steps sequence of the film] is an image that I took as a recurrent motif. Later I learned that Bacon, who had been an important artist for me since the age of twelve or thirteen, had various stills from that same film by Eisenstein in his personal collection. So this was not a citation from the film, which I saw only much later, but from a still that I saw in a booklet about Eisenstein from the

Los hombres collection of Centro Editor. And there is a linkage to my family: Even now I still know very little of my family history, but I do know that my grandparents were from Kiev and I suppose that, like the majority of Russians who migrated to the Río de la Plata, they left from Odessa. So that for me, the descent of that baby carriage is like the departure of my grandparents. That is the source of the title of those works, *El mar dulce* [The Sweet Sea, another name for Río de la Plata]. In this imaginary relationship, the title connects this side of the world with Odessa on the other side. But there is a still darker story, which my family always kept under wraps, and that was the death of my father's sister Sofía as a baby in a difficult situation. At some point I learned that she died from negligence in a horrible accident in the home. That story certainly impressed me, and without thinking of a more appalling image, I just used the loose baby carriage rolling down the stair. In some ways, my family traveled in that carriage, which was the ship that took them out of Odessa.

Q: Like the photos of the Pina Bausch productions, the film still from Eisenstein is an image that condenses a lot of narration into a restrained painting. It is as though you had a sort of catalyst of moments in which other, time-based arts approached painting and you crystallized them into a congealed painting, outside time.

A: Yes, that's correct. Listening to you, I think that I should have known that in painting anything is possible, right? Seeing it that way, the field appears wide open.

The Weight of an Island

An Interview with José Bedia

Nina Menocal

———◆———

From *José Bedia: La Isla en peso* (Mexico City: Galería Nina Menocal, 1993), 14–15.

José Bedia was among the first postrevolutionary Cuban artists to find accep-tance in the international art world. Here, he discusses the politics of art in Havana in the 1980s, his decision to migrate to Mexico in 1991 (he lives today in Florida), and the impact of his Mexican surroundings on his practice.

Q: Is there any difference between Cuban and Mexican avant-garde art?

A: With the exception of a few artists such as Silvia Gruner, Gabriel Orozco, and Diego Gutiérrez, who are working with new proposals, I feel that Mexican art is excessively preoccupied with "painting as painting," aim-ing to demonstrate quality above all. The paintings are filled with good craftsmanship from end to end, what's known as "all-over painting." On the other hand, the Cubans work with ideas, or content, in a clearer and more concise fashion. While the Mexican artist has to keep in mind the bourgeois collector—who wants a painting with a theme, size, tech-nique, and appearance that is easily digested—we state ideas free of pre-conceptions. So we are imposing a different kind of taste and of art appreciation. Our preoccupations are thus not exclusively formal because we don't have to prove our workmanship to anyone.

Q: Where does this Cuban avant-garde come from? Where do you come from?

A: Ever since 1981, after the *Volumen I* exhibition in Havana, American and French artists and critics started to come down. They took interest in our work. They realized, contrary to what they expected, that something very different from the graphic art and posters of the seventies was going on in Cuba. Indeed, the artists of my generation never painted Lenin nor

Che, nor did we paint Fidel talking in the plaza. This wasn't easy. The fact that we made no concessions in art, but did what we should in all honesty, fills me with pride. And then everyone came looking for us. They already had my name, [Arturo] Cuenca's name, [Juan Francisco] Elso's, Ricardo Brey's. We started getting grants and invitations to international events.

Q: Cuba is supposedly a very closed country. What happened to the artists then?

A: It was closed, until after the first Havana Biennial in 1984. My first grant came in 1985; I went to New York for almost four months, invited by the Ford Foundation. Before that moment, to think of a grant was to go to the Soviet Union, or to Hungary or Poland.

Q: So you would say that the Cuban government helped you.

A: It did, in the sense of permitting me to do the work I wanted to do, and sending me to participate in such important events as the Venice and São Paulo Biennials. By chance, at that moment, the directors of the Ministry of Culture had real interest in promoting young talent, so they sent the best Cuban representation to international events. I believe they did it in a fair and reasonable manner. For example, Cuenca was sent out before I was, to the Paris Biennial in 1983. The situation in the Ministry of Culture started to change, however, in 1990. Marcia Leiseca and Beatriz Aulet were replaced when younger artists began to do challenging work, with very critical images referring to social themes and everyday Cuban life.

Q: But were you affected by the government crackdown?

A: I did not belong to that tendency of young artists whose work was almost journalistic, recording daily life, and very localized in one moment of Cuban history. Instead I attempt, along with others from my generation, to work with general and possibly eternal themes, if you can call them that.

Q: You have now been living outside Cuba for two years. Why?

A: The country never came up with the necessary resources for my generation to give all it had to give. This is why almost every artist has left. We had no space [to exhibit] and no studio to paint in. No resources. I was tied to teaching in order to subsist, but I had no interest in it. The Fondo de Bienes Culturales [Cultural Assets Fund] was not selling my work in Cuba because, so it said, it was noncommercial. But it was selling works by other artists who lacked the opportunity, or sufficient skills, to be teachers. There were four parallel powers in the Cuban art world: The Fund, the Ministry of Culture, and the two figures who are still holding onto their posts:

Lilian Llánez from the Wifredo Lam Center and Alfredo Guevara, a prestigious and independent promoter of a group of artists. Each power was always fighting with the other. That's why we artists were always missing something, depending on which power was protecting us. My generation was like a table lacking one leg. Personal hates sprang up among us—divisions, resentments, little groups and teams.

Q: Are they still divided?

A: In a certain way, because of old rancor and misinterpretations.

Q: In these last two years you have become an international star. You have participated in the exhibition organized by MoMA that showed in Seville, Paris, now Cologne, and will end up in New York [*Latin American Artists of the Twentieth Century*]. You have had three solo shows at Frumkin/Adams Gallery in New York. What does Mexico have to do with this process of transformation?

A: Since I've been in Mexico I have many ideas, and I really want to work. I'm especially interested in the northern Indian communities: the Huicholes, the Coras, the Yaquis, the Seris, the Tarahumaras. They are nearer to my spirit and sensibility. They were ancient hunters with a mentality and an artistic-technical heritage that is connected to other things—part of ancestral wisdom—which I intend to reconstruct in time. Both in my Afro-Cuban culture and in the Indian traditions I find parallel points that reaffirm me as bearer of a very old human patrimony. Artists of the beginning of the century paid attention to specific aspects of "primitive" art and wood carving, which allowed them to find Cubist solutions for their work. In my case, I seek a more general knowledge, more sensitive and more inspired. I seek to bring out the presence of the past in the present, much more than any localism. I don't believe that one has to be a Mexican by birth to approach this country with affection, to learn from it, and to leave one's work here.

Q: Would you stay in Mexico?

A: I would like to stay indefinitely. Ninart [Cultural Foundation], above all, has given me the opportunity to establish myself in this country with my wife and son, so that I can work here with seriousness and in comfort. Ninart has been the obvious proof that our work also has a commercial value; that it is accepted and can be promoted with tremendous dignity. Ninart has produced exhibitions such as *Fifteen Cuban Artists*, which was historic at the ideological level. Here, for the first time, two supposedly different groups of Cubans came together. The importance of being only one culture was seen in that exhibition, as also was the mutual recognition between artists . . . Here in Mexico I have the things I need to see every day in order to inform myself and take influence from them.

Q: What are these things?

A: All these art objects from Asia, Oceania, Africa, Latin America, North America. They all form a part of me. They have a meaning that also becomes an aesthetic thing, from an arrow, to a mask, to a shield, to a loincloth: objects that in the end will leave a mark on me and my work.

Q: What do you say of your success in the international press, the *Newsweek* article, and the cover of the January 1993 *Art Nexus*?

A: These are things that have come out, fortunately, because of a situation of coincidences in time and space: that a group of people got together to make a different type of art; that a group of people came to visit our country [Cuba] with the vision to understand that it had value, and with the means to take us and our work overseas; that our age coincided—because we were the new generation—with the Ministry of Culture's proposal to send us to important international events and biennials. Then, the year 1992 marks the five hundredth anniversary of the discovery, or the conquest, or the looting, or the destruction of America. And also the formation of a diverse Latin American culture. This forces our attention onto Latin American art, and on Cuban art as well, not by chance but because this art has a quality already recognized by a lot of people.

Q: Are the Cubans in fashion?

A: More than a fashion, it is a concrete, real thing. If Western eyes are looking at us, this is because we have something that they lack. A sensitivity, a kind of spirituality, cultural richness, and interesting experiences that we have and they, if they once had them, have lost them.

Q: What about your new works for this show *La isla en peso* [*The Island in Weight*]?

A: I liked the title of Virgilio Piñera's [1942 poem for this show] because it is the first exhibition that I have staged outside Cuba while thinking about my country with nostalgia. I liked the idea of carrying the island like a weight upon oneself; of transporting your culture and your things to another place; of all the time having a consciousness of what you are. It is like the mountain that [Cuba's patroness] the Virgin of La Caridad del Cobre sits on, nursing a child. The mountain rises over a little boat, and this in turn rises over the heads of a group of people understood as Cubans. That is the painting *La isla en peso*.

Marks of the Journey

A Conversation with Eugenio Dittborn and Roberto Merino

———

From *Remota: Pinturas aeropostales*
(Santiago: Pública Editores for Museo Nacional de Bellas Artes, 1997), 24–27.

The Airmail Paintings of Eugenio Dittborn raised many issues in the newly globalized art world of the 1980s. Created on thin, nonwoven paper and simply folded and mailed from show to show in flat envelopes, they slipped across borders as if they were letters. At the same time, they called attention to their "peripheral" origins in Chile. That peripheral and contingent status also characterizes much of the imagery in the works. All ellipses here are retained from the original.

October 11, 1989

Q: Regarding your work, much has been said about a certain precariousness of your materials, and a renunciation of profligate ostentation, even though the works are large in format. I see a certain correspondence between such precariousness and necessity. I speak of a principle of necessity in both the media and the techniques. Precariousness, which is also an important component of our national life, is noted in the work, but not explicitly.

A: The precariousness in my work could be seen through the fact that the elements that I connect in my work are connected only provisionally. In the Airmail Paintings, for example, tacking one piece of fabric over another, I can easily unstitch them and move them to another spot. None of the materials that I use allow permanent attachment. This is the provisional character of the inscriptions, and thus of their connections.

Q: So the meaning of a given work seems always to be in a sort of pending state.

A: It's a state that invites both comments and retractions about the work, not a feeling of stable meanings. What is precarious can be dismantled at any time; it seems provisional, and thus fleeting.

Q: There is another question that interests me a lot, which I find very compelling and is one of the points of feeling (or tension) in the work, and it's this: how the journey and its purpose, or the purpose of the journey, is inscribed without explicit markers among the elements of the work. First in the selection of the material (synthetic unwoven fabric), which, as we know, is used for wrapping and shipping, and the matter of the creases, which I relate to the fissures of breakage in the *Large Glass* by Marcel Duchamp.

A: It's a mark of the journey.

Q: The introduction of randomness.

A: In the case of the Airmail Paintings, it's actually the reverse: These marks, the creases, are precisely what makes their journey possible; folding is the precondition for the possibility of shipment.

Q: On the body of the [fifteenth-century Inca] mummy of Cerro el Plomo, which has appeared a few times in your works, there are also unmistakable marks of a journey.

A: Of a final journey. According to what I have read, the child who was mummified had walked about twelve kilometers to arrive at the place of sacrifice, always climbing. This was deduced from the marks on her feet, because the feet show a large amount of blisters, as well as marks from a type of ceremonial shoe, which was a little smaller than the foot. This shoe was continually wounding her throughout the ascent. This is also the case with Duchamp, as we just said. They have marks of a journey. The marks on the mummified skin of this Inca child allow you to deduce the pathway and calculate the distance the mummy traveled.

Q: On another subject: What are the relationships among the faces that appear in your Airmail Painting No. 70, *La VI Historia del Rostro* [*The Sixth History of the Human Face*]? That is, between the pre-pictorial child's drawing, the police sketch, the ID card photos, the pictures of natives, the faces that appear in drawing manuals, faces that appear in reading textbooks, in anonymous drawings, in calendars, notebooks, and magazines?

A: I was looking for faces with the maximum distance between them. There are gulfs and leaps from one type of face to another, between one technique and another, between the method of rendering and method of shipping, and between the places where I found them. Just as each

Airmail Painting traveled, there are "journeys" inside each one, or antipodes joined in abrupt contact.

Q: When I spoke of tension, I meant the way in which that gap to be traveled is inscribed in the work.

A: In a sidelong way. You could speak of the tension of the creases.

Q: Or the tension of the canvas. You remember that we talked about the English word *canvas*, which refers to the linen used for painting, a ship's sail, and the canvas of a boxing ring.

October 16, 1989

Q: Your work travels through space, and it also traverses time and its traces. You could say that for a fairly long time, since 1976–77, you have been developing a system of references in transformation, or a tale of your own references. There is no hint of current fashion, or of the idea of stylistic progress, or of the need to be up to date.

A: Nothing about my work is in fashion. But even that could be in fashion, in a different way.

Q: In the painted caves of France, a few years ago they stopped allowing tourist visits because the carbonic anhydride generated by their exhalations was mutilating the paintings. This news appeared on television, on *Ripley's* [*Believe it or Not*]. On the other hand, a work created for posterity such as *The Last Supper* held out for centuries in that refectory, against the tide of humidity that dampened that place for so long. And during the Napoleonic invasion, French soldiers passed the time throwing bricks at the apostles' heads. Centuries before that, another work of Leonardo, the giant clay horse that was the maquette for the monument to Count [Francesco] Sforza, was also ruined by French soldiers. It is strange when the closed world of a work of art is invaded, or violently infiltrated, by the everyday world. And it's also strange that dust, both domestic and metaphysical, has painted over Rembrandt, making a nocturne out of *The Night Watch*. I imagine that the Airmail Paintings must have some system of defense, since they were created to transit that wide world, to be shipped around and manipulated in it, and to enter its postal system—with its strikes, delays, neglect, and blockages—and still to survive.

A: The fragility of the Airmail Paintings still allows them to pass through the global mail system and arrive on time and in perfect condition for exhibiting. By this I mean that the mail system is not only as you describe, but also the opposite of all that: expedited, efficient, even charming. It always performs the trick of taking the Airmail Paintings to their destination, and then the more difficult trick of bringing them back home. What else can you say about an Airmail Painting resting at 5:15 a.m. in an airport in Papeete, Tahiti inside a Boeing jet of Quantas, UTA, or LAN [airlines], while here in Santiago it's 12:15 the day before, and in Nouméa, the capital of New Caledonia and the work's next stop en route to Sydney, it's 2:15 the next day? Once it arrives, the recipient opens the envelopes, unfolds the works, hangs them on the walls, and exhibits them next to their envelopes. And just then, at that moment, the whole trajectory is visible: when they come to rest. The way bleeding comes only after a cut.

Q: Much has been said about marginality of all kinds in relation to your work: how your work creates a giant gallery of marginalized figures: muggers, thieves, pickpockets, murderers, victims, Indians. In your work there are distinct strategies of choice that allow you to avoid the arrogance of the naturalist, or the devotion of the romantic.

A: By citing photos of criminals from the 1930s to the 1950s, I hope to explore a specific and contradictory relationship: the collision between the police camera, which represents the work of the state in the visual realm, and the faces of the small-time Chilean criminals, both male and female, most of them impoverished peasant migrants. The visual document of this collision is a photograph, which, alongside the subject's full name, false names, aliases, physical traits, and a few biographical facts, constitutes the record of the photographed subject. Such records were then published in *El Detective*, a police magazine of scientific criminology, which the Bureau of Investigations published between about 1925 and 1950. In the case of these records—which do not show vile and outlandish faces, but rather photographic plates annexed to criminal records, brought together by the state in order to solidify its control— what kind of marginality can we be talking about? To put it another way, isn't the power of the state stealing the very marginality from these thieves? Robbed of their marginality and their lives, they proceed to take a leading role, paradoxically, in the only space available to them: the photos on their records. They become the photos on those records. I don't think that this point has been understood. I do not work with marginalized robbers, but rather I work with the precisely frozen moment of their subordination by the photographic power of the state with its printed distribution. Doesn't this instant also represent the abrupt modernization of the face of the criminal?

October 18, 1990

Dittborn: An Airmail Painting is the space in which disparate moments in time can meet each other. In that sense, the hybridization in my work is also temporal. Marks as evidence of diverse and widely separated temporal zones end up there, and the encounter renders them all more visible. This also has to do with their mediations; that is, with that which makes possible the movements, and with that which travels in order to transmit certain questions. For example, in Airmail Painting No. 33 (*Pietá*), the first mediation would be the TV screen on which [welterweight boxer] Benny "the Kid" Paret appeared, mortally knocked out, in the ring at Madison Square Garden [in April 1962]. A United Press International photographer shot the scene which appeared on television, and the UPI sent the picture to the Chilean sports magazine *Gol y Gol*, which printed and distributed it. A copy of that magazine ended up in a used bookstore fifteen years later, where I found it in 1977. I am fascinated by images that show traces of successive transmissions, or marks of a journey, as we said before. Paret televised, photographed, and finally printed: all the mediations that the picture went through in its various versions are there inscribed.

Q: Then the only thing to do is to send this find of yours on another journey in order to keep it intact. The Airmail Paintings are not a final destination, but rather a place where things gather and make themselves visible. But at the same time they must keep on circulating . . .

A: Yes, this has the character of a sentence, so it seems . . .

Q: As a penal sentence . . .

A: Their penalty is to remain forever in motion . . .

Q: Souls in torment have no resting place . . .

A: They have neither a destination nor a home. All destinations become their home . . .

Q: There is one more subject I would like to discuss: The catalog text for the exhibition [of October 1989] at the Australian Center for Photography in

Sydney says that the Airmail Paintings "evade the imperatives of the art market . . . They arrive to unfold and occupy a substantial amount of the hotly contested space of the cultural metropolis." This issue is important: through their airmailed quality, they convert the cultural metropolis into just another place of transit, because from there, the paintings are always in transit to another place that is similarly temporary.

A: What you say is very true; it makes a lot of sense. This means that the Airmail Paintings, in their unassuming envelopes, seem to trick the agents of the customs services in the great cities of Europe, Oceania, and the United States. They ask: Is this a letter? Though it is a little large, yes, of course it's a letter; and they send it on with no problem.

Q: As long as they are letters there is never any problem.

A: The agents say, OK, it's a letter. And when they are opened, unfolded, and exhibited, the Airmail Paintings effectively occupy a substantial amount of the space in the metropolis.

Q: Of the vital space of the metropolis . . .

A: Then probably the Airmail Paintings amount to a stratagem, as [Carl] von Clausewitz defines it [in *On War*]. The stratagem is that the Airmail Paintings are paintings disguised as letters. This allows them to infiltrate. They thus have a viral character; they embody a viral notion of warfare.

Q: What would be the opposite of a viral notion of war?

A: That would be a declared war. Viruses don't declare war.

Q: They just start it.

A: They not only start war, they start it retrospectively [*laughter*]. And then when the Airmail Paintings come back, the agents of the metropolis say, "Aaggh! It's too late." [*Laughter*]

PART TWELVE

Toward a New Century

The Personal and the Political

An Interview with Felix González-Torres

Robert Storr

———

Part I from "Etre un Espion," *Artpress*, January 1995, 24–32; Part II from
Felix González-Torres, Roni Horn (Munich: Goetz Collection, 1995), 30–34.

*A leading conceptual artist here addresses the question of what political art is.
He also mentions the pain he felt in his personal life when his partner, Ross
Laycock, died of AIDS-related illnesses in 1991. The two themes intersect in
many of his pieces, especially* Untitled (Placebo), *which is discussed here. The
work consists of 1,200 pounds of silver-wrapped candies on the floor of the
gallery, which viewers are free to take, thereby causing the work to disappear
for later replenishment. Also considered is his series* Stacks, *which comprised
stacks of large, identically printed sheets of paper that viewers could take home
with them. The long interview was originally published in two disparate places,
here brought together and excerpted.*

Part I

Q: When you say what you and some of the people of your generation have
done is to deal with the elements of conceptualism that can be used for
a political or a social end, how do you define the political or social
dimension of art? What do you think the parameters are?

A: I'm glad that this question came up. I realize again how successful ideology is and how easy it was for me to fall into that trap, calling this sociopolitical art. All art and all cultural production is political. I'll just give
you an example. When you raise the question of political or art, people
immediately jump and say, Barbara Kruger, Louise Lawler, Leon Golub,
Nancy Spero, those are political artists. Then who are the nonpolitical
artists, as if that was possible at this point in history? Let's look at
abstraction, and let's consider the most successful of those political

artists, Helen Frankenthaler. Why are they [the abstract artists] the most successful political artists, even more than [Joseph] Kosuth, much more than Hans Haacke, much more than Nancy and Leon or Barbara Kruger? Because they [the abstract artists] don't look political! And as we know it's all about looking natural, it's all about being the normative aspect of whatever segment of culture we're dealing with, of life. That's where someone like Frankenthaler is the most politically successful artist when it comes to the political agenda that those works entail, because she serves a very clear agenda of the Right. For example, here is something the [US] State Department sent to me in 1989, asking me to submit work to the Art and Embassy Program. It has this wonderful quote from George Bernard Shaw, which says, "Besides torture, art is the most persuasive weapon." And I said I didn't know that the State Department had given up on torture—they're probably not giving up on torture—but they're using both. Anyway, look at this letter, because in case you missed the point they reproduce a Franz Kline, which explains very well what they want in this program. It's a very interesting letter, because it's so transparent. Another example: when you have a show with white male straight painters, you don't call it that; that would be absurd, right? That's just not "natural." But if you have four Black lesbian sculptors from Brooklyn, that's exactly what you call it, "Four African-American Lesbians from Brooklyn."

Q: What's your agenda? Who are you trying to reach?

A: When people ask me, "Who is your public?" I say honestly, without skipping a beat, Ross [Laycock]. The public was Ross. The rest of the people just come to the work. In my recent show at the Hirshhorn, which is one of the best experiences I have had in a long time, the guards were really in it. Because I talked to them, I dealt with them. They're going to be here eight hours with this stuff. And I never see guards as guards, I see guards as the public. Because the other answer to the question "Who's the public?" is, well, the people who are around you, which includes the guards. In Washington people asked me, "Did I train the guards, did I give them a lecture?" I said, "No, I just talk to them when I'm doing the work." They said, "You know, we have never been to an exhibit where the guards go up to the viewers and tell them what to do, and where to go, what to look at, what it means." But again, that division of labor, that division of function is always there in place to serve someone's agenda.

When I was at the Hirshhorn and saw the show, there was one

particular guard who was standing with the big candy floor piece *Untitled (Placebo)*, and she was amazing. There was this suburban, white, middle-class mother with two young sons who came in the room and in thirty seconds, this woman—who was a black, maybe churchgoing civil servant in Washington, in the middle of all this reactionary pressure about the arts—there she was explaining to this mother and kids about AIDS and what this piece represented, what a placebo was, and how there was no cure and so on. Then the boys started to fill their pockets with candies and she sort of looked at them like a schoolmistress and said, "You're only supposed to take one." Just as their faces fell and they tossed back all but a few she suddenly smiled again and said, "Well maybe two." And she won them over completely! The whole thing worked because then they got the piece, they got the interaction, they got the generosity and they got her. It was great.

Q: Do you think there's a way to break the intellectual habits that result from generations of moralizing protest art?

A: Such work is based on the idea that the artist is there to enlighten a socially benighted world; along with that comes the expectation that the artist personally be a beacon of virtue so that if, at any point, they are shown to be less than pure, then everything they say is subsequently dismissed as bogus. This has happened over and over, as if the social content of art were limited to individual ethical exercises rather than thinking of art as a political and cultural probe. Let's go to the political arena—I'll say, the real political arena—and say that some politicians have not been "good," yet they have done some very wonderful things for everyone, improving the quality of life for a lot of us in a very tangible way and at the most intimate personal levels. Like some of the programs John F. Kennedy started. I'm a product of that. I went to school because of what that man started. Womanizers and drunks and all that stuff, guys with mob connections made all these changes possible so that someone like me could get loans and go to school. That's just one simple example from life. Let's move forward to a certain degree, in terms of the kind of protest art that says all Capital is bad, Benetton is bad. We know that! We really do know that. We don't need a gallery space to find out something we read in the news.

Q: What about ideas of a puritan antiaesthetic?

A: I don't want that. No, between the Monet and [conceptual artist] Victor Burgin, give me the Monet. But as we know, aesthetics are politics.

They're not even about politics, they are politics. Because when you ask who is defining aesthetics, at what particular point—what social class, what kind of background these people have—you realize quickly again that the most effective ideological constructions are the ones that don't look like it. If you say, "I'm political, I'm ideological," that is not going to work, because people know where you are coming from. But if you say, "Hi! My name is Bob and this is it," then they say, "That's not political." It's invisible and it really works. I think certain elements of beauty used to attract the viewer are indispensable. I don't want to make art just for people who can read [poststructuralist art critic] Fredric Jameson sitting upright on a [Charles Rennie] Mackintosh chair. I want to make art for people who watch *The Golden Girls* [TV show] and sit in a big, brown, La-Z-Boy chair. They're part of my public, too, I hope. In the same way that that woman and the guard are part of my public.

Q: We've touched on this already, but you came up in a generation where young artists read a lot of theory and out of that has come a great deal of work that refers back to theory in an often daunting or detached way. And that has put off many people. In effect, they've reacted against the basic ideas because they've gotten sick of the often pretentious manner in which those ideas were rephrased artistically.

A: It's a liberating aspect of the way that most of my generation does art, but it also makes it more difficult because you have to justify so much of what you do. If we were making, let's say, a more formalist work, work that includes less of a social and cultural critique of whatever type, it would be really wonderful. Either you make a good painting or you make a bad one, but that's it. When you read [Clement] Greenberg you can get lost in page after page on how a line ends at the edge of the canvas, which is very fascinating. I love that; I can get into that, too. But when some of us, especially in the younger generation, get involved with social issues, we are put under a microscope. We really are and we have to perform that role, which includes everything. It includes the way we dress and where we are seen eating.

Those things don't come up in the same way if you are interested in the beautiful abstractions that have nothing to do with the social or cultural questions. It's part of the social construction but it has less involvement in trying to tell you what's wrong or what's right. These are two plates on a canvas, take it or leave it. What you see is what you get. Which is very beautiful, too; I like that.

After doing all these shows, I've become burnt out with trying to have some kind of personal presence in the work. Because I'm not my art. It's not the form and it's not the shape, not the way these things function that's being put into question. What is being put into question is me. I made *Untitled (Placebo)* because I needed to make it. There was no other consideration involved except that I wanted to make artwork that could disappear, that never existed, and it was a metaphor for when Ross was dying. So it was a metaphor that I would abandon this work before this work abandoned me. I'm going to destroy it before it destroys me. That was my little amount of power when it came to this work. I didn't want it to last, because then it couldn't hurt me.

From the very beginning it was not even there; I made something that doesn't exist. I control the pain. That's really what it is. That's one of the parts of this work. Of course, it has to do with all the bullshit of seduction and the art of authenticity. I know that stuff, but on the other side, it has a personal level that is very real. It's not about being a con artist. It's also about excess, about the excess of pleasure. It's like a child who wants a landscape of candies. First and foremost it's about Ross. Then I wanted to please myself and then everybody.

Part II

Q: I want to focus on the aesthetic dimension of your work. What you do has a very pronounced aesthetic tone. It's not a formal system, it is a tone. I wonder if that distinction makes sense to you.

A: I think it is a system and it is also a tone. I don't want to spell out everything that I'm doing to myself, although I'm always engaged in these question-and-answer sessions with myself. That's why I don't make that much work because, if I really ask a lot of questions, I won't make it. I'll say, "Why make it?" and then it's not needed. But in terms of the tone, I think it all has to do with going to extremes. I always enjoy extremes, I always like the fringes. Or you might call it the margins. For instance, when I recently finished the big bead curtain piece in San Antonio [*Untitled (Beginning)*], I said, "This is beautiful, but this is also pretty extreme stuff, since there's really nothing else there, in the middle of this room." There is a screen, that is all, a screen that people can go through. People were actually playing a lot with it, with the sound. I get into narrative that is not written, but it is there. It's kind of a blood memory thing. The system has been there from day one, and it is a system that has to do with creating things that are not necessary.

Q: The fact of the matter is that your work is quite accessible, and it is accessible because it does not go straight at the subject; nor does it go directly against what people already think. It gets them from the sides. There's no detail that is extraneous, there's nothing that's sloppy, and it is very calm. That completeness or simplicity and that calm is what I mean when I talk about the consistent tone shared by the different kinds of work you've done.

A: That's how a good metaphor works. When I'm dealing with issues of, let's say, the body, to me it is much more exciting to have a stack of blue paper that I name *The Body* and/or name *The Loverboy*—that's Ross—than to have a sculpture there that is a body. Because that sculpture of the body may not be just about the body: it may be about wax and how good I am at putting hair on wax, or plaster. But that is not the way the body is constituted in our culture; it is constituted through language. Yet there is something that looks like a body. There's a whole bunch of cells that make up a body. I think in terms of art bringing that to the attention of the viewer, at least for me as a viewer, doing that is much more exciting than just having a body. That is really not a metaphor. When you take these pieces of paper out of the stack and the stack disappears, I think that is a very beautiful and poignant metaphor for the body, which is always decaying and disappearing. It's always leaving. At the same time, because of the formal characteristics of the work it can always be redone or replenished. It is a metaphor that can keep coming back. As long as there is someone there supporting the work, someone responsible, i.e., the collector, the piece will always exist as something that I named *The Body*. Now, that was my own language, my own brand-new idea of what a body could be, and can be; it's just paper. When most people die, all they leave is paper—photos, books, and letters and stuff like that—that's it.

If there is a tone to the work, the tone has a lot to do with being tough on myself. I am always saying, "Is it really needed? Is it something new? Is this moving us somewhere?" One of the reasons why I stopped making the stacks is because I think I had said something that I needed to say very badly and that was it. I did it, so now let the people deal with it. That poses some problems, because people like you to do something for ten or twelve years. Signature work has to go on and on, but I have rejected so many shows that asked for new stacks. I tell them that I don't do stacks anymore. I said what I had to say; what else can I do with a stack? . . .

One thing that I want to emphasize as much as I can with my students is, "Who is your public? What are you making this for?" That is better than trying to get some signature form or look or way of working. I think the tone is about not having anything extra but only what's necessary. I believe with all my heart in the economy of means. You just reach a point when you know that's it. One page: that is all you need. Same thing with Emily Dickinson, who used very simple language. That's all you need. Poetry is the toughest. Just pick a line and that is all you need. It is funny because now that I have been taking all of these pictures of birds flying away and swirling, I have started seeing poems that are about birds all over, from [Pier Paolo] Pasolini to Elizabeth Bishop. My favorite poem about birds is Pasolini's "I Work All Day," where he tells about his consciousness being a bird that sees everything. I've always been aware of birds, but I had never really *seen* them. Then one day, I saw birds, and suddenly they became an obsession, a total fascination. The last time I was in Miami on the beach. I started seeing the brown pelicans like I've never seen them before, and I said, "I'm thirty-seven years old and I've never seen that beauty that was right in front of my eyes." And it is just beautiful, to see a simple V-line of sixteen to eighteen pelicans flying south. They have always gone south and north, for how many millions of years. When I look at art that moves me it's about learning to see. When I see a [Robert] Ryman or when I saw that Roni Horn piece *Images on a Gold Field*, I let my imagination fly, just like a bird. Conceptually those objects are so simple, because that is what they are. And that is all you need to start, to push you forward.

Q: Let's go back to the question of tone, which is different from a signature style or method. It is a way of approaching things. In your work, you are always very present, no matter how much you shift the ground or format. You're there in the stacks, and you're there in the photos of birds, even though they at first seem more traditional than your situational pieces.

A: I insist and I repeat: I am a big sucker for formalism and I would never have done those pictures if I didn't think they were formalist. They are total exercises in formalism. There is really nothing there; it's just grey sky. I think these new, less-dramatic ones are the most successful photos I have done. They are very antiphotographic: it is just the camera looking straight up and shooting at birds that happen to be very far away. Then you print the image as twenty-by-twenty-four[-inch] photos and suddenly it becomes so abstract and intriguing. I test my work by putting these images up on the wall and I look at them to see how I feel a week later, and if I still feel very excited, then I take them to the gallery to see the reaction in people's faces. Because there is a certain kind of reaction that people cannot fake. Like when people go up to you and say, "What the fuck is this?" and then they get into it. People who know me, like Bob Nickas, walked in and said, "That's Felix's work," even though he had never seen it before. I said to him, "How do you know?" and he said it was just obvious.

Of course there has to be a method because I don't want to make it look like it's natural, because it is not natural. It depends on a lot of reading and doing and on having a very specific vision of what you want to put out. But this thing about tone is very interesting. It's a really funky question that I never thought about because I do things that I think are necessary. I try to say, "OK, I've done this portrait; what else can I do to make it more complete, to make it more effective?" Because people just don't remember, especially our culture; we have an explosion of information, but an implosion of meaning. It is like [the movie] *Casablanca* where Humphrey Bogart said, "A long time ago, last night." People don't remember last night.

Q: Perhaps preoccupation with memory and with loss is what I've been trying to get at. It's the constant in so much of your work, the fingerprints that you leave on all of it, rather than the signature style.

A: And I try to break that. I try to break that signature as much as I can. Like I said at the very beginning of the conversation, I get a lot of pleasure from jeopardizing my own career, my own way of thinking things. I think it has to do with reinventing myself. There has always been so much fragility.

Printing Shadows

An Interview with Graciela Sacco

Marguerite Feitlowitz

Excerpted from *Bomb*, Winter 2001–2002, 23–28.

This interview begins with the artist's roots in Rosario, Argentina, and then touches on some of her innovative ways of working with imagery, particularly heliography. The impact of her work is conditioned not only by the source and method of the imagery, but also by the site and the event where she installs it. Such questions of public address are important to a great deal of Latin American modern art, dating back to the mural movement.

Q: Rosario has always struck me as one of those provincial cities right out of a Balzac novel.

A: [*laughter*] Totally, yes. Completely.

Q: Nonetheless, it has spawned avant-garde art and literary movements at political flashpoints in Argentina's history. You are often associated with one of Rosario's—indeed Argentina's—most illustrious artists, Antonio Berni. I ask because I don't think of your work as narrative, while Berni's is very strongly so, especially his graphic series on the innocent Ramona and her hair-raising descent into prostitution and "the lower depths," as Maxim Gorky would say. Were you conscious of Berni as an early influence on you as an artist?

A: Berni was certainly part of what I would call my artistic horizons. But he was not the definitive influence. Let me say that while Berni had an extremely strong narrative period, in which he mostly made prints, his greatest strength was in the use of materials. That, I think, is what liberates him from being didactic, and enables him to transcend the tired label *Berni el bueno* [Berni the Good]. I was much more influenced by what is commonly called *arte popular*: Mexican *corridos*, [José Guadalupe]

Posada, the Brazilian practice of decorating town squares with sheets of drawings or poetry set to hang like laundry drying in the sun. When you walk into a chapel covered with objects and offerings, you are caught up in a dialogue where art is totally entwined with daily life. I think that from a conceptual standpoint, my work has a lot to do with this. The site is always integral to my work. This is something the Mexican muralists understood very well. Their works were intended to be social events, places of meeting on various levels. They were also narrative, of course, but that isn't what attracts me to them . . .

Q: You would have been a student in the late '60s and early '70s—

A: I began university in '75 and dropped out in '76. It was impossible to be at university during the dictatorship. Those were terrible times. Even before the 1976 coup, the schools were a battleground. A bomb would go off: Was it the military? The Triple A [Argentine Anticommunist Alliance]? The [leftist] guerrillas? You couldn't be sure. It was very complicated, very dangerous. As you know, people were being disappeared, others were underground, everyone was burning books. And in terms of studying, it was a trap. Art was restricted to working from the live model.

Q: How did you manage to read texts that were of personal importance to you?

A: Photocopies. There wasn't much at the time, but what there was got passed around. Hideous, horrible times. Nothing romantic about it. Shortly before I'd left university, I'd married, had a child. But I never stopped working, and gave art classes at advanced levels. I went back to the National University of Rosario in 1980, and have taught there ever since.

Q: And you still offer special seminars on the problematic of Latin American twentieth century art. The subject intrigues me. What does it mean to you? A close friend who is a writer always insists, "Theory is real, it's concrete." What do you think of that?

A: If we look at this in the conservative sense, it has to do with how you arrive at form, how you take a problem and materialize it. Any reading of a work radiates from the form. All artistic production has theory behind it. What changes is how that theory is made legible. That's where the specificity of technique comes in—if it's language or painting or video or sound. But the essential problem remains the same. It's a search for form, for a way to *materialize* our questions, conflicts, quests, and discoveries.

Q: You've always been fascinated with multiple images.

A: For some reason, I've always wanted to transfer images from one surface to another. And yes, I've often used multiple images of the same event, or used the same image over and over. I've also made images with hand-made paper. Once I recycled newspapers and made them into sheets of paper that still had little vestiges of headlines and news stories . . .

Q: You also printed on the paper you made.

A: Yes, I printed postage stamps, which I made myself. I also made the lino-leum or woodblocks used for transferring the images. Conceptually, I was working with transformation, and so sometimes there was no image as such, only the gestural surface of the homemade paper. I wanted to juxtapose the material itself with the act of making paper. For me, that alone was aesthetically very strong. And I discovered that you could make paper from a whole host of things—asparagus, for example. And I made paper from all kinds of things—celery leaves, lettuce, onion, banana leaves . . . When you make paper, you're working with the pro-cess of putrefaction. Natural chemical reactions: water, rain, heat. You wash the vegetable, get down to the fiber, that's what gives the paper consistency, body. I got hooked. This observation of the physical world got transformed into a physical activity. I moved on to make dyes—the seed of an avocado gives you a violet color you can hardly believe . . .

Q: Have you always kept your studio at home?

A: No . . . And when I started with heliography, there too it began from necessity. I was doing a project that had to do with the city of Rosario and it had to be sent to a number of places. I love chemical processes, they fascinate, they delight me. I don't know if it's the transformation that gets me thinking, or if I'm always thinking about transformation. Whatever. I found these papers, the kind used for making architectural plans. These papers are photosensitive: the light attacks, passes through, the image is revealed. Well, I loved the idea. All you need is the sun. It's like photographing without a lens. But there were chemical limitations. So once I got the papers, I called the factory to see if I could buy the product they'd used to treat the paper. They'd hang up on me like I was some sort of crackpot. Until finally one day, I reached a young woman who said, "Look, I have to tell you I have no idea what you're talking about, but there's a chemist here, I'll pass you to him!" So I got passed to this very lovely, elderly gentleman who said, "Well, fine, why don't you come by?" Now I live in Rosario, and this factory was in Temperley, just outside Buenos Aires, almost four hours by bus! Early the next morning,

I was at the bus stop. I had these huge sheets of paper—two by three meters—on which I'd begun to work. The chemist couldn't believe it. The products only have a life of about six hours, he told me, by the time you get home, they won't work very well. But I insisted and finally he gave me the chemicals like someone offering alms. I have to tell you, I could feel my blood start to flow in a different direction. I just knew it would work. Within a month, I went back to show him what I'd done, and the factory gave me money to do a publication showing the use of their materials in the making of art.

Q: What a wonderful story. So you started painting—if we can put it that way—with these chemicals.

A: Exactly. Well, first you have to prepare the surfaces. And then I made special camera-like things to guide the passage of light and reveal the images. And then I started giving classes in this technique. And I wrote a book about it. [*Escrituras solares: la heliografía en el campo artístico*]

Q: Is it a fast process?

A: It has its quirks. It's not the most complicated, or the most simple. The technique existed before photography as we know it. And it had only continued to exist in the form of an industrial secret.

Q: So you didn't begin with the idea of recovering a lost technique . . .

A: No, not at all. For me, it was about solving a problem. How to transfer an image from one surface to another. This technique was used for making city plans. That too has a connection for me. So you can look at it in very practical, historical, or poetic terms. But I wasn't thinking about any of that in the beginning. Later, at the São Paulo Biennial I was asked by some German critics how I'd made these things. When I explained, they told me that this was a pre-photographic technique. And that was incredible to learn. But no, I hadn't started with the idea of salvaging a lost technique. I did this in the same spirit as my experiments with vegetables for making paper. Or the work with shadows. How was I going to be able to print shadows? You can only print if you've got a surface impregnated by light. With heliography, all you need for printing on the sidewalk is the chemical and the sun. With photoserigraphy, you start with the thrown shadow on a transparent sheet of Plexiglas. Although the image is imprinted on the Plexiglas, it's essentially invisible until light passes through the sheet. In reality, the imprinted image blocks the passage of light. What you actually see is not the image itself, but its shadow. But with both techniques, the sensation is the same. Suddenly you can see! Literally. And of course there's a whole metaphorical change as well.

Q: Quite a lot has been written about the poetics of heliography. I've read a number of articles that posit your use of this technique as a way of recuperating history, making the past palpable in your art-making. It's coherent. Especially now that you know the history of heliography.

A: Yes, but that interpretation is not completely right. While the choice of a technique is never innocent, and technique is always integral to the sense of a work, the images have their own history, and so does the artist, and all this derives, at least in part, from the medium. But I have no interest in nostalgia, or in exploring nostalgia. The pieces I make are inscribed in the present.

Q: You have heliographed open mouths on spoons and postage stamps, on sidewalks and city walls, even on top of election posters. The combination of the image—communicating hunger, outrage, fear, or shock—and its site make for a shifting resonance. In a gallery, the suspended heliographed spoons create a very quiet, glowing space. I've seen visitors gather round, and remain there, quiet and thoughtful. In another installation, you had these spoons in plastic cases, like laboratory specimens. And while walking down the street it must be an unsettling experience to realize you've just stepped on one of these mouths.

A: It would be, yes . . .

Q: Which brings us back to the importance of the site.

A: The space is always integral to the work, and sometimes in ways that go beyond one's original intentions. *El combate perpetuo* [*The Perpetual Combat*], which shows a popular demonstration with a man in front throwing a stone toward the viewer, was first exhibited at the sixth Havana Biennial, in 1997. At the next Havana Biennial, I was assigned to a cell in La Fortaleza, which was the jail for political prisoners. So there—as part of a different installation—the image of the man throwing a stone had a much more specific charge, a whole different frame of reference. As a viewer, inside the cell, it was like a photographer's darkroom. You saw nothing, until you approached the flashlight hanging from the ceiling in the middle of the room. I'd put eyes all over the walls, all over the ceiling. They were photoserigraphs, but you only saw this when you got close to the light. When you started to see, the first sensation was one of presence. Of being looked at. What I didn't know was that this space was the very cell that had been occupied by the writer Reinaldo Arenas.

Q: Really!

A: It was incredibly strong. And the power of it was beyond my control.

Q: Did you know Arenas? Had you read his work?

A: I didn't know him personally. I'd only read a few short things, but was deeply impressed.

Q: You've said that you think of objects in a primitive way, as things that have a great deal of life within them.

A: I was walking down the street one day and saw this soccer ball, collapsed, dirty, discarded. How terrible, I thought, an object that was made to be kicked until it's no good anymore. In Latin America, as you know, the soccer ball has a social and political resonance. There's a whole history of art right there. So I took the ball home and printed a big mouth on it with the words, *Ay, de mi!* [Woe is me]. I try to imprint images in a way that makes it seem as though they arise from within the object. In *Cuerpo a cuerpo* [*Body to Body*], I appropriated a photograph of the May '68 demonstrations in Paris and heliographed it onto jagged wooden sticks. The sticks are leaned up against one another, nailed to the wall. It's the crowd and the barricades, the barricades and the crowd.

Q: The faces, clothes, and bodies in this work are so distinct and immediate. The separation of the sticks, which are rough and of unequal sizes, intensifies a sense of movement, of things breaking apart.

A: I hope so. I've also used images from Prague Spring, the Intifada, and other uprisings, and no matter where I exhibit them, viewers associate what they see with events from their own city. In Rosario, people thought of the food riots of 1989 and 1999; in Córdoba, they flashed on the *Cordobazo* [uprising in 1969, which sparked similar events all over Argentina]. It happens every time.

Q: You've also done works on paper, as opposed to nontraditional materials. Does working in two dimensions change anything for you?

A: No, it really doesn't. Because I work from the image. It's essentially the same process. I manipulate the images, of course, as in *Cities of Fear*, where I burned out facial details to lend the tumultuous street scenes a certain anonymity. And many times I work with images from the newspapers. I think it has to do with a conception of what is available firsthand. The sources make it impossible to say, "There is no war in the Middle East," or "There is no ethnic cleansing in Bosnia." Even if you weren't there, you saw it on television, the images came into your house. This is a valid form of knowing and mustn't be denied.

Q: But isn't there another layer here? These images are also projections, they're framed, an interpretation of what happened. The news is never the event itself, it's always a version of the story.

A: I totally agree. You know I've been asked why I don't cite the photographer of the original picture. Which seems to me a completely wrongheaded question, since what I'm after with the use of these images is something we've experienced in common. And as you were just saying, the photographer chooses what to shoot, sends it to his agency, which sells it to a newspaper, which does its own framing. So who am I supposed to credit? The news is a construction. A photograph as well. We can ask, what is the starting point of this photograph, where did the work begin? In what reality? In whose reality? The actual event is a fragment of a fragment of a much larger story. When does one ever apprehend a totality? The field is trimmed, the optic set, the image arranged and recomposed. At every stage, something new is evoked, something new gets seen. Art too is a construction, if not a fiction. So in that sense, who am I supposed to cite?

Q: Have you had legal problems arising from this?

A: No, actually, I haven't.

Q: You did have a problem with an intervention you did last year in Israel, a work you called *Borders*. Here again you used shadows of eyes on city walls, and included a passage from Heidegger: "A border is not the line where something stops, but the place where something begins to manifest its essence."

A: I did this same intervention in Jordan and in Egypt. Because, in all these places, I was working with the theme of shadows, I chose a site where the sun would pass, project light, and then pass on. An argument in Israel broke out over the text by Heidegger, raised by a man who had been in one of the concentration camps. I understand where this gentleman was coming from, given that Heidegger was apparently a member of the Nazi Party. For that gentleman, I have only respect. But Heidegger has an undeniable place in the history of ideas, and what he is saying in this passage is very important: "A boundary is not the line where something stops, but the place where something begins to manifest its essence." The objective was to enact this drama about boundaries physically, through art. The fact that I'd appropriated the text and was using people's shadows provoked the questions: Where is the boundary? Where does the art begin? Whose shadow is it? Everyone has a shadow; all shadows fall, or don't fall, in the same way according to the light . . .

Q: May I ask—as a non-Israeli, as someone who is not from the very trou-
bled Middle East—what right do you have to insert yourself in such a
way?

A: Good question. I actually don't think that I do insert myself. I insert an
idea. In general, working the street is the same everywhere. Unless it's a
biennial, in which case it becomes a kind of official action, which is different. It's always good to find out later what it provoked for people. But
working the street isn't really very different from appropriating an image
from the newspaper. I interact with a public space. It's an attempt to go
from the intimate to the public. I never occupy a public space in the
sense of making a statement. Rather, every space is for asking questions.
Every image should start a dialogue.

Q: Is that what you mean by making art that is "engaged"?

A: For me the definition of engaged is the genuine intention to inscribe oneself in a different place. To question one's own boundaries, or limits.

Q: So we're back to your passion for transformation.

A: For observation and discovery.

Art, Ideology, and Violence

A Conversation with Doris Salcedo and Rocío Londoño Botero

———

From *El arte es marcadamente ideológico*, a video produced by
Fundación Razón Pública, Bogotá, March 2013

Here, a leading installation artist reflects on her motives and goals. The memory of violence is her principal subject, including how art can usefully depict violence. The interviewer asks about a famous performance in which the artist commemorated a 1985 guerrilla assault on the National Justice Ministry of Colombia. The original assault lasted twenty-seven hours and led to ninety-eight deaths, among them eleven of the fifteen Supreme Court justices. For the performance, the artist in 2002 enlisted ninety-eight assistants who each ascended to the roof of the same building and lowered that number of empty chairs with ropes, slowly, down the façade of the building, over the same time span as the assault.

A: I believe that all good art is, in itself, political. Because it is always opening up unknown pathways or unknown spaces, and it's always markedly ideological. It always lines up against some establishment or in favor of some other side of things. In my case, I am interested in political art because my entire output is centered on political violence, and what it means for those who are in power to destroy the lives of their fellow humans. All of the works and installations that I create are closely bound to that. At the base of each work is a testimony, always a testimony. I begin with a testimony, and from there I build something that is not exactly about that victim, but rather takes in a more broad remembrance of those kinds of events.

Q: *Which works of yours have had the most impact?*

A: I think that you can't speak of impact with art: much less a social impact, certainly not a political impact, but rather a small, somewhat weak impact on aesthetics. I think that all of my works do attempt to define a specific situation of victimhood, perhaps through displacement, or torture, or any of the awful horrors that we have in this country. Each of my works attempts in some way to show the specific marks that these types of crimes leave on their victims. It is like showing the texture of violence: not so much recounting an event, or narrating what happened, but rather showing how the victims were marked, and to work with the forgetfulness of society, entering the space of the horror of these victims, and there, right there in that space, to implant an image. To implant the image; that is what I am doing.

Q: *Beyond impact, let's talk about the effect of your works, such as the installation on the façade of the Palace of Justice in 2002.*

A: I think that what art can do, and it undoubtedly did in that case, is to create a type of emotional relationship; it can communicate some sense of the victim's experience. It is as if the shattered lives of those victims—which were truncated at the moment of their murders—those lives can in some fashion continue in the experience of the viewer. At the point that the viewer gives the work a moment of silent reflection, in that moment the emotional relationship that I am speaking of can exist. And it does happen. I could not say which work of mine has more effect than another, among all the works that I have created. And although I have been working with the same themes consistently throughout my career, each work creates a different space. What is most important is that the work marks absence, that it implants itself, and that it confronts. Violence creates its images; it is always creating images. And we all have these terrible images in our minds, such as, for example, of people dismembered, monstrous images. Violence is giving this society a huge quantity of images. I think that the function of art is to create images in opposition to those images, and in that way to create a counterbalance to the barbarity that occurs in this country. Here is an example of this idea: Guernica is one of many cities that suffered aerial bombardment, but the one that we remember is Guernica because an image exists that humanizes the completely inhumane act that was that bombardment. That image works. Not that it retells exactly what happened, not that it consoles the victims, nor aids them in their mourning, no; it creates meaning for all human beings. Therefore it is a memory, but more specifically, it is a memorial . . .

Q: *The Colombian victims' law, among other measures devoted to reparations, orders the creation of a memorial museum.*

A: When we speak of art, we must remember that we are in the land of paradox. Art has nothing to do with literal truth, nor with declarations of certainty. Regarding the symbolic reparations that art can pay to victims, I do think that this can happen, but it happens in a more discreet and indirect way than what the victims themselves may wish for. We are in two realms. One is the realm of the monument. A monument is a space that society creates in order to remember, or in some cases to celebrate, or to commemorate. A great many monuments exist to preserve memories in ways that have absolutely nothing to do with art. I think that for many bereaved persons, the presence of the names or pictures of their lost loved ones is very important. Therefore the bereaved always have photos of their loved ones, and ways of keeping their names. This goes somewhat beyond the realm of art. The realm of art, by contrast, is indirect. The realm of art is not in retelling a story or a direct experience. What it narrates, or what it approaches from the other side, is the void. Art presents absence. For many who grieve, this will not be sufficient, because it is not sufficiently direct. The function of art is undoubtedly to preserve a memory, but not in an immediate way; it can refer to what happened in the past, or even to events that will occur in the future. It will not be as precise as the sufferers may hope for. I think it absolutely essential for us as a society to humanize ourselves through the images that only art can provide. One thing is documentation of what has happened to the loved ones of the thousands of individual victims that we have had. And another thing is what we need to do as a society. We have a story to tell, events that we must preserve and attempt to keep in our minds.

In order to represent violence as such—to represent violence and to be faithful to the violence that actually occurred—what you would have to do would be to re-present it, almost to reenact it. How could you, for example, represent for today a Nazi concentration camp? Any image will always be weak. It will always omit millions of aspects, and it will be insufficient for the survivors of that camp, always. Thus, art cannot truly represent violence, because the only way to represent it would be by restaging the violent act; that would do it. But I do not believe that violence is present in any image: not religious violence, nor political, nor even artistic violence. I believe that an image is not the same as a blow. We have many artists who attempt to give us blows, but I do not believe in this. There is a beautiful phrase of Jorge Luis Borges that can help to define this idea: He said that art is the imminence of something that will never happen. Representing violence in art, without violence, is like that.

It is the imminence of what does not happen. It is not described, it is not narrated. Art cannot do this because to do so would require passing over to the realm of violence. Artists work under a rubric, and that rubric prevents them from undertaking the repetition of violence, which would be very dangerous . . .

I believe that art has a function similar to that of a eulogy at a funeral. At the very moment when the subject cannot hear you, you address that person and take leave of that person. I believe that this shows the essence of the human being, who is capable of enduring the pain of burying someone and still speak to that person who can no longer hear, and will never come back. Such an act dignifies us. It dignifies the bereaved and also the memory of the one who is buried; it is a wonderful thing. I think art is very similar to this, to a eulogy. All of the public artworks that I have created in Bogotá are acts of mourning, which unites them with our Colombian reality . . .

I think that art allows us a moment of pause. It allows a hiatus, a pause in the awful torment of transformation, for thinking, for understanding the suffering of others, for sharing the suffering of others, for understanding that in this world we are all here, sharing a country and sharing a space. We have to take account of them. Thus, to that extent, I believe that these pauses in the conflict allow us to think and to reflect on it all. We have such a quantity of terrible events that keep accumulating, one atop another and another, that we do not have time to stop and reflect on them. And that's why they keep occurring.

Shades of the Tropics

A Conversation with Beatriz Milhazes and Arto Lindsay

From *Patek Philippe: The International Magazine*, Spring 2012, 42–47.

Here, the artist discusses her identification with Tropicalism, the movement in popular music of the late 1960s that commented sarcastically on Brazil's tropical climate and third-world status. She also reflects on her relationship to Tarsila do Amaral, one of Brazil's founding modernists. Other subjects include dance, cannibalism, and the validity of a global culture.

Q: In what way are you connected to the Tropicalistas?

A: I feel extremely connected to Tropicalism, but I have not studied it formally. To some extent, I'd say I've deliberately left it alone, or allowed it to act on me. I saw shows by the Tropicalistas as a child with my parents, but this was in the seventies after the Tropicalism movement as such was over.

Q: What about the bossa nova?

A: I have loved the bossa nova all my life. Where Tropicalism is a set of ideas, bossa nova is a musical expression. Tropicalism was a movement with manifestos. Often the lyrics seemed more important than the music. Bossa nova was based on new feelings and a new possibility for rhythm to exist without any lyrics at all. I see Tropicalism as essentially the possibility of intelligence in the tropics. But I'm a romantic. I like love songs. And to take long walks on the beach. My romanticism can at times seem elegant and chic, or it can come across as sentimental and corny. Music defines the notion of soul for me, and bossa nova is without a doubt the soul of Rio.

Q: Does music represent a kind of reverie for you? A kind of daydreaming, a way to begin to think [about] or enter into your work?

A: Actually, in the studio I prefer silence. I prefer the rhythm of the painting as I'm working on it; I like to listen only to it, and without distraction.

Q: Where does the sensuality lie in your work? Do you analyze it or quantify it? Or do you avoid thinking about it altogether?

A: Everyone considers my work to be very sensual. Perhaps this is because my forms develop organically. I don't like brusque interruptions in my compositions. Motifs are transformed from one to another in "natural" movements. Lately I've begun to use stripes and squares, which have a way of providing a resting place for the eye within the painting. My work is a lot about geometry and how geometry structures life.

Q: I remember reading somewhere that you don't feel particularly close to literature, that you judge it to be too close to life itself. Too realistic. Not sufficiently abstract. But I feel something literary in your paintings. Perhaps it's in the combination of the flat surface and the conflicting planes. Perhaps it's in the work's claustrophobia. Or the way a single canvas develops. The amount of time you spend on it. The way layers supersede each other but don't disappear. The way these layers form a narrative.

A: If you mean the narrative of the work itself, then yes, I would agree that there is a story happening. My work is a lot about process, and process is its own narrative. And mine, I would say, is a particularly rational process. I might start painting with a washy green field and every step thereafter will remain in conversation with that green. But the conversation is also an expression of a deeper conflict.

Q: You speak of claustrophobia in your work. Care to elaborate?

A: Excess, even when balanced and/or structured, can be suffocating. Yves Klein once said that when you add one color to another you start an endless conflict. That is exactly what I wanted from relations between colors: a conflict! And for there to be no winners. It can be claustrophobic sometimes.

Q: Do you feel that your work is connected to miscegenation?

A: All of Brazilian modernism is based on the theory of "a culture eating a culture." Tarsila do Amaral, who was perhaps the most important painter in Brazil at the time, is a central reference in my work. Painting came to Brazil from Europe and later from North America. This I was well aware of, and yet ever since I first wanted to be a painter I have always wanted to work with elements of my own culture. In my work, I continue to ask some of the same questions that the Brazilian modernists asked in the past. How can one speak the international language of painting using the Brazilian cultural experience?

Q: Do you classify Brazil as a Western country?

A: Yes, but it is not generally considered a Western country. Western culture is determined by Europe and North America. Brazil is not part of this hegemony. Things are changing, but I don't believe in the idea of a "global culture." I think artists are more interested in looking to their own culture even if it is not a culture that features prominently in Western art. Andy Warhol created an art that is all about his culture. He probably wouldn't have made the same work had he grown up in Bangladesh. I'm an abstract painter and I speak an international language, but my interest is in things and behaviors that can only be found in Brazil. I'm Brazilian. I grew up in Rio de Janeiro and studied painting here with a teacher who was Scottish. My paintings address all of these influences, so yes, [they are] "culture eating culture."

Q: When did you realize that you wanted to paint?

A: My mother realized it for me. She's an art historian and university professor and my father is a lawyer. Both are intellectuals and share an interest in culture. I originally wanted to be a journalist and even received a degree in journalism. But in my second year of college, when it became clear that communications wasn't the subject I really wanted to devote my life to, my mother suggested art school. So I went there, and found skills that I did want to develop.

Q: What about your involvement with other media? Your sets for your sister's dance company [Marcia Milhazes Dança Contemporánea], your collages?

A: Up until 1996, I was exclusively a painter, and painting remains at the center of my art. But I cannot paint all the time. I need to take breaks, though I never like to stop painting altogether. In 1996, I started making prints with Durham Press, and I still work with them. In 2002, my first artist's book, Coisa Linda [Something Beautiful], was published by the Museum of Modern Art in New York. In 2003, I received my first commission to create a glass façade for the Selfridges and Co. department store in Manchester, England. The scale was gigantic: seven stories high. It was an enormous challenge, not just due to the scale but also because I had to draw on an architectural plan, which I hadn't done before. I have never made sketches or preliminary drawings for my paintings. Ordinarily I work directly on the piece, whatever its scale may be. To make an architecturally scaled drawing was quite difficult but exciting. The technique is a kind of collage with vinyl. Nothing is printed; each shape is cut out and applied.

I felt that it was a success. I found I could provide a very different experience from that of viewing a painting by placing my images in a public space, where they become part of the architecture: around, not merely in front of, the public. The images become part of that space and people cannot get away form them. I've been invited to do others. Like the set design work I have done in the past for my sister: it has brought a new perspective to my art. As attracted as I am to the blank white canvas, it can also be very scary sometimes. It can be inspiring to work with different media that, in turn, bring new questions back to painting. I feel very lucky that I am able to work well in a variety of media; it helps maintain my interest in painting.

Autoconstrucción, or Self-Construction

Abraham Cruzvillegas

———⋆———

From *Autoconstrucción: The Book*
(Los Angeles, CA: Roy and Edna Disney/CalArts Theater, 2009), n.p.

This essay relates the artist's three-dimensional assemblages to the process of building his family home outside Mexico City. A deeper symbolic meaning lies in the construction and exposure of an identity, and his work conflates the three (sculpture, house, identity) in a poetic way. The artist's citation of art historian Aby Warburg as an influence is also noteworthy. Warburg arranged pictures of objects into panels, guided, he said, by "elective affinities" between the disparate items rather than visual similarities. With both the house and the artwork, the goal is "to create awareness of how human action generates forms."

During the first twenty years of my life, I witnessed the slow construction of the house my family lived in; we all participated in this process. The context was a massive invasion of immigrants from the countryside who had immediate needs such as housing. The construction of my house and my neighborhood began in the 1960s, in an area strewn with volcanic rock south of Mexico City that lay outside any urban plan.

The materials and techniques they used were completely improvised, depending on the specific circumstances and immediate surroundings, in the midst of widespread social and economic instability in Mexico and probably across the world. Every solution answered a pressing situation or need, such as how to add a new room, to modify a roof, or to improve, alter, or eliminate a certain space. Because its construction lacked both a budget and input from architects, the house today looks chaotic and almost useless; however, every corner and detail has its reason for being there. The house is an authentic labyrinth, polished to a patina by simultaneous construction, use, and destruction.

This self-construction, to use the generic term for this type of building, should be seen as a fluid process in which cooperation among neighbors and family members is very important, not only in terms of their collaboration as such, with shared investments, but also as an enriching and educational environment for any individual member of the community, to understand his own circumstances.

The series of artworks that make up the self-construction project start from observing the house as a whole. Its details and techniques were improvised or developed out of an organic imperative to arrange for a home, a space that arises through a spontaneous, contradictory, and unstable process. The references in the works that reflect the house become, also in an unstable manner, like obstacles, blockages, leaps, jumps, shakings, irregularities, separations, rebounds, breakups, or cancellations. They refer to the house as they express a bodily awareness of the immediate, the urgent, of physical presence in multiple and simultaneous times and spaces. Many of these works show my desire to juxtapose two or more radically different economic systems, bringing about hybridized marriages and unexpected mixtures of materials and techniques.

There is no way of representing the technical details of each construction; there is only a reproduction of the diverse dynamics involved, viewing its social and economic surroundings as the arena in which I operate. Even when some isolated sculptural works may figuratively recall the basic structure of a house, my principal task, beyond simply showing maquettes of poor buildings, is to create awareness of how human action generates forms, as I try to renew a vehicle of meaning for invention and creation.

In addition, like an underlying soundtrack in time and space, alongside the sculptures that I make, there is an equally contradictory parallel accumulation of information translated into drawings, photos, moving images, and sounds, all appropriated from books, music, other images, and my life experiences. Collections of movie posters, images cut out from magazines and postcards, strips of video, ballads and songs, texts taken from my reading: these all make up some of the conglomerations that I share as I exhibit my world. All of these fragments are the handmade bricks and stones that shape the walls, ceilings, and floors of my house.

For the realization of this total image of my personality, I collect and display objects after the manner of the *Mnemosyne Atlas* of Aby Warburg, a cumulative and affective search for expressive signs in all places. Buckminster Fuller said that materials are organized according to their sympathies, an idea that applies to my collections of objects, images, and sounds, just as for my three-dimensional work. Through its minimal transformations, without anecdotes or narratives, and perhaps without any skills whatsoever, my work is the proof that I exist. In my work, the transformation of information, materials, and objects makes up as well the definitely unfinished construction of my own identity, as an approximation of reality through deeds.

Real and Virtual Light of Relational Architecture

An Interview with Rafael Lozano-Hemmer

Geert Lovink

Excerpted from *Alzado vectorial: Arquitectura relacional* no. 4.
Mexico City: Conaculta, 2000.

This interview deals with two important pieces in Lozano-Hemmer's output: Displaced Emperors *invited viewers to project discordant and subversive imagery onto a European palace in 1997;* Vectorial Elevation *enabled viewers to program a dramatic searchlight display on the central square of Mexico City for six seconds each in 1999–2000. Describing these works takes the artist into several other regions, including some technical explanations, the history of high-tech artwork in Mexico, and whether these works are too connected to the culture of international capitalism.*

Q: The way you use [light] is very high-tech. For me it is almost an abstract category. Very metaphysical, holy, it is the sphere of the gods. You seem to be able to use it in very different ways, to make historical and political references, like you did in your installation in Linz [*Displaced Emperors*] and for the media and architecture festival in Graz. This was about projection, colonialism, and interaction, both technically and from the narrative point-of-view complex installations. And funny, too. How do you put these stories together and what is the role of the light as a virtual reality element in this?

A: My installation projects, done in collaboration with Will Bauer, are within a field that I call Relational Architecture, which can be defined as "the technological actualization of buildings with alien memory." Here, alien memory refers to something that does not belong, that is out of place, while technological actualization means the use of hyperlinks, aliasing, special effects, and telepresence.

In relational architecture, buildings are activated so that the input of the people in the street can provide narrative implications apart from those envisioned by the architects, developers, or dwellers. The pieces use sensors, networks, and audiovisual technologies to transform the buildings. In particular, light projections are used because they can achieve the desired monumental scale and can be changed in real time, and their immateriality makes their deployment more logistically feasible.

I like to make a clear distinction between work in relational architecture and virtual reality pieces. For me, virtual architecture could be differentiated from relational architecture in that the former is based on simulation while the latter is based on dissimulation. Virtual buildings are data constructs that strive for realism, asking the participant to "suspend disbelief" and "play along" with the environment; relational buildings, on the other hand, are real buildings pretending to be something other than themselves, masquerading as that which they might become, asking participants to "suspend faith" and probe, interact, and experiment with the false construct. Virtual architecture tends to miniaturize buildings to the participant's scale—for example, through virtual reality peripherals such as head-mounted displays or automatic virtual environments—while relational architecture amplifies the participant to the building's scale, or emphasizes the relationship between urban and personal scale. In this sense, virtual architecture tends to dematerialize the body, while relational architecture tends to dematerialize the environment. This is not to say that virtual and relational architectures are opposing practices, nor that they are mutually exclusive.

Cicero, [Winston] Churchill, and a dozen others have been quoted as saying "we make buildings and buildings make us." This is far from the current urban situation; buildings no longer represent a city's inhabitants. As [architect Rem] Koolhaas and others have noted, most new architecture consists of generic, de-featured buildings that reflect market forces and not local specificity. I call these "default buildings." A housing project in Kuala Lumpur is bound to be quite similar to one in Mexico, Cleveland, or Athens. On the other hand, we have what the Spanish architect Emilio López-Galiacho calls "vampire buildings," which are emblematic buildings that are not allowed to have a natural death, that are kept alive artificially through restoration, citation, and virtual simulation. Vampire buildings are forced to be immortal due to "architectural correctness," a cultural, political, and economic conservative tendency to assign a representative role to a select number of buildings. Vampire buildings, while culturally incestuous and necrophilic (or perhaps because of it), will always remain protected from erosion, gravity, war, crawling vines, graffiti, and the like.

So, one important aspect of Relational Architecture is to produce a performative context where default buildings may take on temporary specificity and vampire buildings may decline their role in their established, prevailing identification.

Having said this, I am interested in distancing my practice from the notion of the "site-specific," particularly from the postmodern attempts to find and deconstruct essential constituent characteristics of a particular space. I am very committed to the idea that a site consists of an indeterminate number of intersecting imaginary, sociopolitical, physical, and telepresent spaces. Therefore, I like to use the term "relationship-specific" to describe the uniqueness of a discreet interaction between participants, different planes of experience, and the relational building(s). What is specific is the new behaviors that might emerge during interaction.

Q: Yes, let's go to the messy reality of Mexico City, in this case, where you have just finished a pearly piece of relational architecture [*Vectorial Elevation*]. Do you see the high-tech equipment you have been using there clashing with rampant poverty, a low-intensity civil war in Chiapas, in general the huge social divides in Mexico, or this is just another Western cliché? I suppose you have just intensively enjoyed doing it, overcoming all sorts of difficulties connected with such a complicated setup. Tell us all about the everyday contradictions you have encountered, compared to the Spanish or Austrian bureaucracies and formalities.

A: The piece in Mexico City was commissioned by the National Council for Culture and the Arts, for the millennium celebrations. The president of the Council saw my work in Austria, which questioned the notion of heritage and "cultural property," and asked me to use Mexican history as a departure point for a spectacular installation in the Zócalo Square. Now, most Mexican art this century has had a very didactic, historicist bent that is clearly evident in the *Neue Sachlichkeit* [New Objectivity] work of the muralists. Modern masters adopted a "revolutionary" aesthetic that was characterized by a problematic romanticization of indigenous peoples, a militant patriotism, and a fascination with linear models of history. Perhaps what could have been expected is to have a new kind of virtual muralism, consisting of projections of parading national heroes. The last thing I wanted to do is to repeat these mono-logic mantras. Fortunately, contemporary Mexican art departed long ago from this vision, starting with Octavio Paz, who challenged the concept of "progress" almost forty years ago, and José Luis Cuevas, who denounced muralism as a "cactus curtain" that was blocking the transit of ideas in and out of Mexico.

In any case, the problem of large-scale monologic representation is not only a Mexican phenomenon. Most millennium shows throughout the world consisted of *son et lumière* [sound and light] spectacles that defined a linear historicist narrative of "representative" moments or actors in history. Each of those narratives must be analyzed in terms of their exclusions of so-called minor histories, because there can never be a comprehensive, exhaustive, nor neutral representation, and what is shown is always a profile of the current elite. There is a very close connection between representation and repression, particularly when it is applied to what Edward Said calls "identitarian" narratives. Elites have always used such narratives to homogenize and control what are otherwise complex, dynamic social fabrics. The millennium was the first chance to see the widespread impact of new technologies of representation on the scale and insidiousness of identitarian power affirmation (although it could be argued that they were already evident, for instance, in Pokémon consumerism or the "special effects" capitalism of dot-com corporations).

From the very beginning of the design process, I knew that the piece had to incorporate interactivity as a way of avoiding historical representation and [Andre] Lurçat- and [Albert] Speer-like [Nazi] spectacles. I wanted the main protagonist of the piece to be the participants themselves. Because the minister had asked me to look at Mexican history to find a departure point for the piece, I investigated the largely undocumented history of Mexican technological culture. I found several useful precedents that serve as a legitimate backdrop for electronic art projects, from the research of [Guillermo] González Camarena on color TV to the popularization of electronic music by Luis Pérez Esquivel. One discovery was incredibly useful: the theory of cybernetics was postulated by

Norbert Wiener and Arturo Rosenblueth at the Mexican Institute of Cardiology to explain self-regulation in the heart. Since I became aware of this, I have joked that cyber art is a native Mexican practice!

But seriously, to answer your question regarding the potential clash between high-tech equipment and the appalling economic situation of many Mexicans, I have to say that Mexico is a very complex, hetero-geneous society that is full of contradictions. There is an almost feudal society in regions of Chiapas that continues to systematically impover-ish indigenous people; at the same time, Subcomandante Marcos is a networked revolutionary leader who understands and uses the subver-sive power of "high technology." This is not to say that social inequality and technology do not clash; of course they do, for example, in the high-tech *maquiladora* factories in the border towns, where management and technology come from the US and the underpaid work force, raw mate-rials, and space come from Mexico. My position is that technology is an inevitable aspect of society and it is a key challenge for the media artist to develop or misuse it to break the stereotypes and create new techno-logical languages. One of the reasons I like to quote the precedents of Mexican technological culture is precisely because I like to think that technological development is not necessarily exclusive to "developed" countries. Think of the software industry in India or the Nortec elec-tronic music movement in Tijuana.

The piece was done in the Zócalo Plaza, which is the world's third-largest square, measuring 240 by 220 meters and holding over two hun-dred thousand people. The Zócalo's monumental size makes the human scale seem insignificant, a fact that some Mexican scholars consider an emblem of a monolithic political legacy; there are almost one thousand protests a year in this site and yet its scale drowns most of them. In order to have an impact on this square it was necessary to deploy very powerful equipment: we placed eighteen robotic searchlights with a total of 126,000 watts of power on the rooftops of surrounding build-ings like the National Palace, the City Government headquarters, and the hotels. On a clear night the searchlight beams could be seen from a twenty-kilometer radius and covered the entire historic center of the city, including landmarks such as the Metropolitan Cathedral, the Supreme Court of Justice, and the Templo Mayor Aztec ruins. Despite the power of the installation, my intention was not to do a cathartic millennium show but a quiet, slowly fluctuating space for reflection.

The concept for the piece was for people on the internet to design light sculptures using a 3D interface [and] submit them to Mexico where they would be queued, rendered by the searchlights in the plaza, and finally documented in a digital archive. We connected the searchlights with hundreds of meters of data cable and measured their location with GPS trackers. Custom software was written to interface a virtual reality modeling language simulation of the Zócalo to the servers that could control the searchlights. Three webcams placed in the National Palace, a hotel, and a skyscraper would document participants' designs and also stream live video feeds. As with any event that I have ever done in public space, the logistics were intense: we filed several reports to the department of National Security, obtained permits from air traffic control, installed coaxial internet feeds through the hotel's bathroom ventilation, stopped street traffic while cranes lifted the searchlights, and so on.

Q: I have seen the video you produced that documents the Zócalo installation. It is truly amazing. You have just won the Prix Ars Electronica prize in the category of interactive installations. Congratulations. What struck me in the video was the poetry of the searchlights, which are usually only set up to mimic military searchlights, scanning the night sky for suspicious objects. The movements of the ever-changing grids seemed so elastic. This must be a visual trick because the hardware and software you managed to bring together looked so massive. The scale of works you are doing really has transcended from the museum and gallery into large-scale urban spaces. Did you run this art project as a military operation, or rather like a business, a theatre show? Does the virtual spectacle you staged resemble some elements of the big, orchestrated fireworks, pop concerts, and rave parties?

A: The elasticity that you are referring to is in fact the effect that I was looking for the most when designing this project. The smooth morphing between different submitted designs was crucial to evoke a sense of constant transformation and flow. The transitions between positions were as important as the positions themselves.

My original notion was for the searchlights to render a new design every second, both to fit as many participants as possible and to match the tempo of a slow heart beat. In the end, six to eight seconds were needed per design to allow the searchlights to position themselves and for the three webcams to take pictures. In retrospect, I am very glad that we used this slower pace because it invited contemplation, and anything faster would have been too aggressive in a city that does not need any more aggression.

As you mention, historically searchlights have been used for military antiaircraft surveillance, and their vocabulary of movements has been limited to coordinated "sky scanning" patterns. These patterns have a very different interpretation in Europe, where bombings wiped out entire cities, than in America, where they became associated with celebration, thanks in part to the use of searchlights in WWII victory parades. Once searchlights were adopted by Hollywood-style events, the movements became largely randomized. The searchlights were used to attract people to a single point from which the light beams were originating. In *Vectorial Elevation* the light beams were always in a coordinated state of mutation as they positioned themselves to render participants' designs. The movement was "purposeful" in that every six seconds a unique static pattern would emerge and then dissolve into the next one. The theatrics of power used by Speer and others was also avoided to an extent by the lack of linear narrative: the piece was in operation from dusk to dawn for two weeks, becoming more of an urban fixture than a time-based event. Although I am conscious that the scale was "spectacular" I am happier to compare the work to a public fountain or to a park bench than to a *son et lumière* [sound and light] show.

The piece was developed by a large number of programmers, designers, and technicians in four countries. Even though I was commissioned to design the project in March 1998, we only got to work a few months before the opening. The Internet connection in the control room was installed four days before going live! So it was a pretty tight development schedule. The physical setup was done by a Mexican company that normally presents large rock concerts and musical theatre, so to them the scale was not a problem. Logistically, I have always thought that my work is more akin to the performing arts than to the visual arts. The installations tend to be ephemeral interventions where the public becomes an actor through interactivity, and they are closer to perpetration than to preservation. I am also particularly interested in the fact that theatre, concerts, and performance art are direct, shared experiences where people actively assume different roles, thanks to the "wideband" feedback that is possible with collective closeness. Composer Frederic Rzewski called this essential pleasure of the performing arts "coming together."

Q: Could you tell us about the special software that has been developed for the Zócalo? Will there be any spinoffs, used in other installations? Will the software, for example, be available as open source? If you work on this level, what experiences do you have concerning innovative and creative further development of certain technologies? Are you optimistic about the role that this kind of new media arts can play? Through your work within the Spanish telecom giant Telefónica you would probably agree [with digital media theorist Peter Lunenfeld] that "digital art is the product of transnational corporate capitalism." Could this type of work possibly influence the direction technology is taking? Or shall we, with Lunenfeld, say that the "Demo or Die" essence of electronic arts is to perform corporate technologies?

A: We had twenty computers in the control room running mostly custom-made software: Linux/Apache servers, video reflectors, watermarking processors, DMX control boxes, etc. The main design specification was that the interface should be accessible across platforms, across browsers, and without the need for any plug-ins. We turned to Java as the solution but even it had to be tweaked heavily to achieve this goal. Most of the software is too specialized to be useful in other contexts but now it will be very easy to make new versions of *Vectorial Elevation* for other cities. The only piece of software that may find itself repurposed in some form is a video streaming system that the programmers called "kyxpyx" and which is released as open source. We wanted to have a cheap (free!) alternative to the current video streaming solutions from Microsoft, Apple, and Real, and that worked without plug-ins.

I agree that digital art is the product of transnational corporate capitalism. So is the environment we live in and our identity itself. Many years ago I wrote an essay for *Leonardo* magazine called "Perverting Technological Correctness" where I outlined some strategies artists deploy to corrupt the inevitability of corporate technologies. Among them, I included the simulation of technology itself, the use of pain, ephemeral intervention, misuse of technology, nondigital approaches to virtuality, and resistance to what I call the "effect" effect. I believe that artists have been and can be at the forefront of technological development. For media arts, the usual example that gets cited is the development of the data glove by Dan Sandin, Tom DeFanti, and Gary Sayers under a grant from the National Endowment for the Arts in 1977. But there are many other examples. Will Bauer, my collaborator for the past twelve years, has been developing a wireless 3D tracking system that we have incorporated into many of our pieces. This integration has been very beneficial to both the artistic and technological developments and we find it hard to distinguish what comes first, if anything. Of course, I am aware that most technology is developed for and by the military-economic complex, but I am enamored by the romantic illusion that if art had the military's budget we would create more jobs than they do and develop more interesting technology (including great art bombs!).

Index

abstract art, xiii, xv, 99, 102, 136, 177, 183
abstract artists, 258
abstractionism, and functionalism, 135
abstractionist architecture: International Style, 132–33, 136–39; International Style and capitalism, 136–37; realist architecture and, 132–38
abstract painting, in Argentina, 183
Abu Ghraib prison, 197, 198
Actions of Art Collective (CADA), 208
Africans: in Cuba, 85; enslavement, 85; sculpture, 85
Airmail Paintings, 248–53
Akhenaten, 79, 80
Almeida, Guilherme de, 17
Almeida, Tácito de, 17
Almost-Still Life, 195
Alzado vectorial: Arquitectura relacional (Lovink), 284–92
Amaral, Tarsila do. *See* Tarsila do Amaral
Amauta, 52
Amenhotep IV, 79, 80
America: artwork of, 9–10; new art of, 95–98
Americanism, 95, 96
Andrade, Guilherme de, 16–18
Andrade, Mário de, 16–19
Andrade, Oswald de, 16–19; *Anthropophagite Manifesto*, 20–23
animals, 72
Anthropophagite Manifesto, 20–23
anthropophagy, 20–23
Anti-Aesthetic (Noé), 183
Antonioni, Michelangelo, 87
Apex, 95
Apostroph' Apocalypse, 82–83
Apu Inca Atawallpamam, 110–11
Aragon, Louis, 58

Aranha, Graça, 18, 19
architectural space, 127–28, 134, 145, 146, 286
architecture: abstractionist, 132–39; artists and architects, 214–15; Baroque, 121, 122, 131; color and, 130–31; construction materials, 131; emotional, 139–41; engineering and, 127, 133; European modern, 127; functionalism and, 133–36, 139–40; integration of arts, 127–31, 145, 146; International Style, 132–33, 136–39; light and, 284–92; Maya, 219, 220; mechanism and, 133, 134; painting and, 127–30, 139; realist, 132–38; regionalism in, 132, 133; relational, 284–92; sculpture and, 127–30, 139, 141, 145, 146; social conditions and, 136; virtual, 285–86, 289. *See also* modern architecture
Arden Quin, Carmelo, 105
Ardévol, José, 83
Arenas, Reinaldo, 269–70
Argentina, 236; abstract painting, 183; Federalists and Unitarians, 184; New Figuration, 181–88; Rosario, 265, 266, 267, 270
Arguedas, José María, 110, 111
Arp, Jean, 123
"La arquitectura moderna de México: ¿Qué significa socialmente?" (O'Gorman), 132–38
art: abstract, xiii, xv, 99, 102, 136, 177, 183; artistic language, 129; artwork of America, 9–10; autochthonous, 95, 97; capitalism and, 53; change and, 211–16; collective, 48, 115; communication and, 213, 216; consideration of, 115; culture and, 127; decadence and,

Mexican art (*continued*)
colonialism and foreign current of, 138;
high-tech artwork, 284; historicist bent
of modern, 286–87; Mexico City art
scene, 1950s, 176–80; nationalism and,
173–75, 179; popular and realist, 137;
protest and nonconformity, 173–75;
selling, 173; study, 169–73
Mexican modern architecture: abstractionist architecture in International
Style and, 132–33, 136–38; capitalism
and, 137; colonialism and, 137; realist
architecture and, 137; social significance, 132–38
Mexican mural painters, 114, 170–75, 266;
mural movement, 50, 169; struggle
against military coup, 37–39
Mexican painters, 47
Mexican Revolution, 38, 39, 41, 50
Mexico, 247, 281; attempted military coup,
37–39; Indian communities, 246; pov-
erty, 288; technological culture, 287–88
Mexico City: art scene, 1950s, 176–80; gal-
leries, 176–80; National Council for
Culture and the Arts, 286; relational
architecture, 286; *Vectorial Elevation*
show, 284, 286–91; Zócalo Square
installation, 286, 288–91
Meza, Mundo, 224, 225–26
Michelangelo, 128
Middle East, 272
*Midnight Puppets [Fantoches da Meia-
Noite]*, 15
Milhazes, Beatriz, 277–80
millennium exhibitions, 287
Milliet, Sérgio, 17
Ministry of Education building, Brazil,
119–20, 123
Minorista (Minority) Group manifesto,
28–31
Minujín, Marta, xi, 189–91
Miró Quesada, Luis, 110
Mnemosyne Atlas (Warburg), 283
modern architecture: functionalism and,
133–36, 139–40; International Style,
132–33, 136–39. *See also* Latin American
modern architecture
modern art: artists and, 58–61; public and,
58–59. *See also* Latin American modern art

Modern Art Week: Di Cavalcanti on,
15–19; program, 13–14
modernism, xiii; European, 20; post-
modernism, 122. *See also* Latin
American modernism
MoMA. *See* Museum of Modern Art
Mondrian, Piet, 158, 186
Monet, Claude, 259
monologic representation, 287
Monroe, Marilyn, 165–66
Mont, Daniel, 139
monuments: art and, 275; Maya, 217–20
Las moradas, 110
Morales, Armando, 110
Moreira, Jorge, 120
Moro, César, 65–69, 107
Moses, 78–80
Moses and Monotheism (Freud), 78, 79,
80, 81
Muchnik, Carolina, 184
Municipal Theater (São Paulo), 13
muralism: East L.A., 228, 229; virtual, 287
muralists: New Objectivity work of, 286–
87. *See also* Mexican mural painters
mural movement, 265; Chicano, 231, 233;
Mexican mural painters and, 50, 169
mural painting: Chicano, 233–34; collec-
tive, 48; easel painting and, 46; Mexi-
can, 37–39, 50, 114, 169–75, 266
*The Murdered Student [El estudiante
asesinado]*, 113
Murillo, Gerardo. *See* Atl, Dr.
Museo Experimental El Eco, 139, 140
Museum of Fine Arts (Houston), xii
Museum of Modern Art (MoMA), xii–
xiii, 122, 242, 246
museums, 74
music interpretation, 165–66
Mussolini, Benito, 53

La Nación Revista, 197
*Nadie olvida nada [Nobody Forgets Any-
thing]*, 240
National Autonomous University of
Mexico library, 132
National Gallery, 74, 75
nationalism, 24
nationalistic art, 173–75, 179, 183–84
Nazis, 82, 83, 275
neoconcrete art, 163; manifesto, 157–60

www.ingramcontent.com/pod-product-compliance
Lightning Source LLC
Chambersburg PA
CBHW020854180526
45163CB00007B/2504